# Elad Lassry

# Table of Contents

# Inhaltsverzeichnis

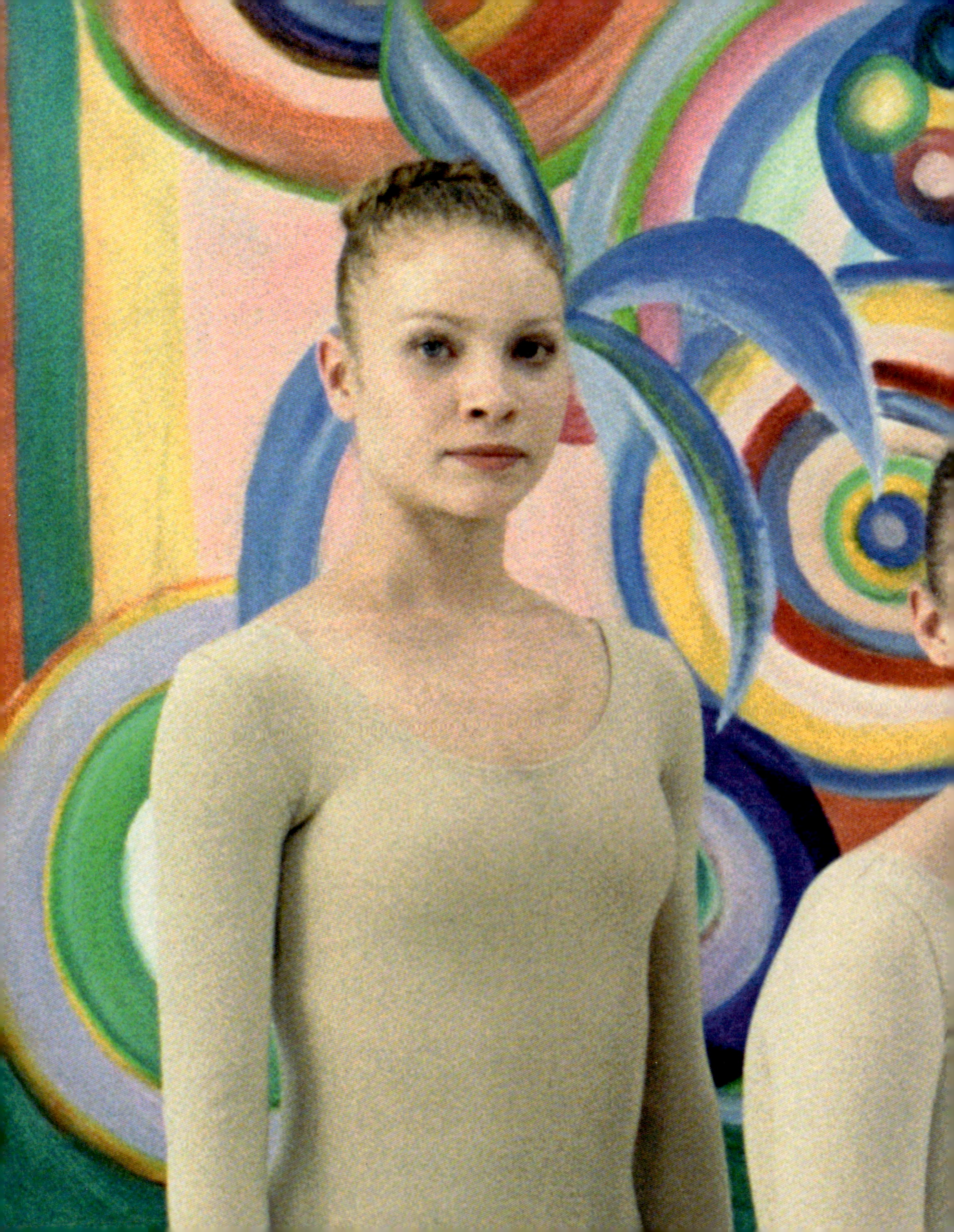

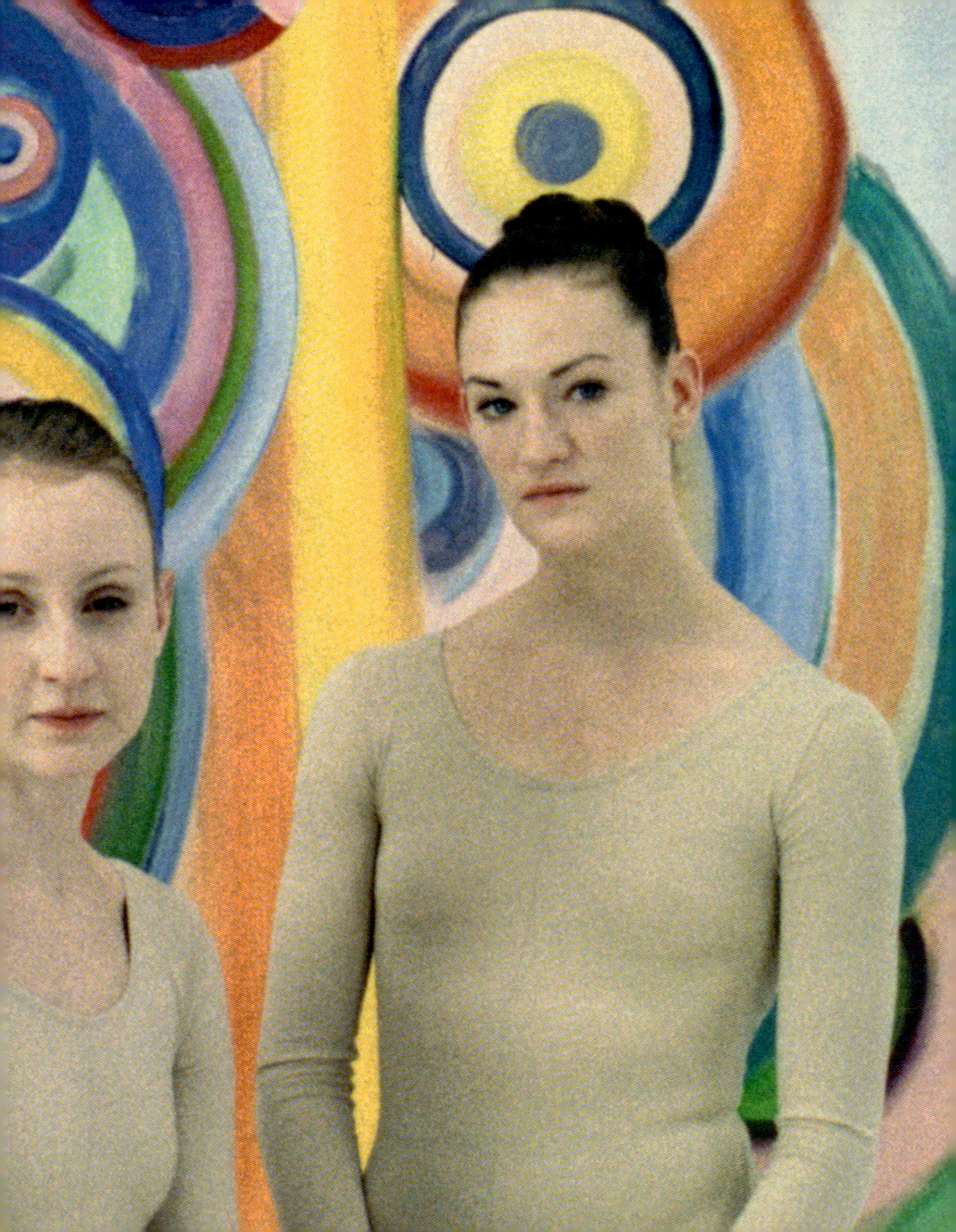

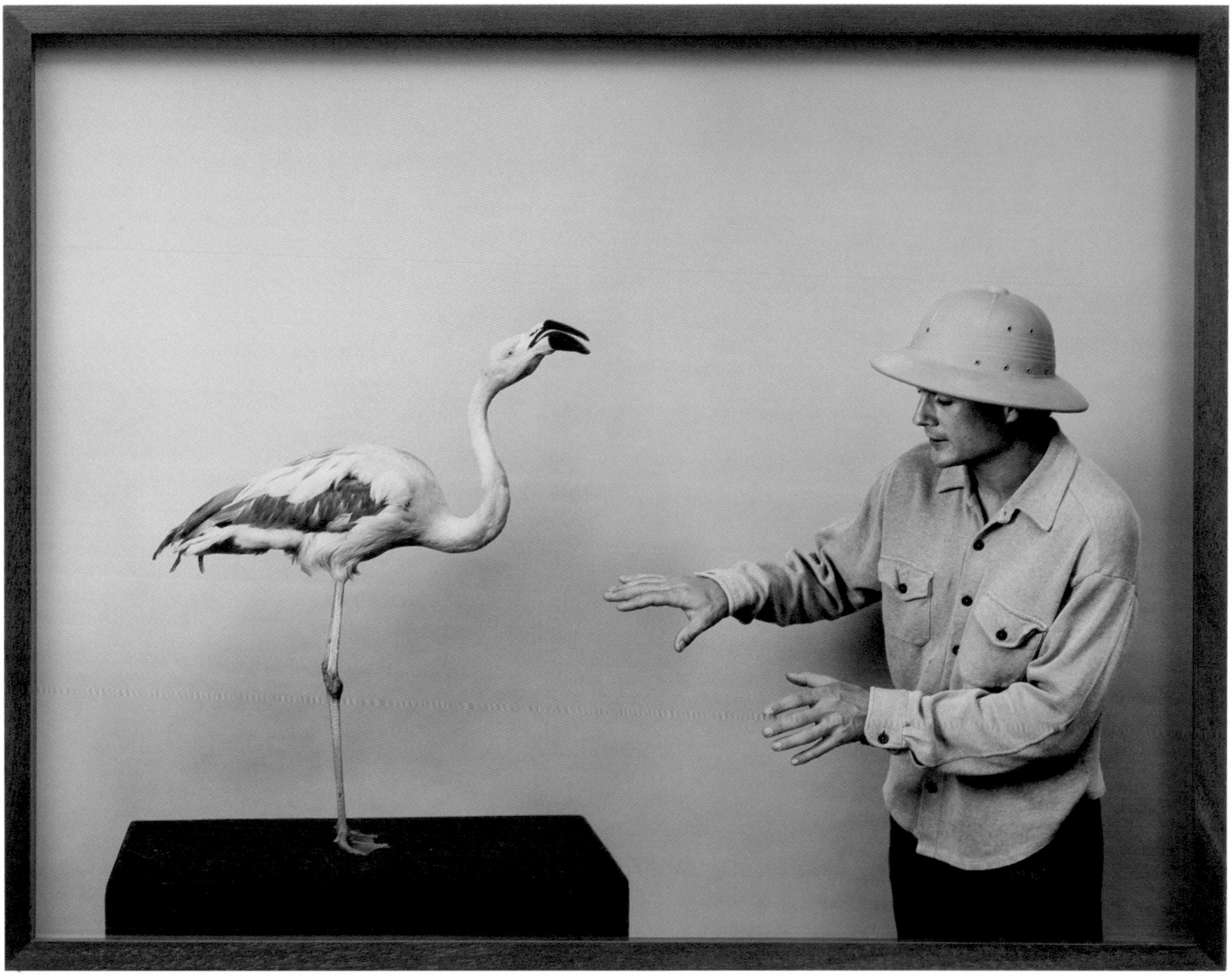

← *Untitled (Passacaglia)*, 2010

*Travis Parker and Chilean Flamingo, 90028*, 2008

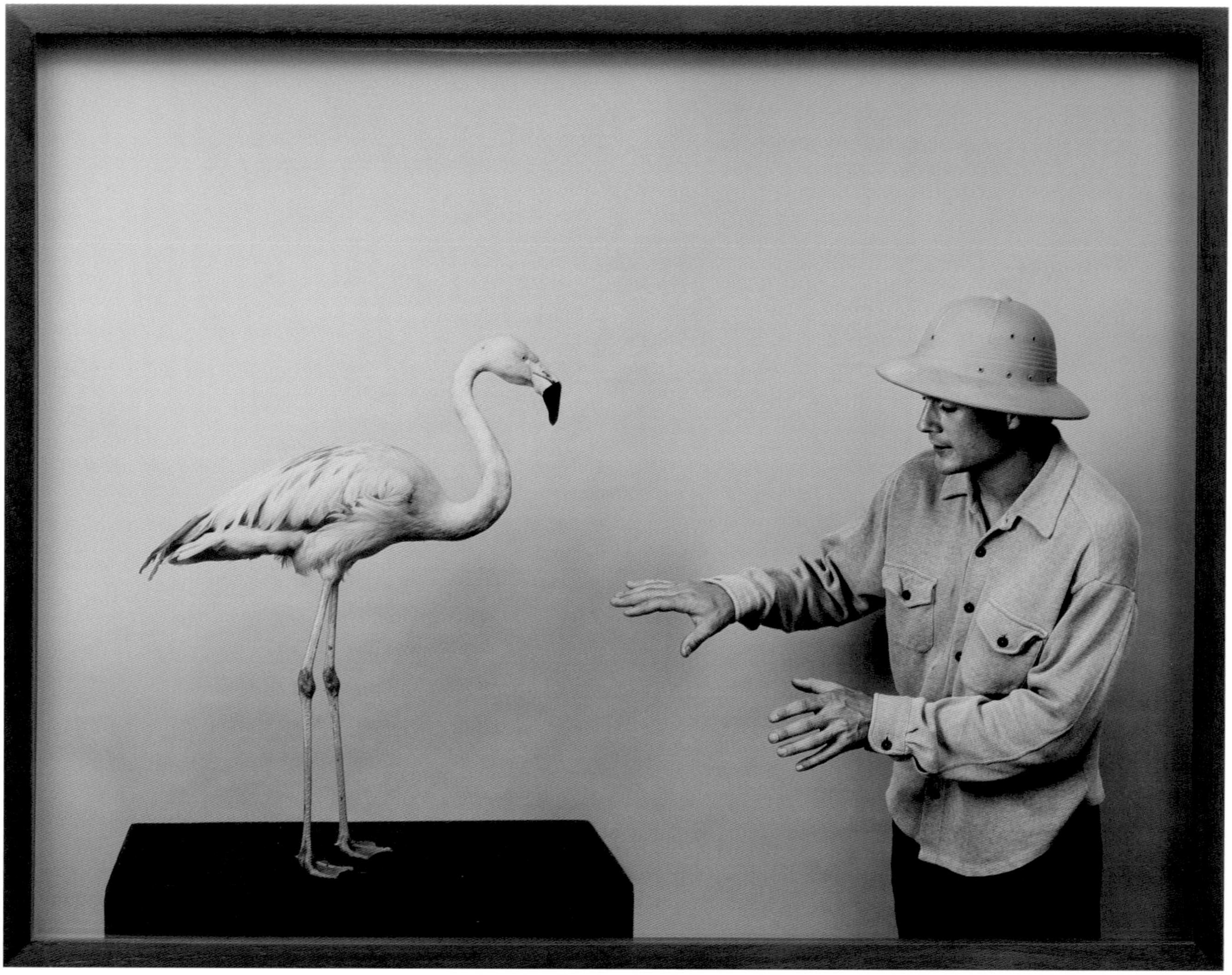

*Travis Parker and Chilean Flamingo, 90028*, 2008

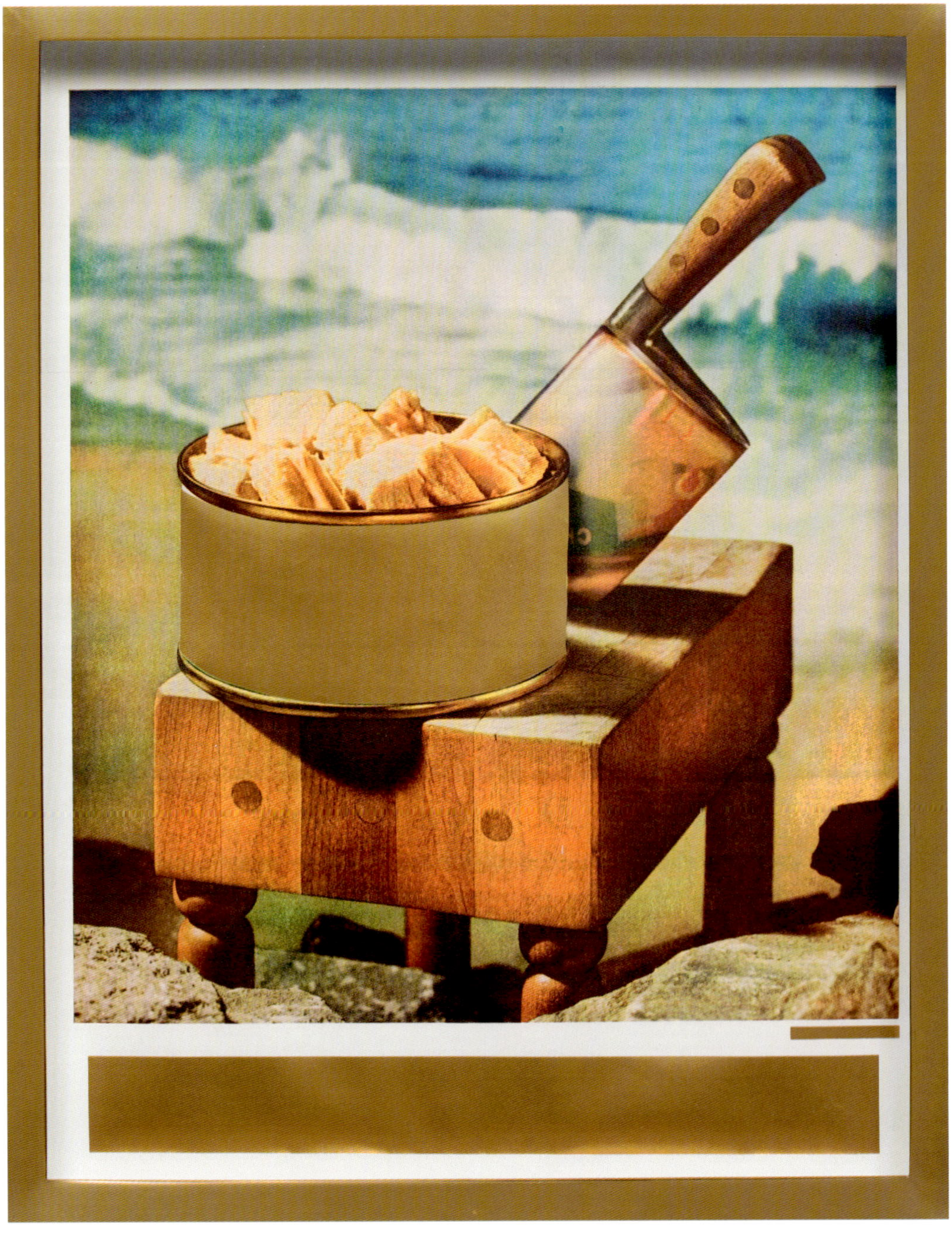

*Tuna Can*, 2009

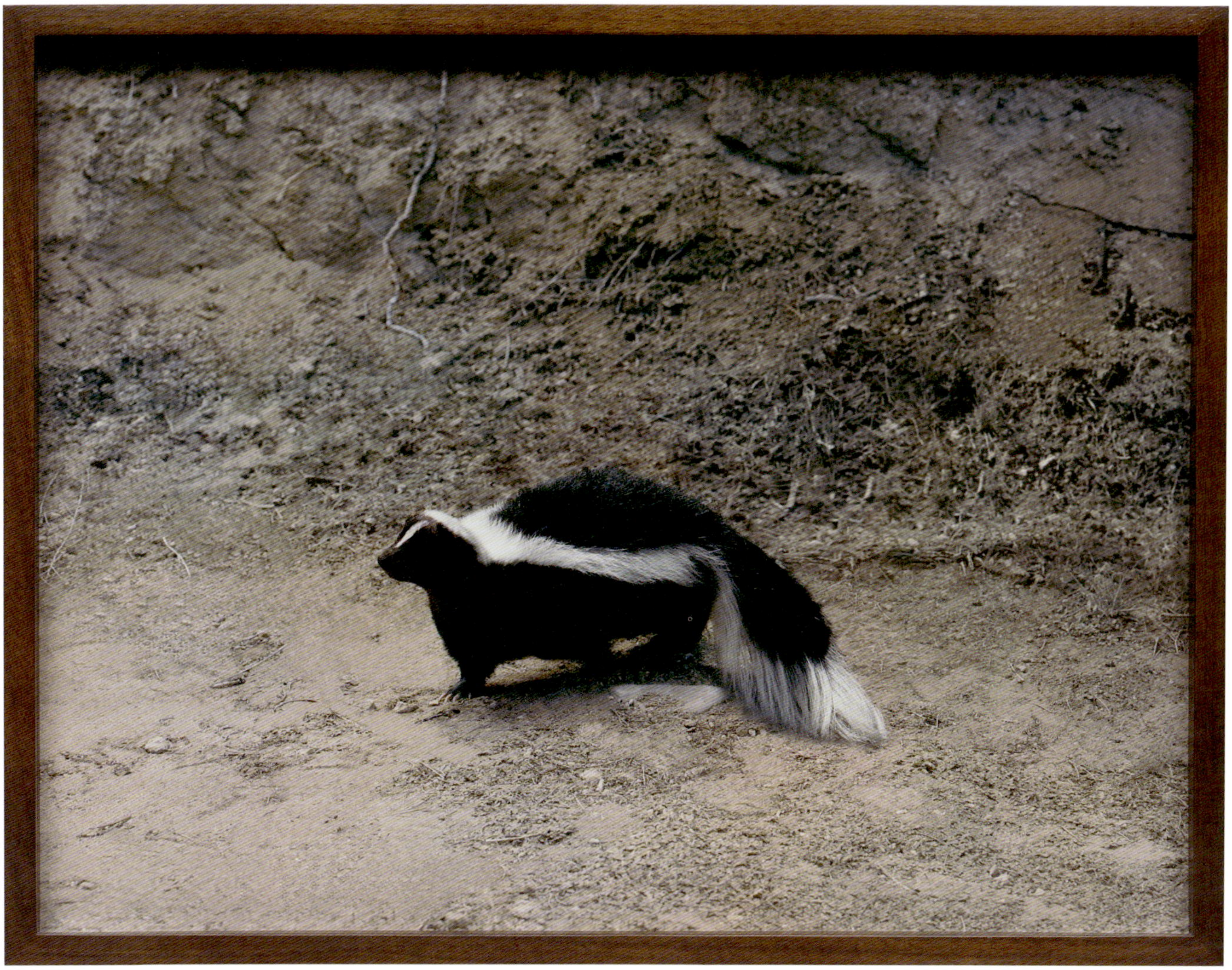

*Skunk*, 2009

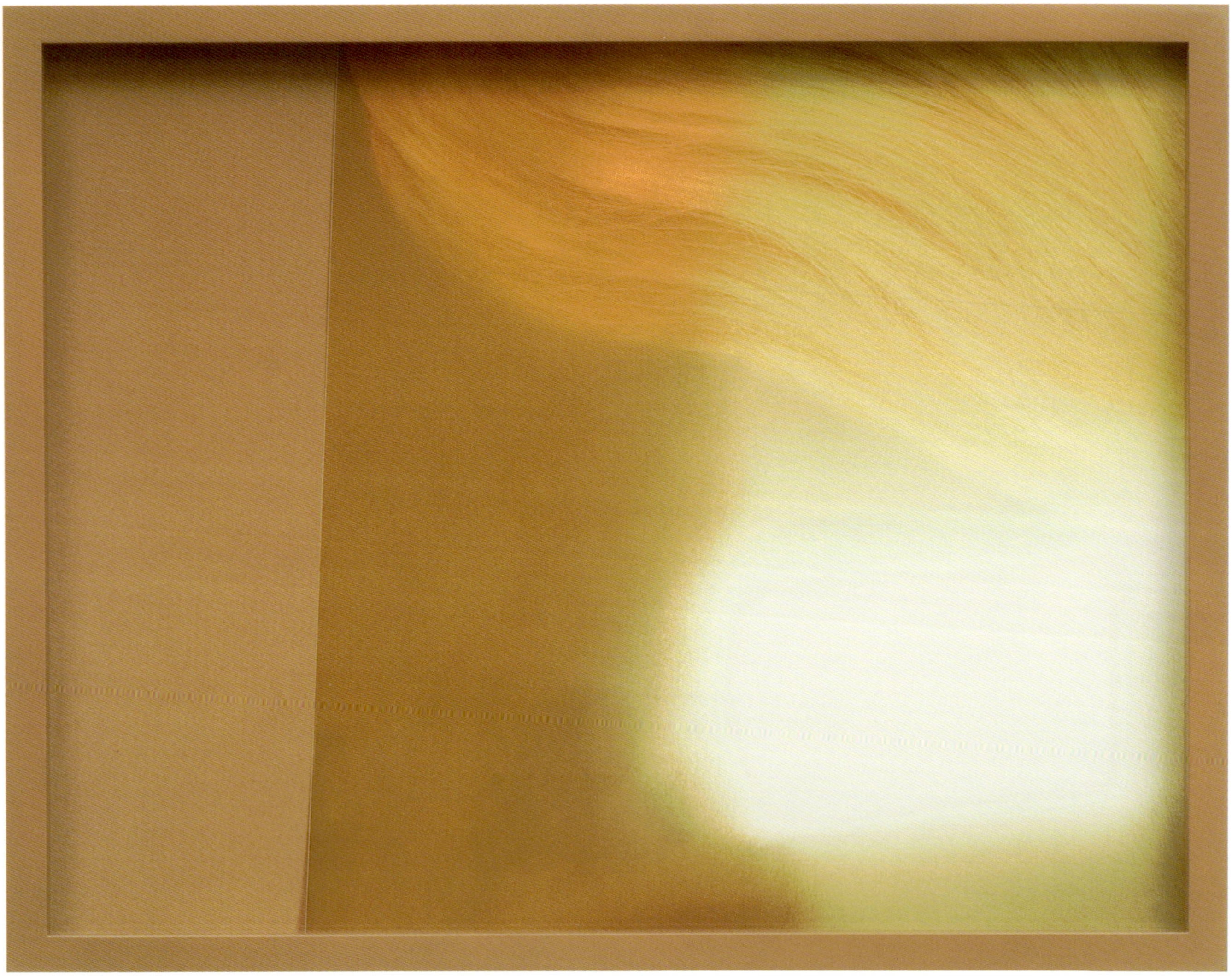

*Cardboard, Platinum Blond Wig, Gold Reflector*, 2007

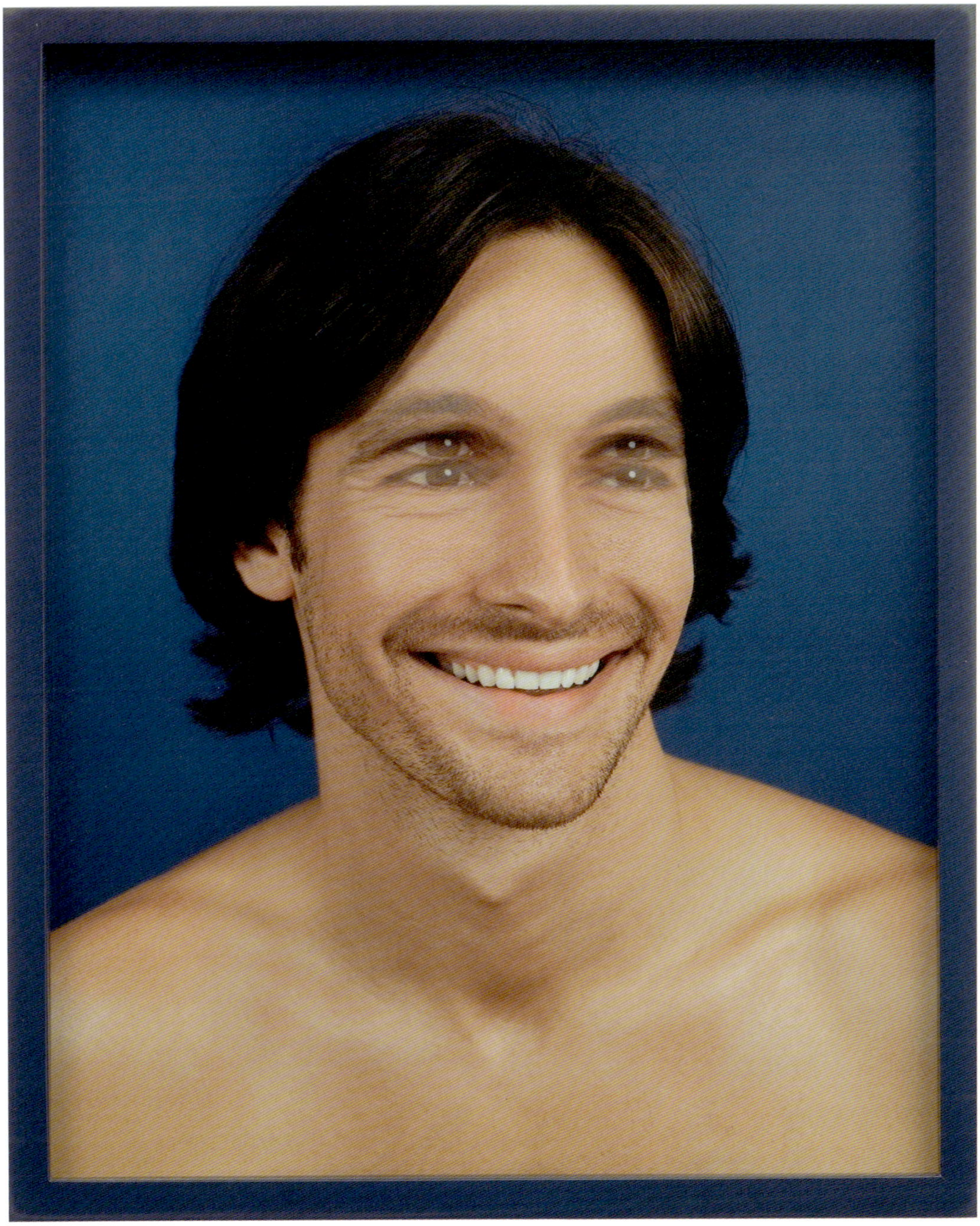

*Man 071*, 2007

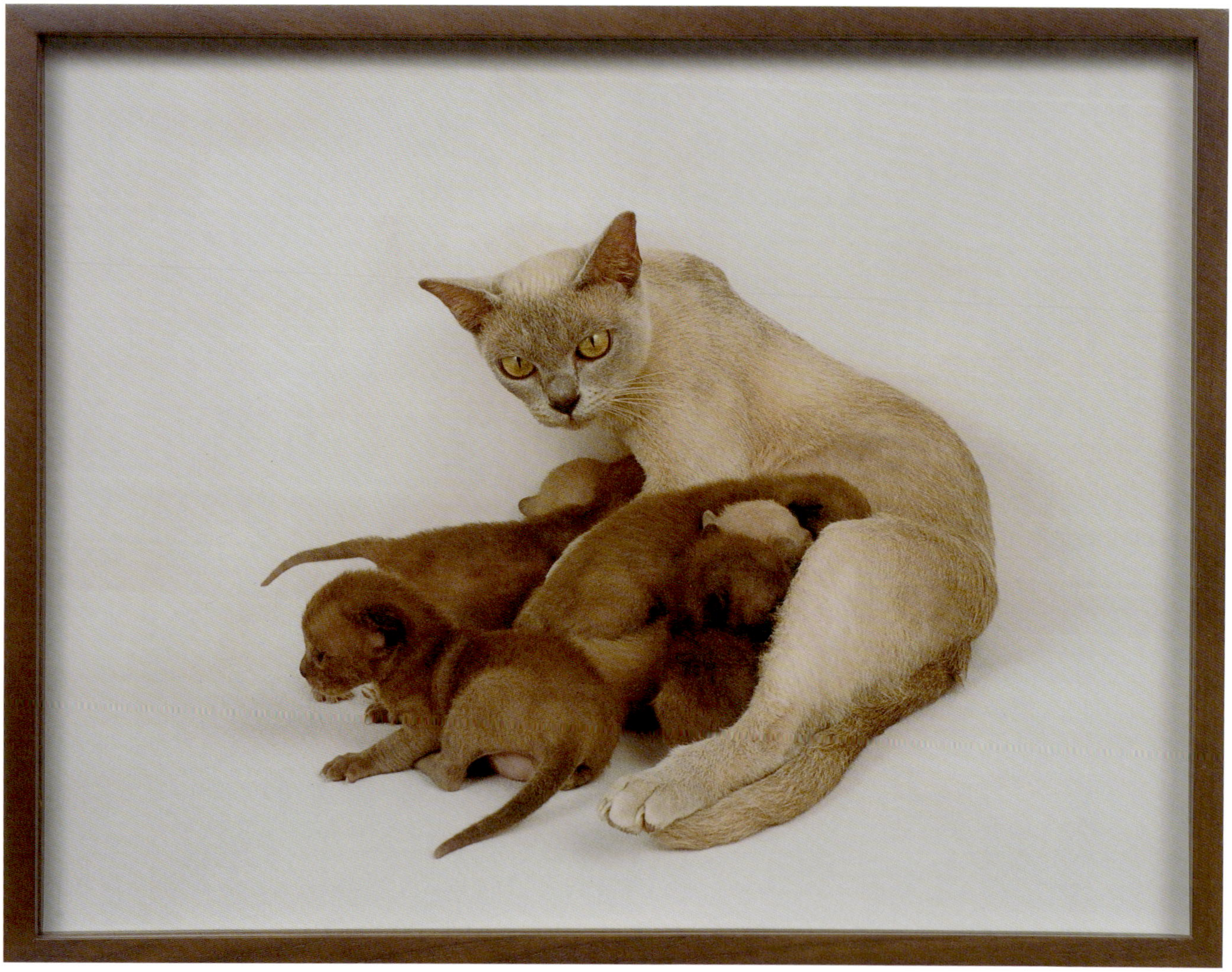

*Burmese Mother, Kittens*, 2008

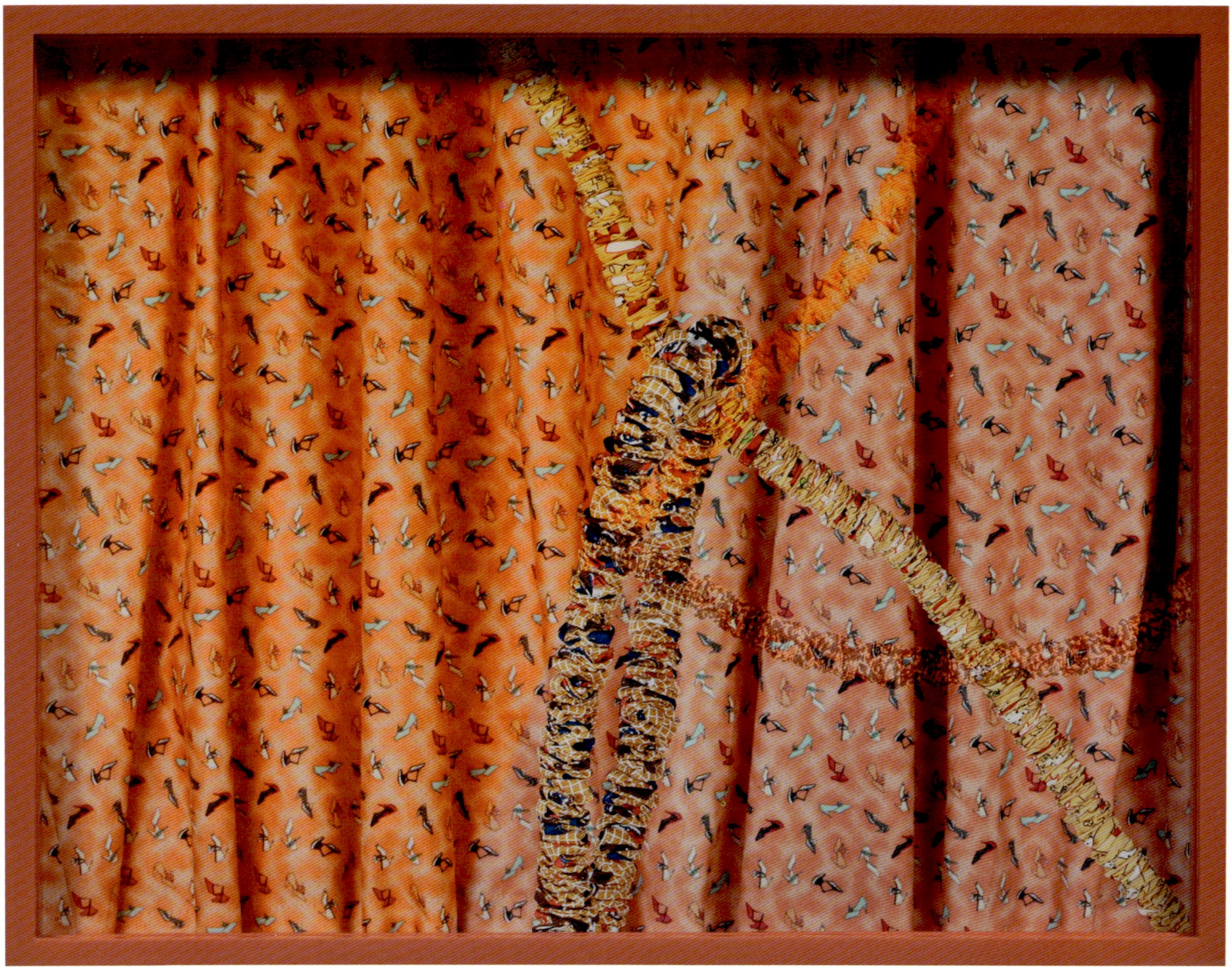

*Shoes, Ropes*, 2009

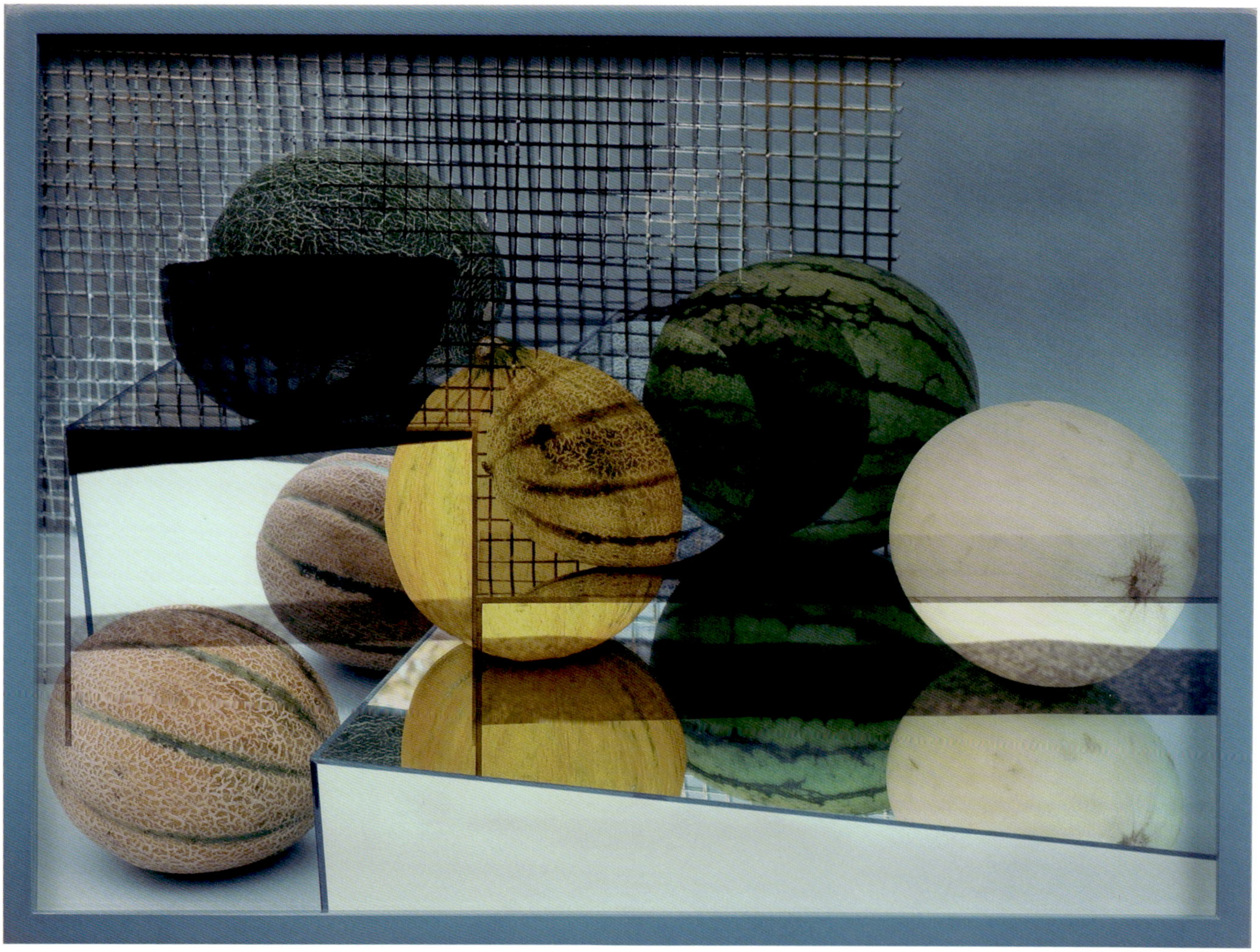

*Circles and Squares (A Tasteful Organic Melons Arrangement) 2*, 2007

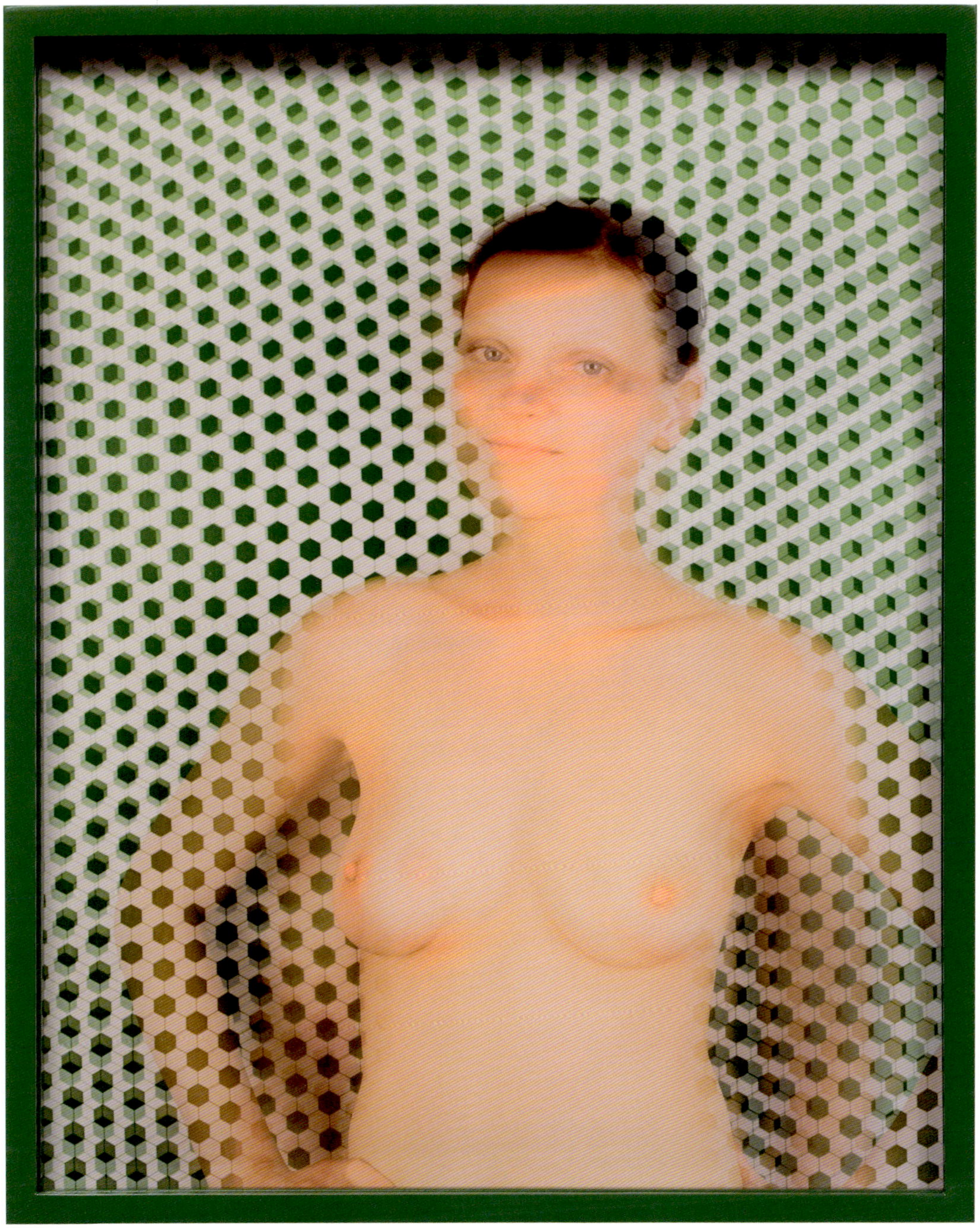

*Guinevere (Green)*, 2009

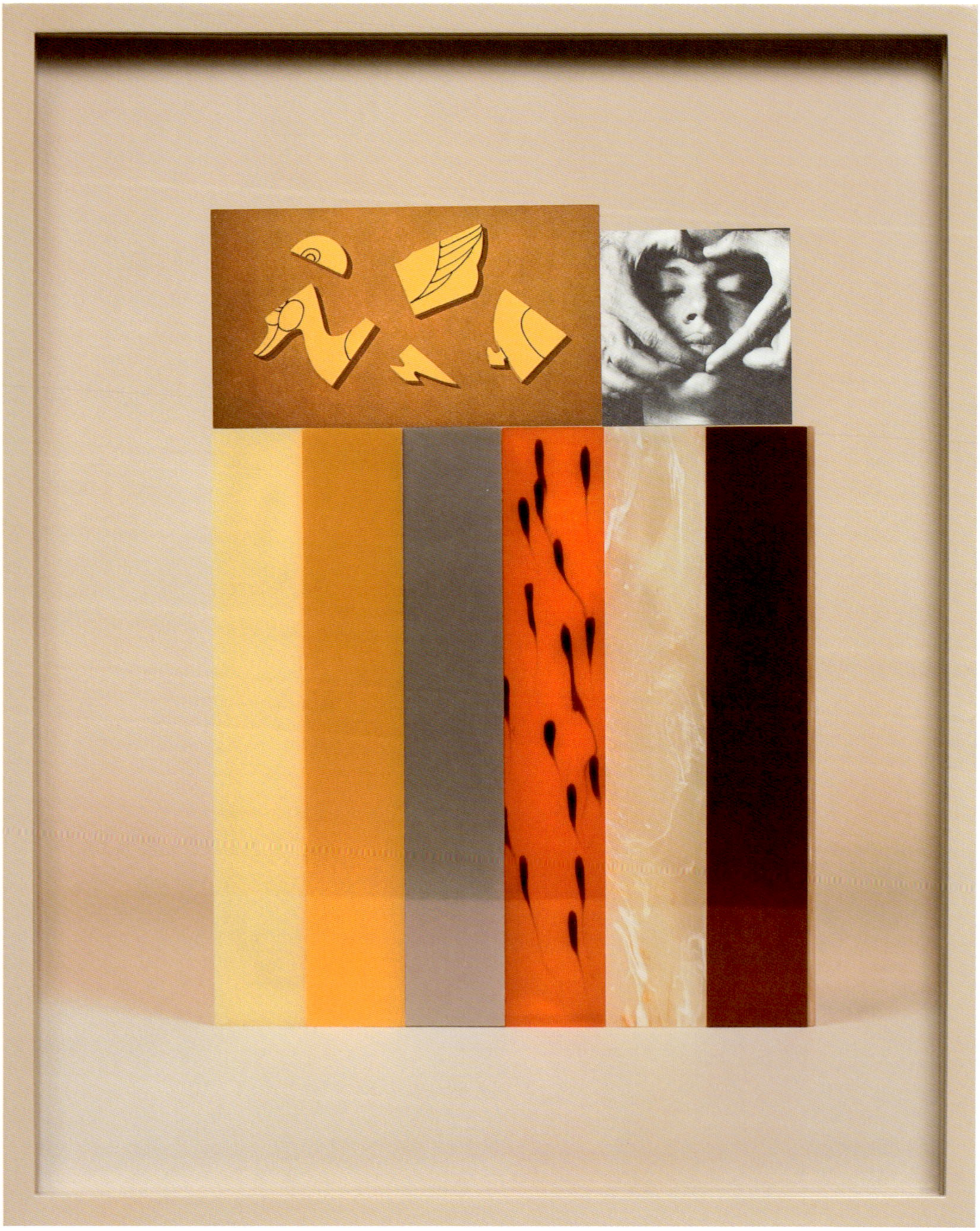

*Laminated Structure (For Test and Heart)*, 2009

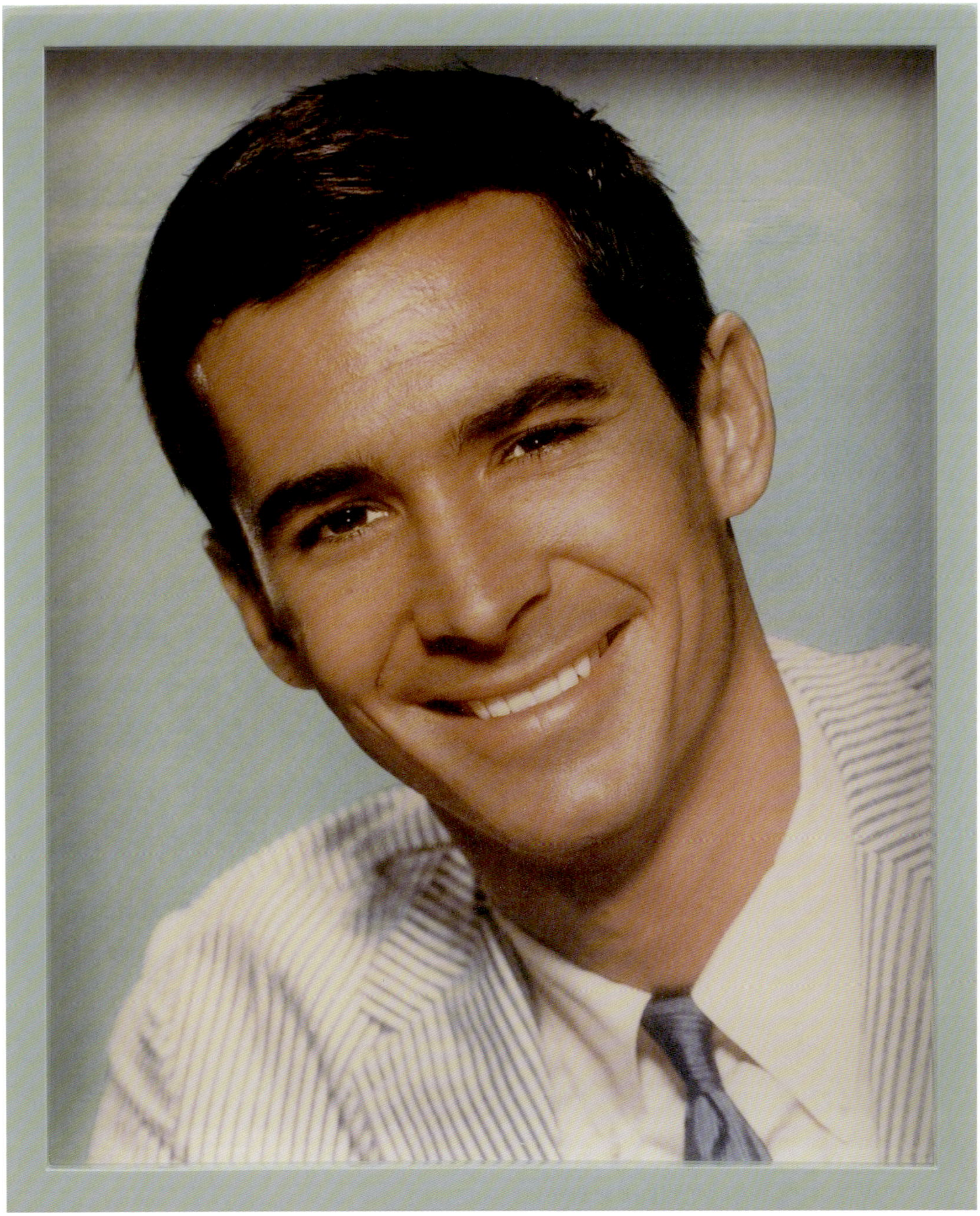

*Portrait, Navy Blue*, 2008

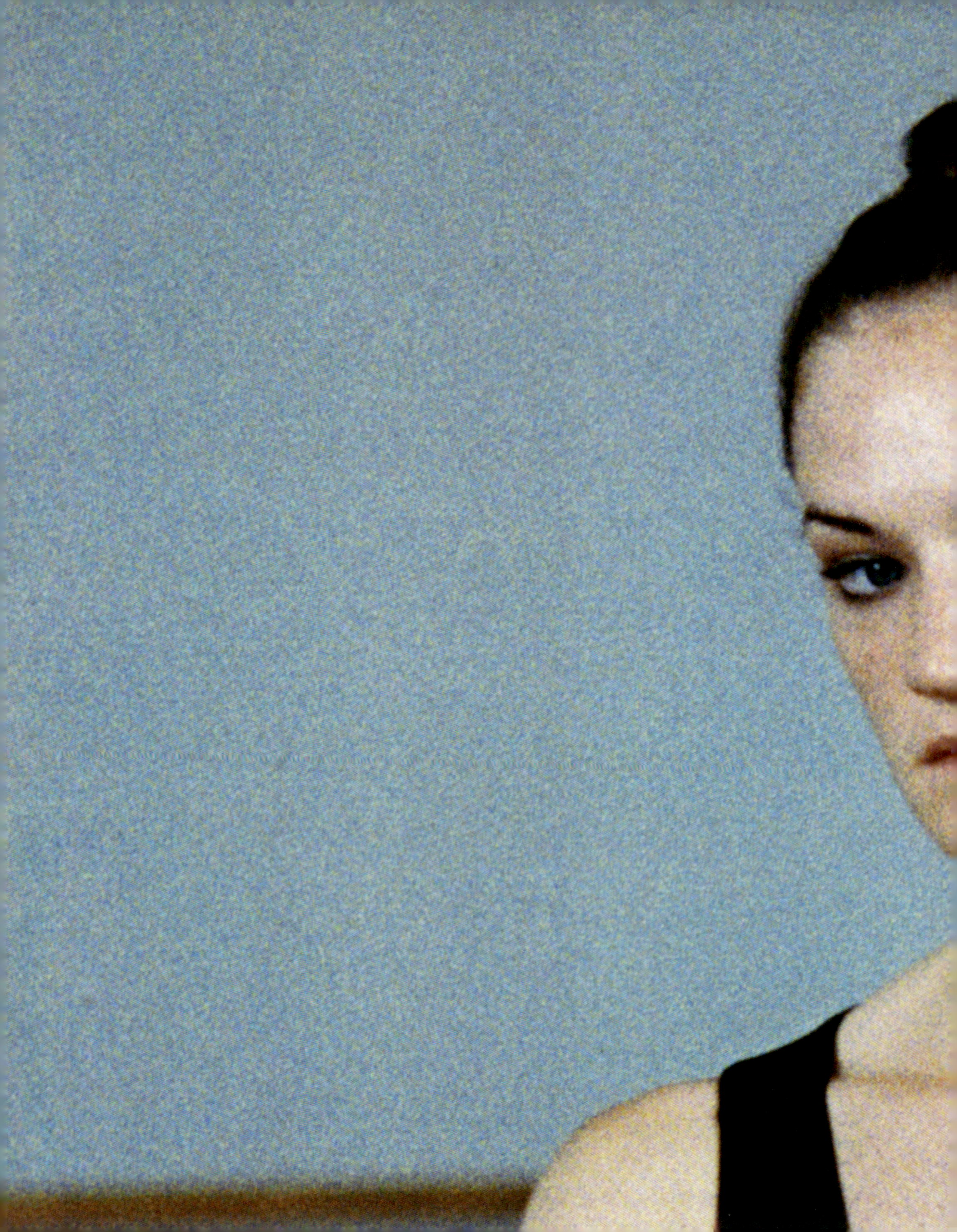

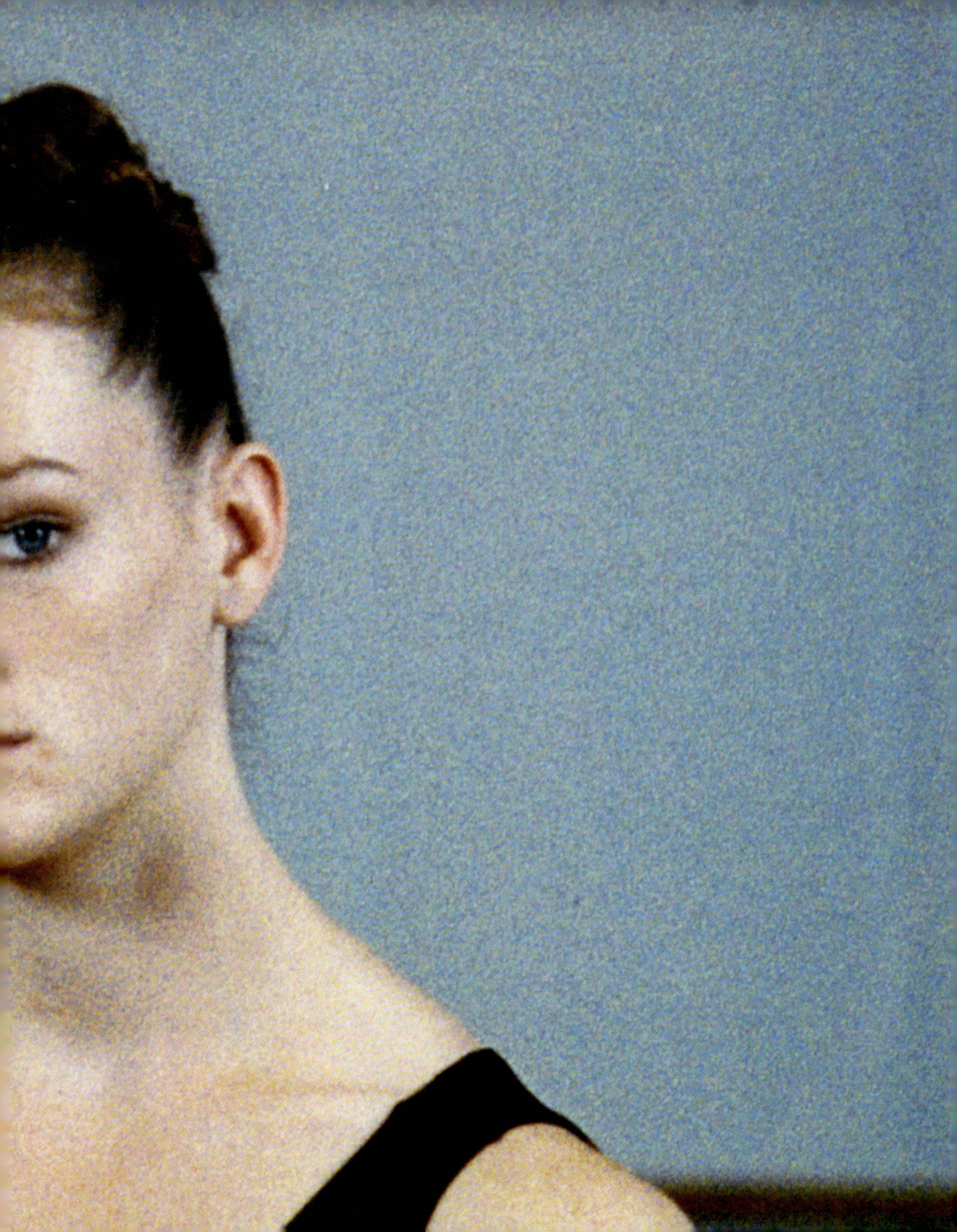

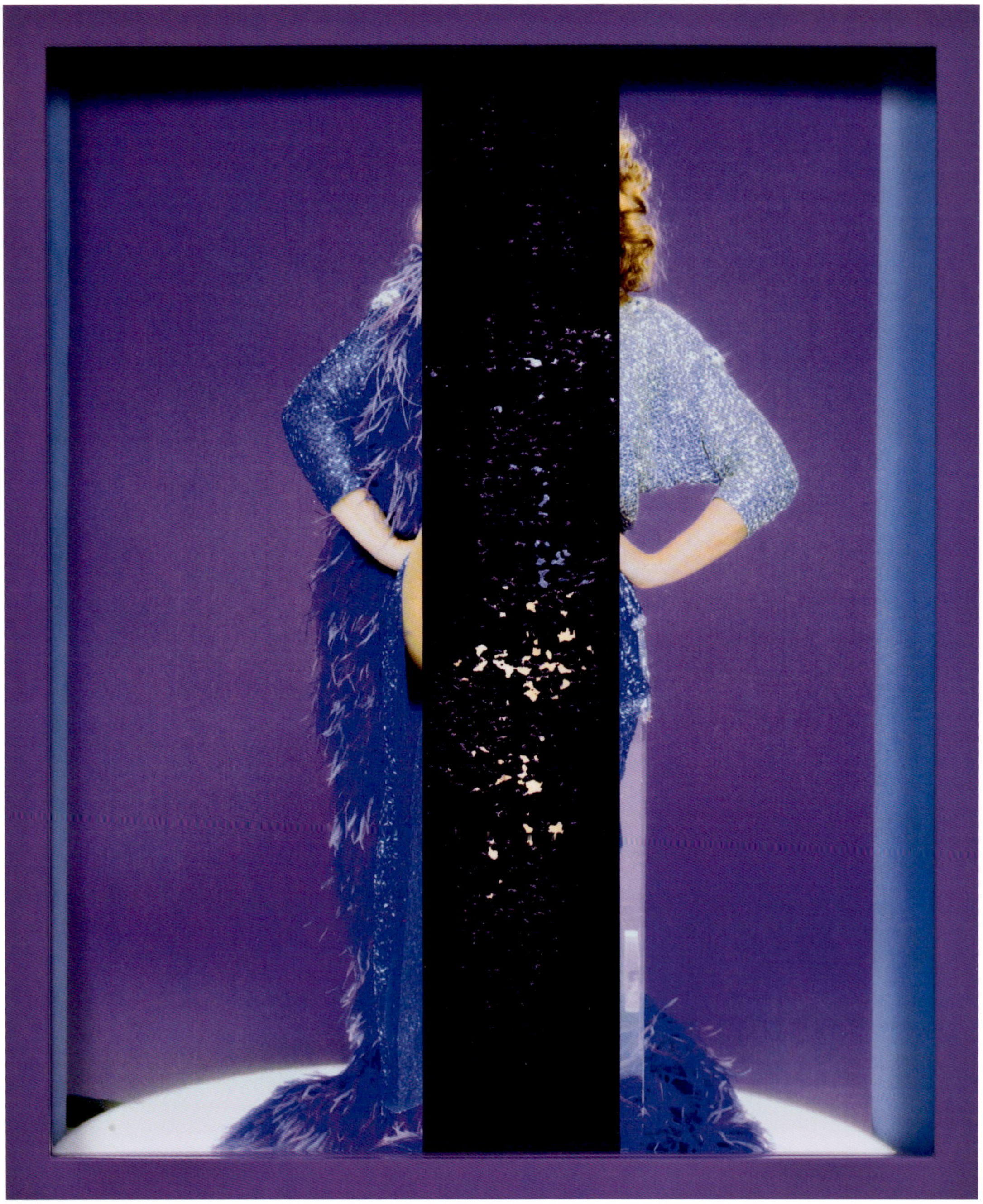

← *Untitled*, 2007

*Untitled (Purple Bar)*, 2009

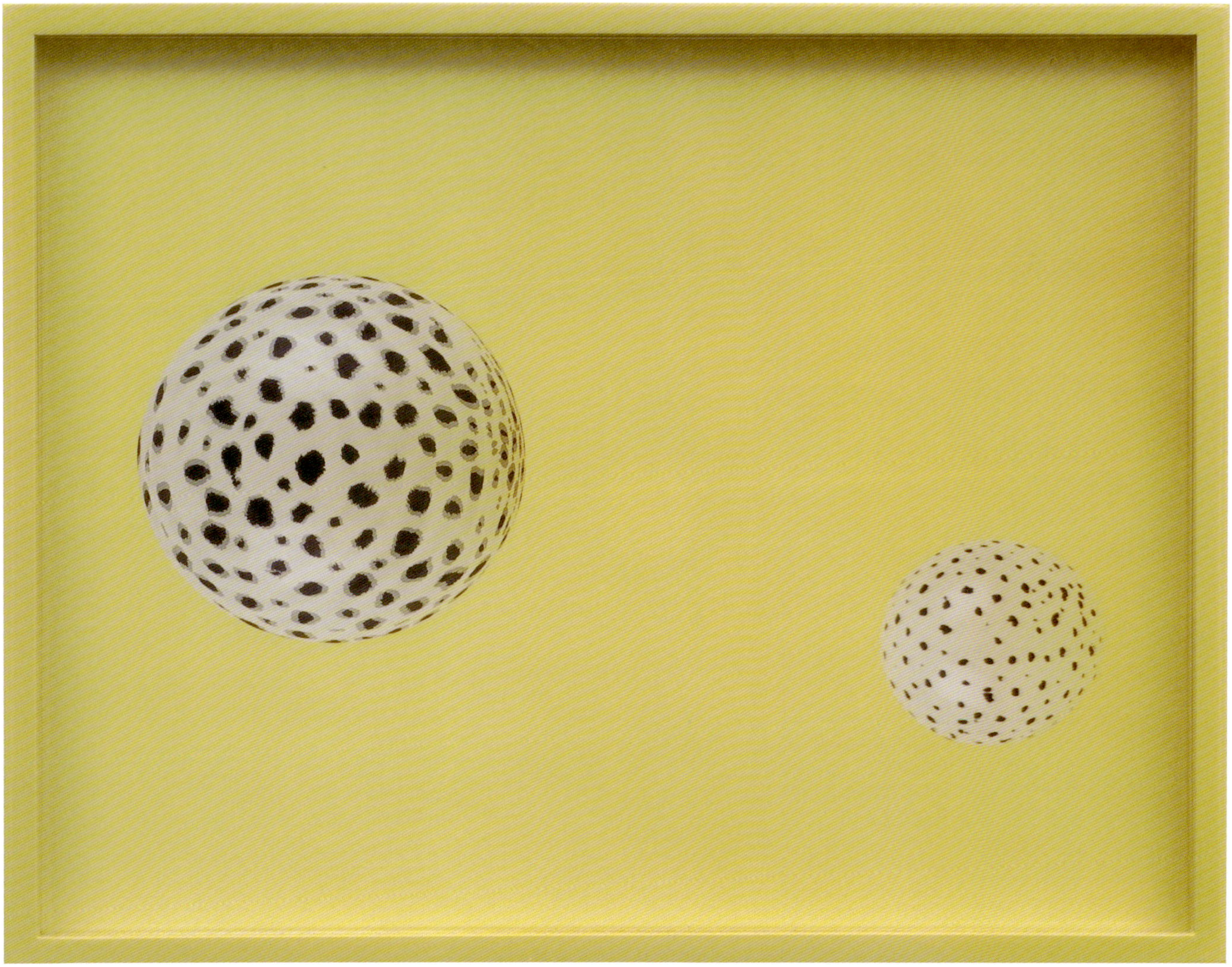

*Untitled (Cheetah)*, 2008

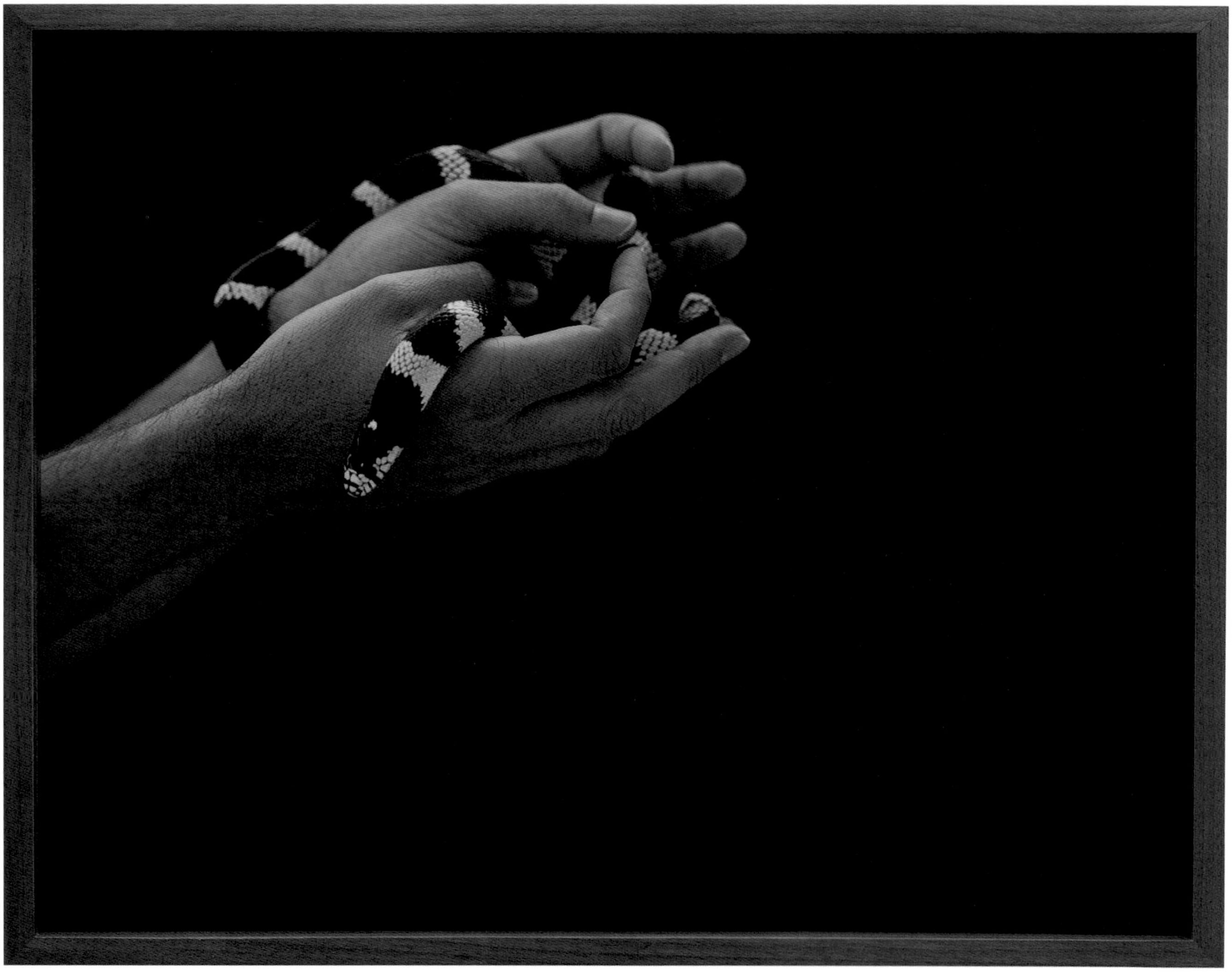

*California King Snake, CKS*, 2007

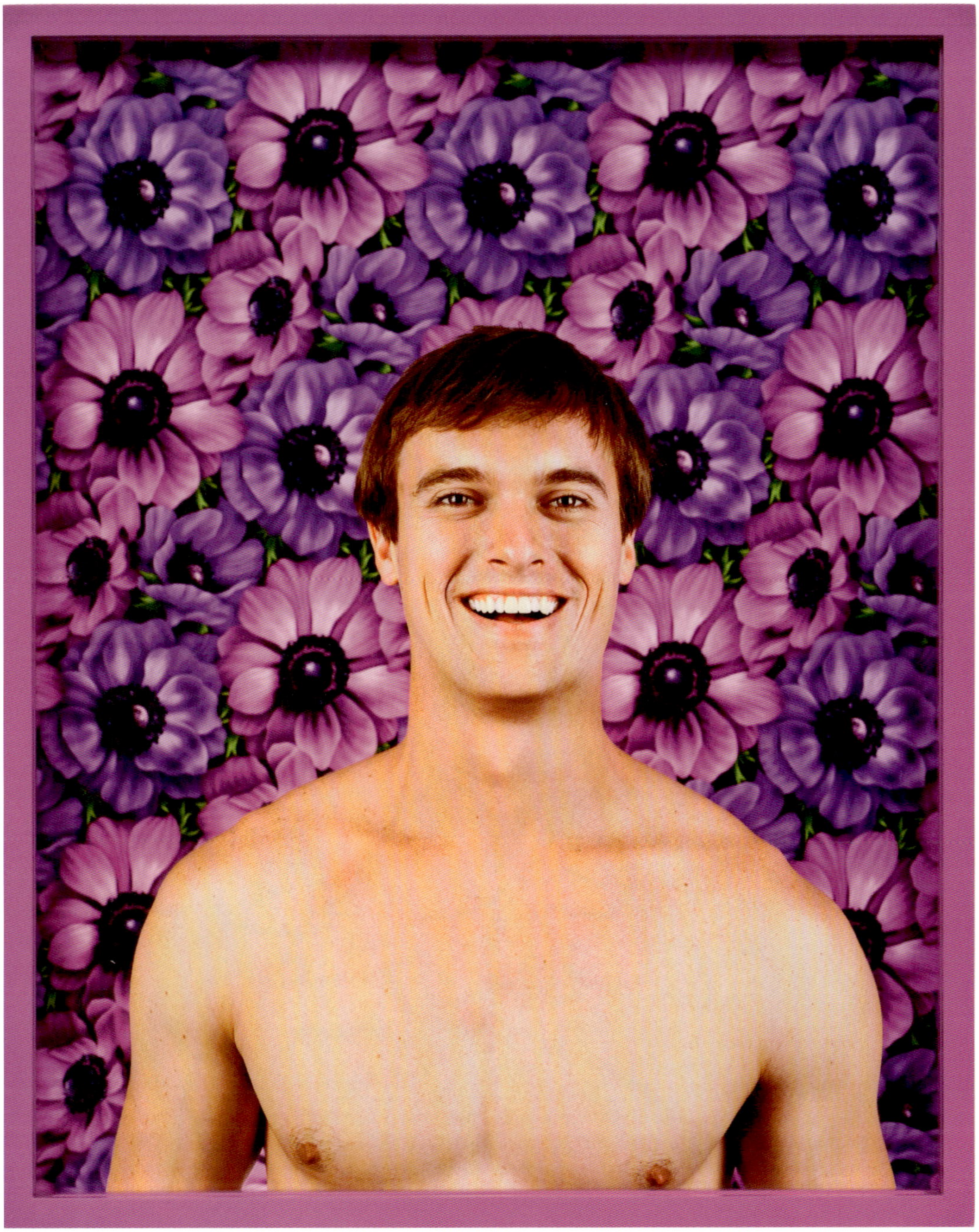

*Philip Pruitt*, 2009

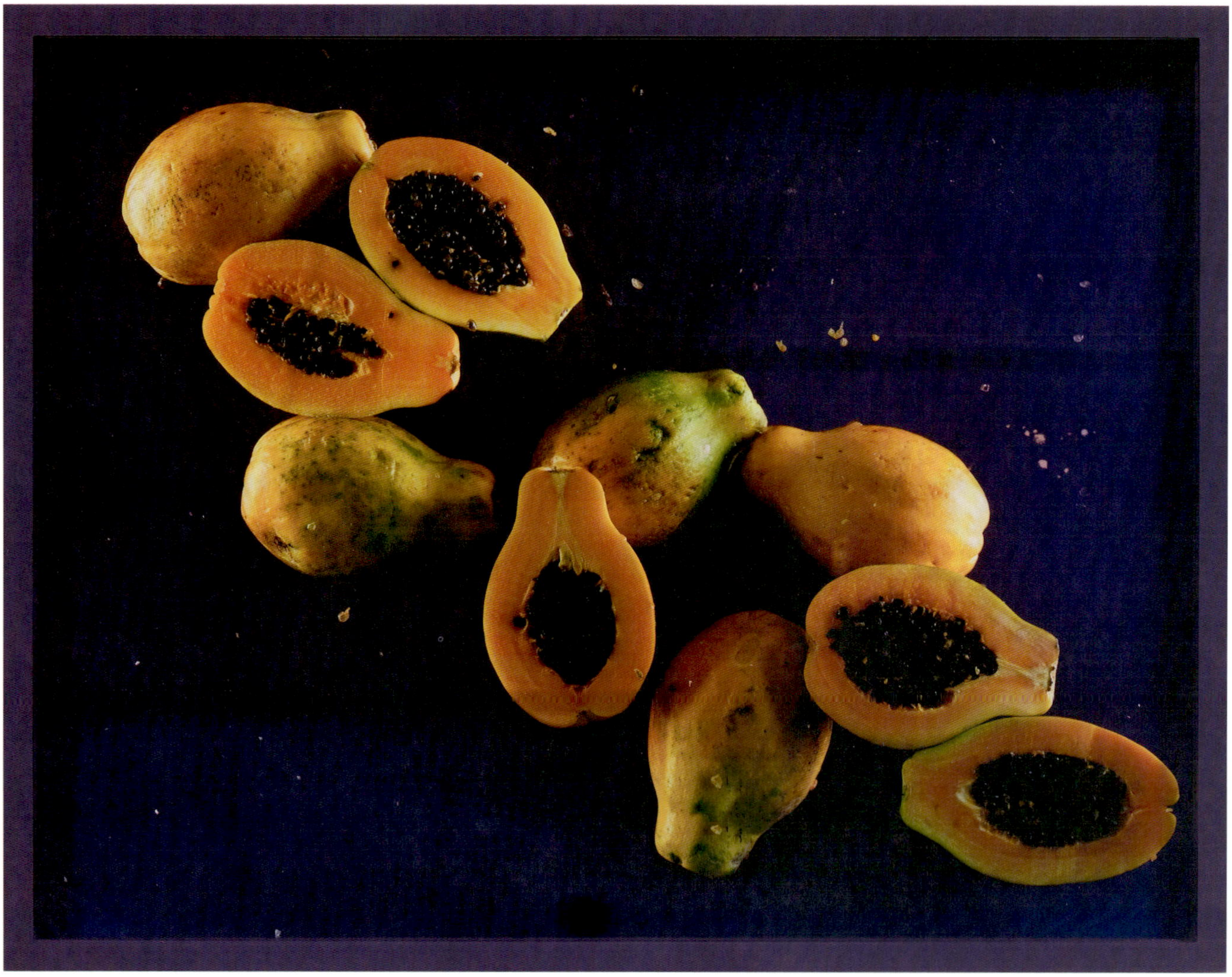

*Papayas*, 2009

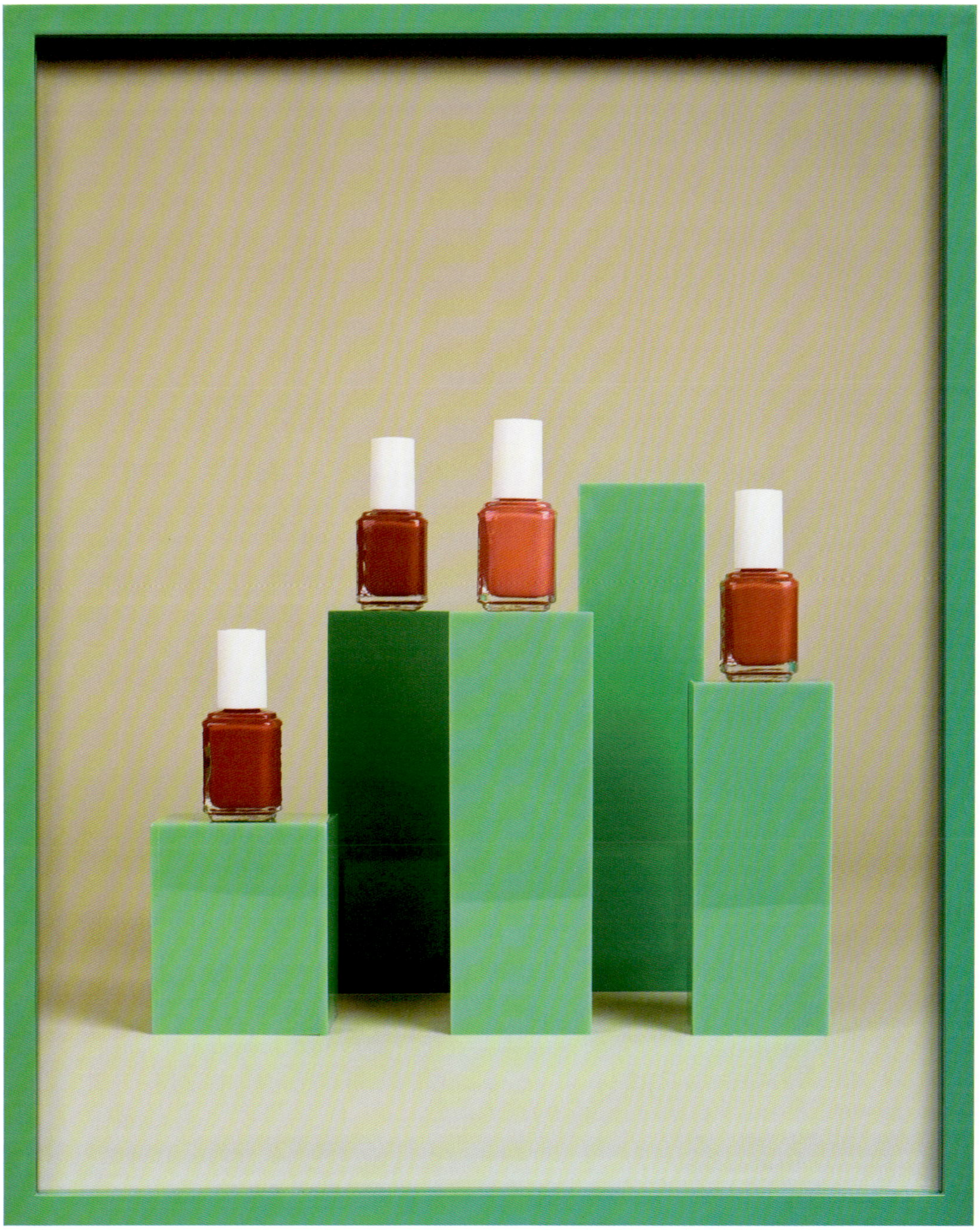

*Nail Polish*, 2009

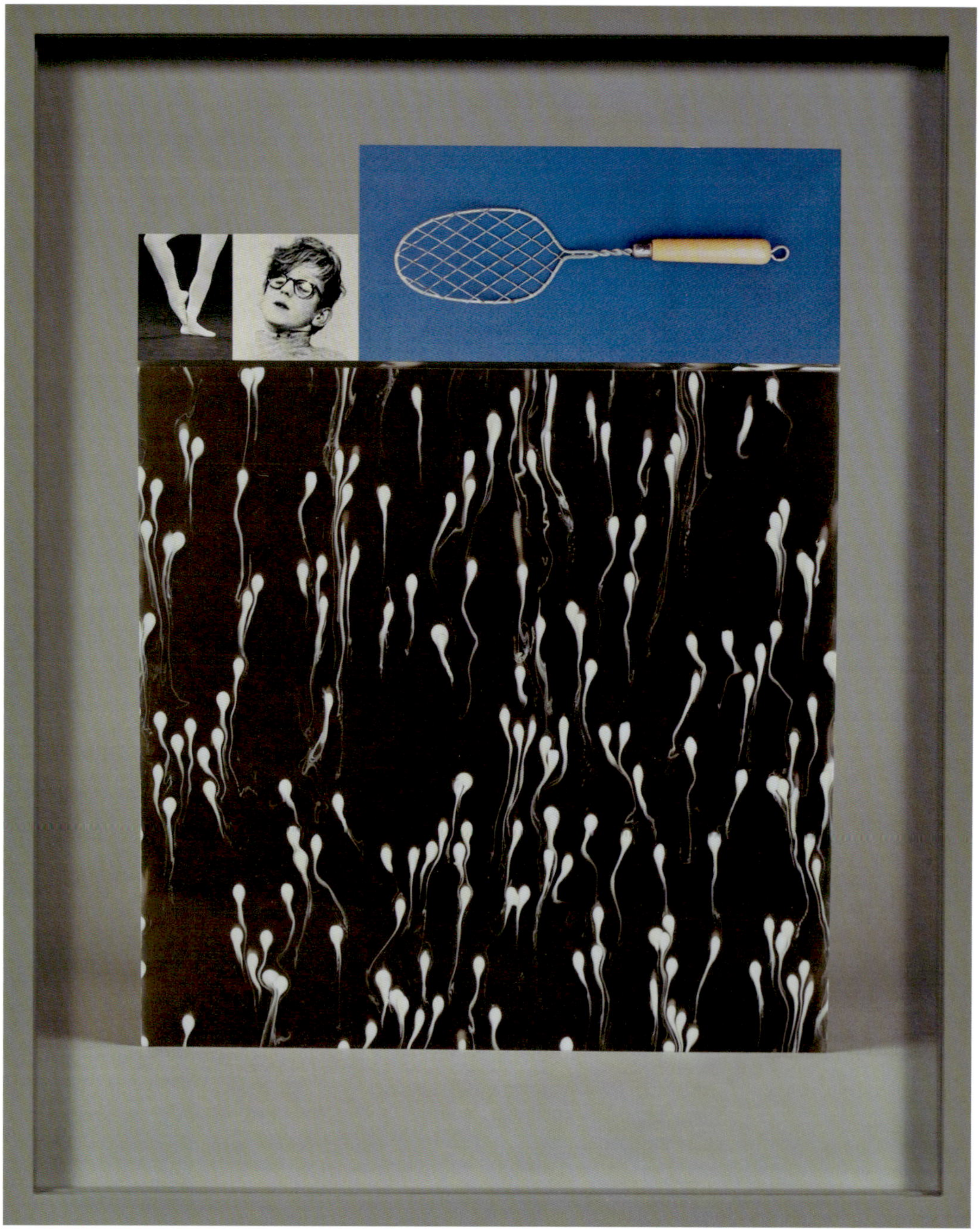

*Tadpole Structure (For Dancer, Boy and Collectable)*, 2009

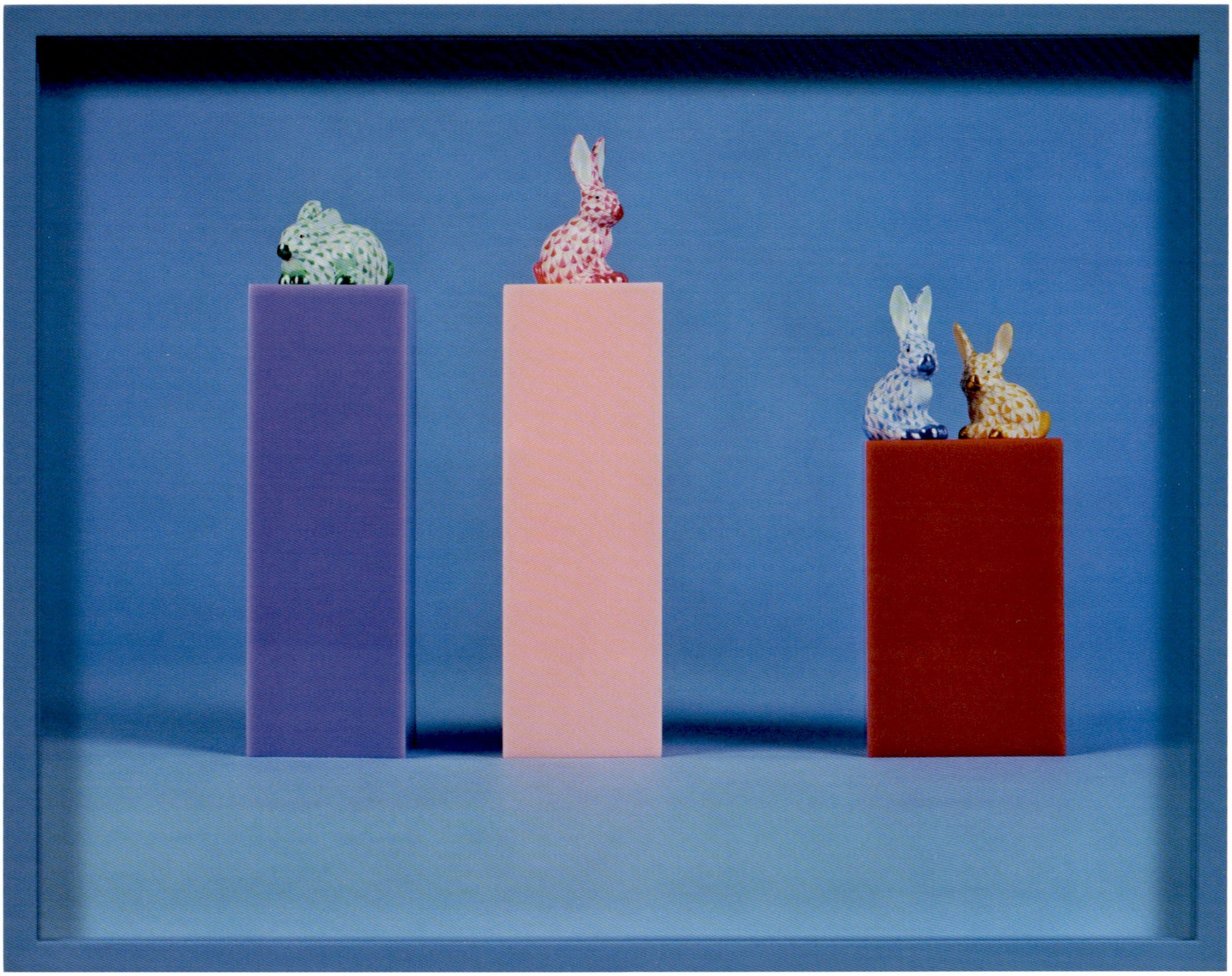

*Bunnies*, 2009

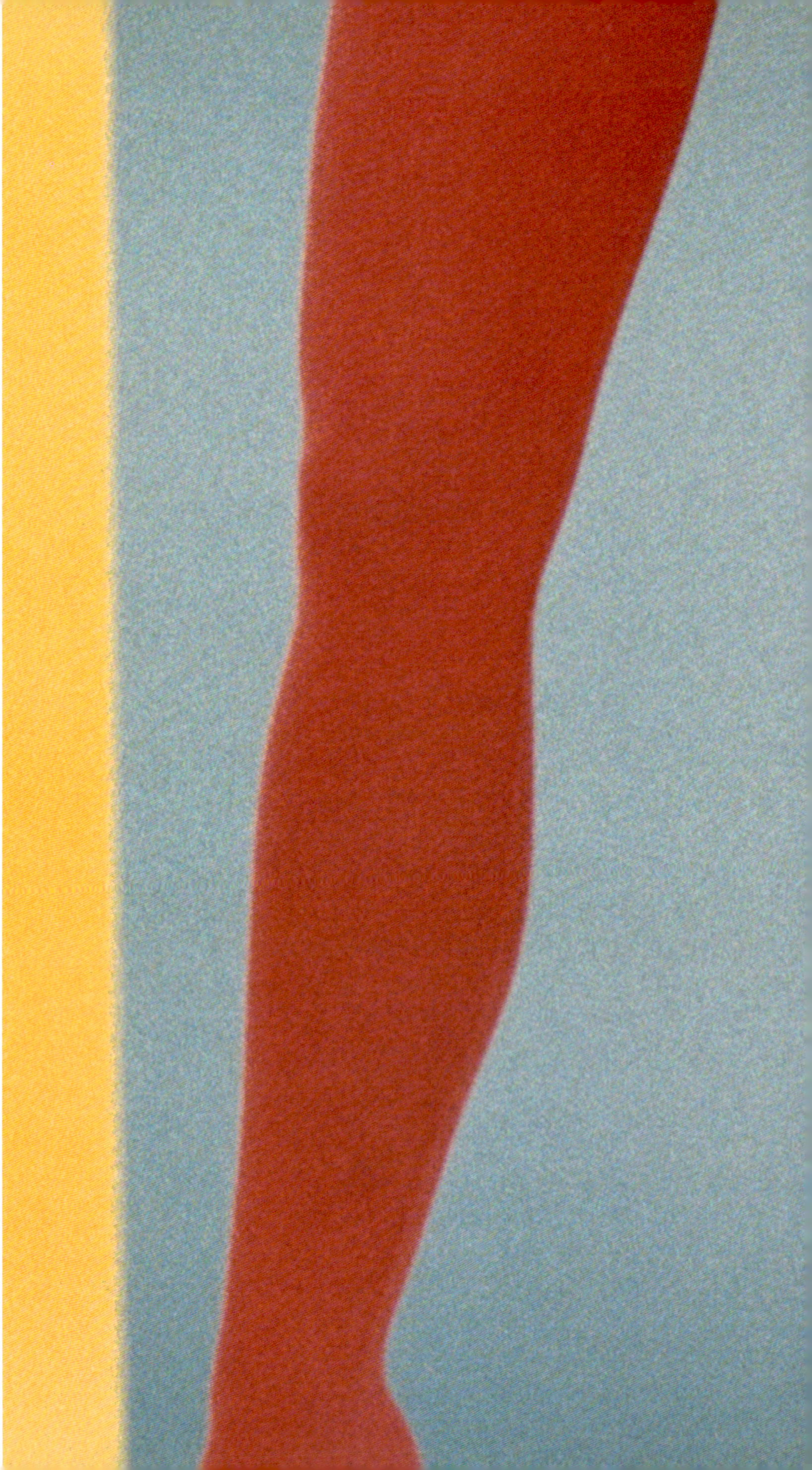

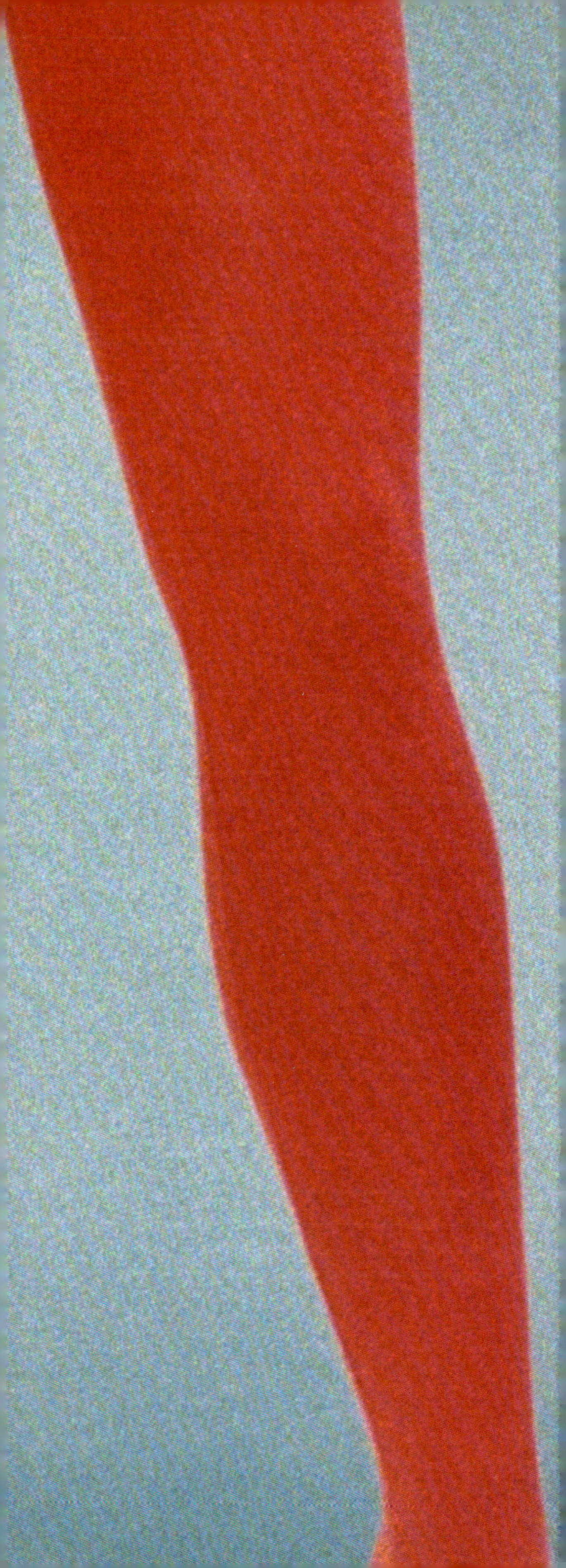

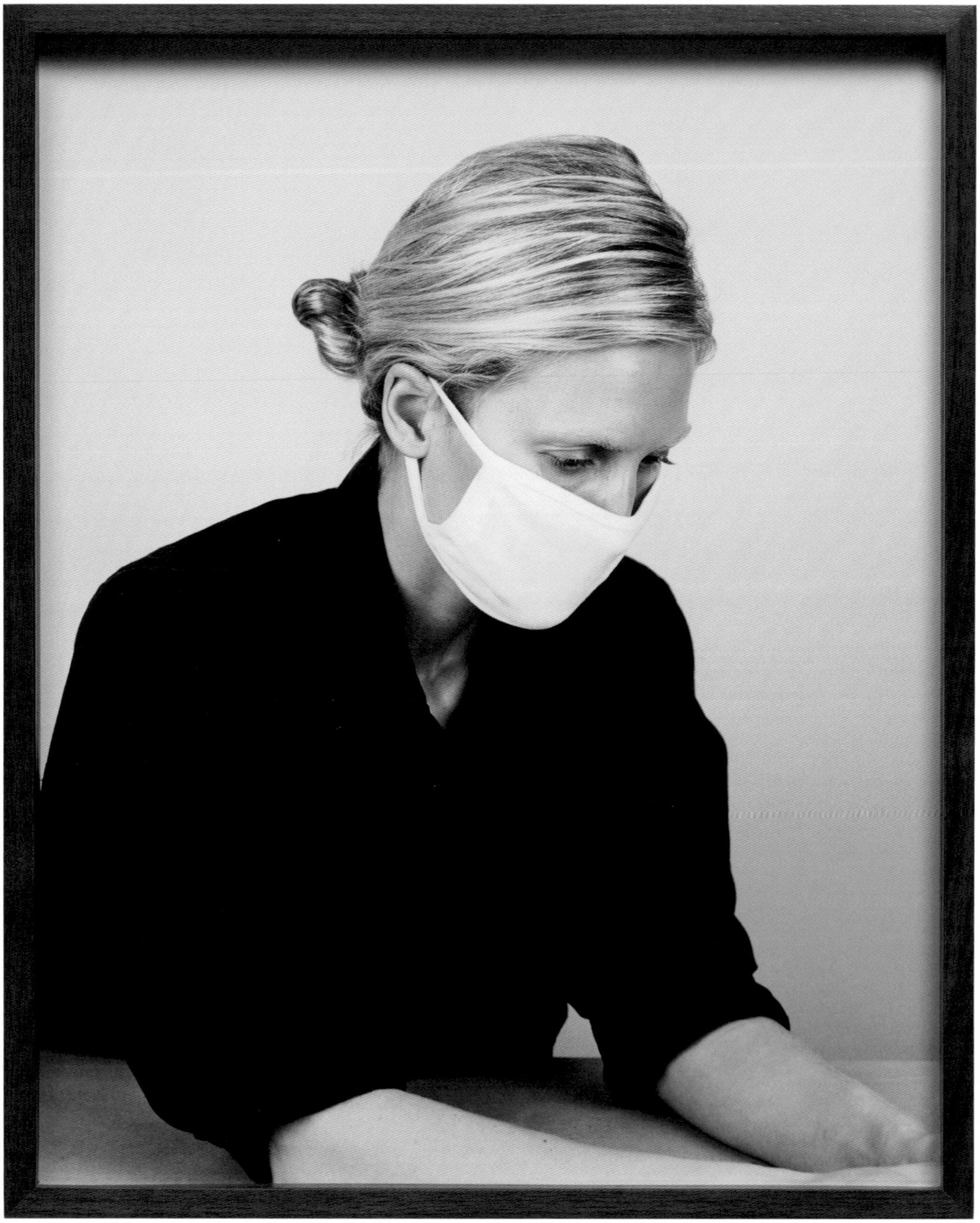

← *Untitled*, 2009

*Blonde Girl*, 2009

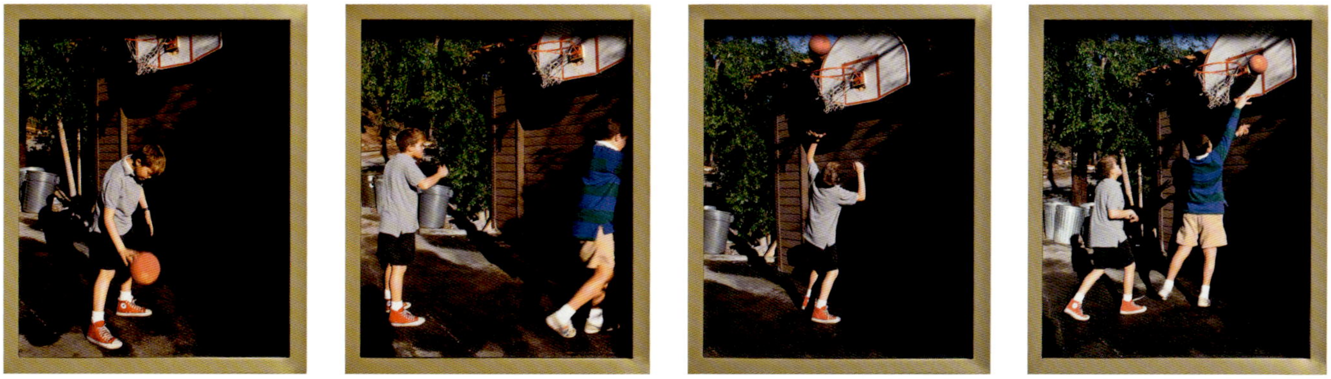

*Laurel Canyon*, 2009

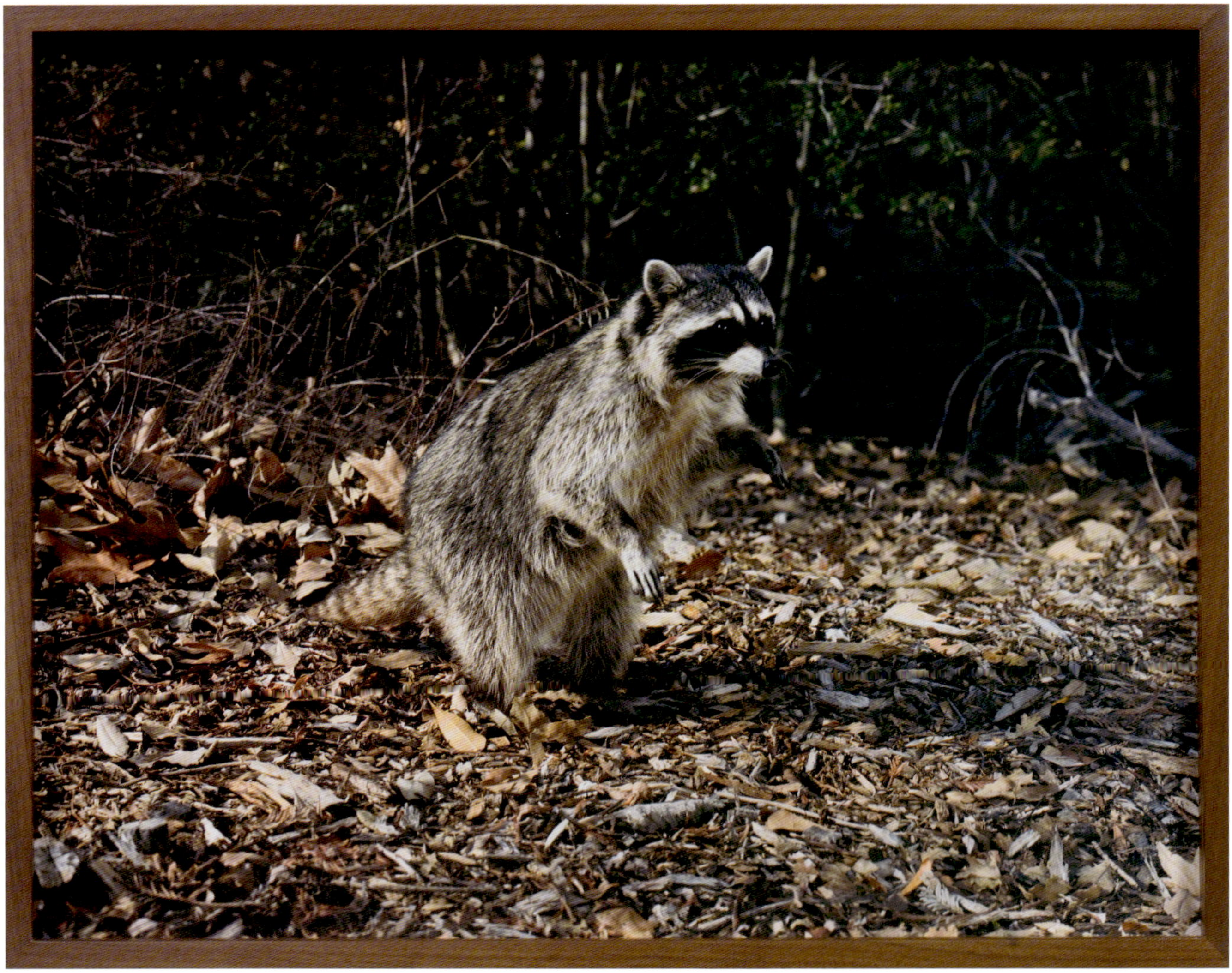

*Raccoon B*, 2010

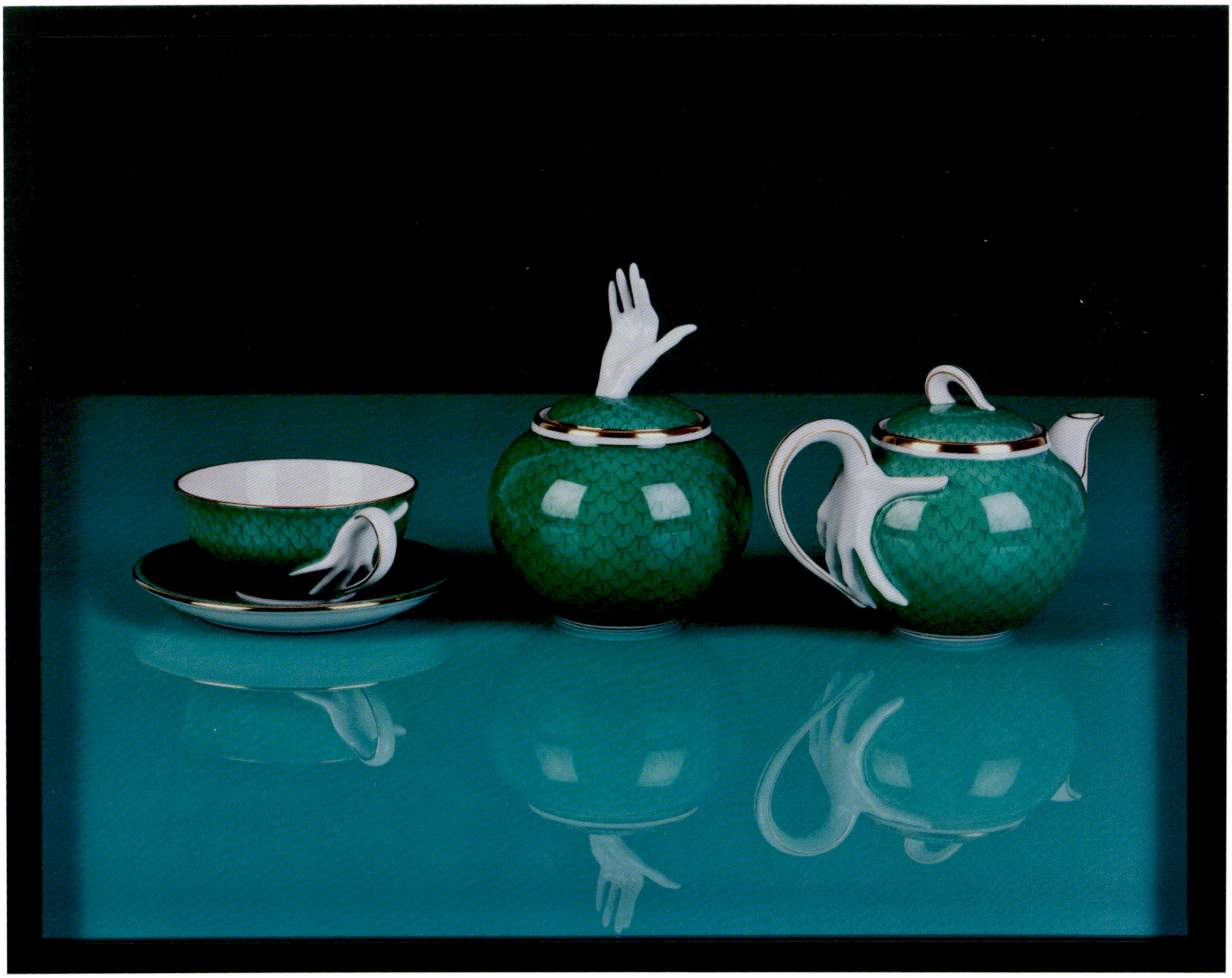

*Melocco*, 2009

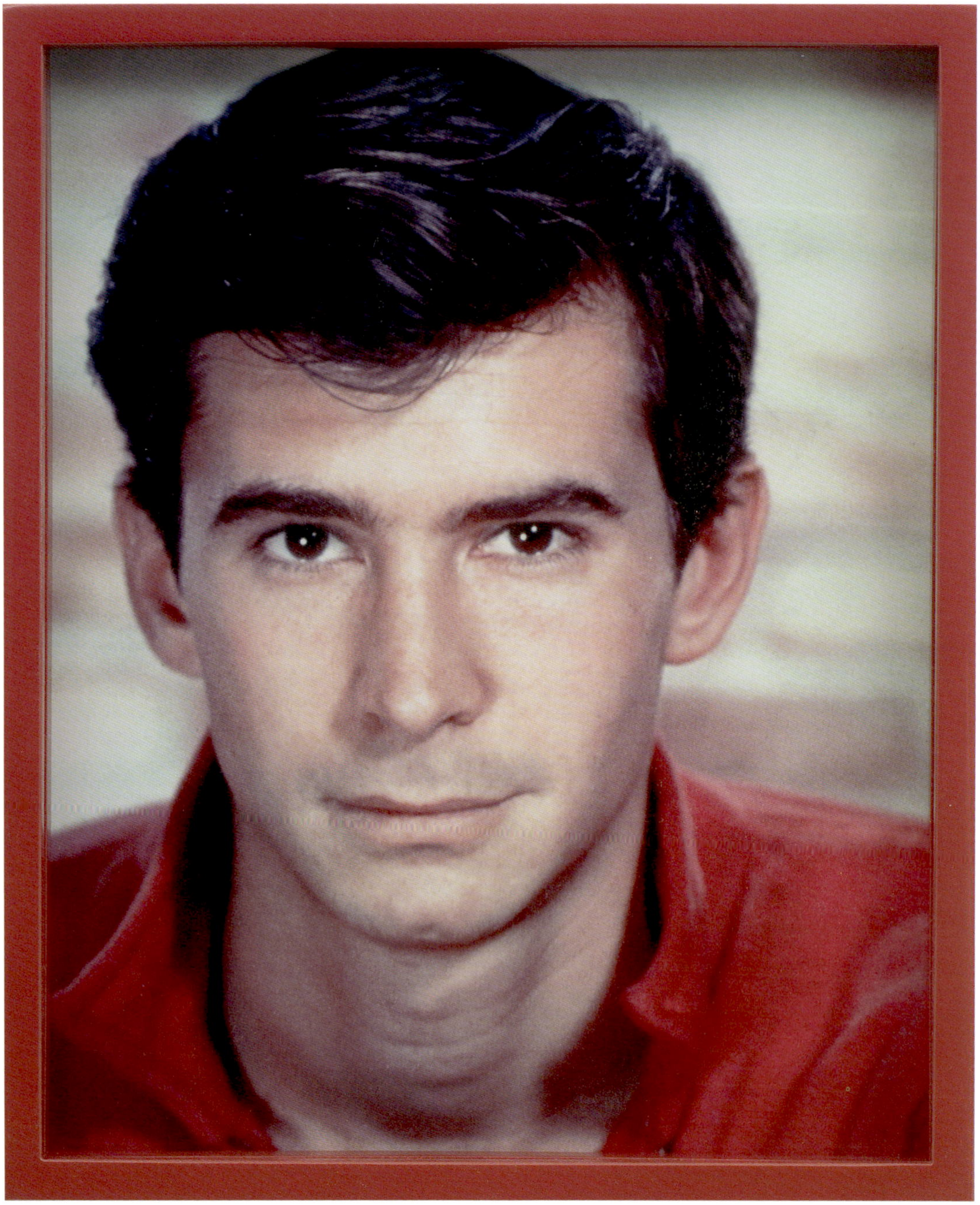

*Portrait, Amarant Red*, 2008

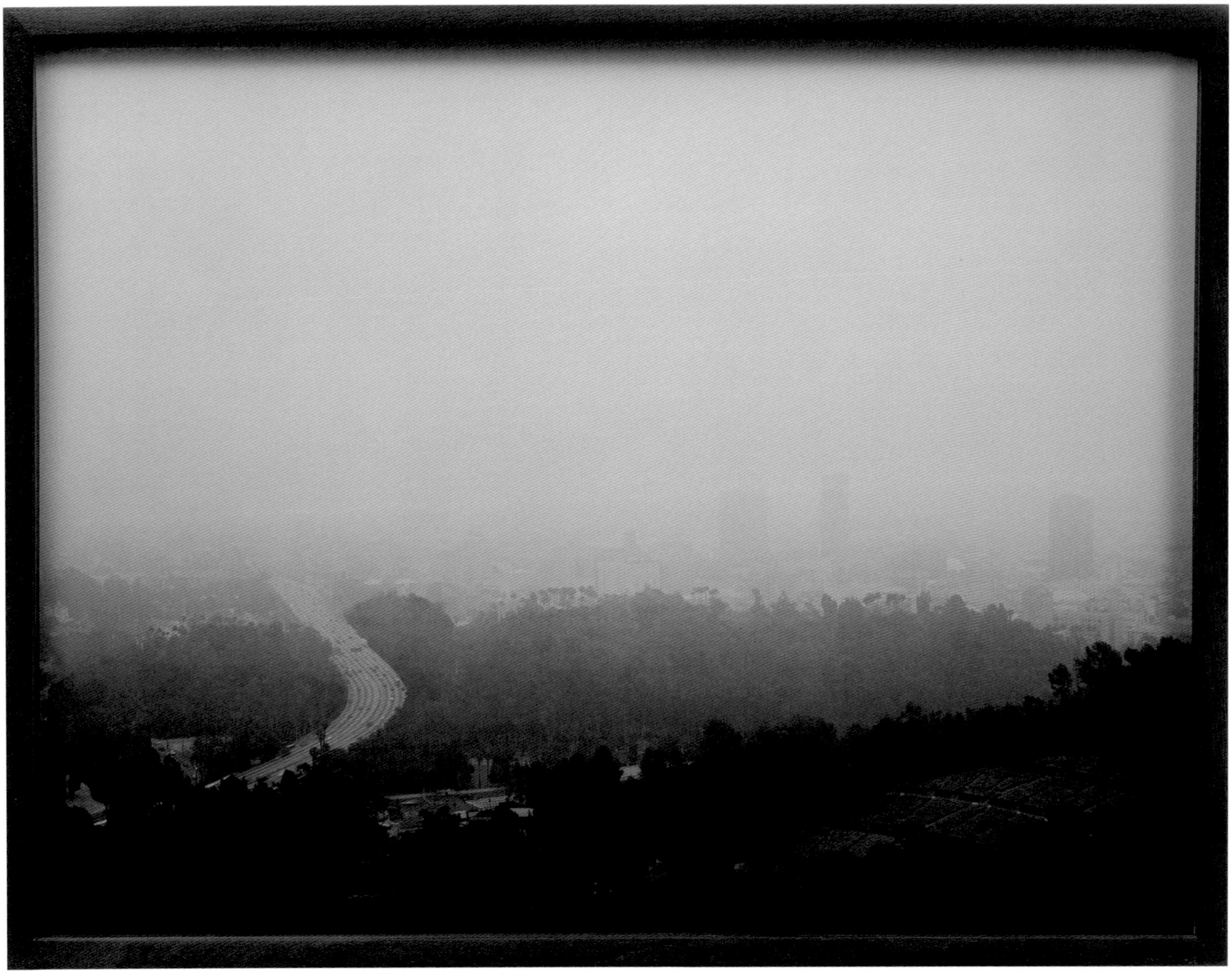

*Hollywood Bowl, Fog*, 2007

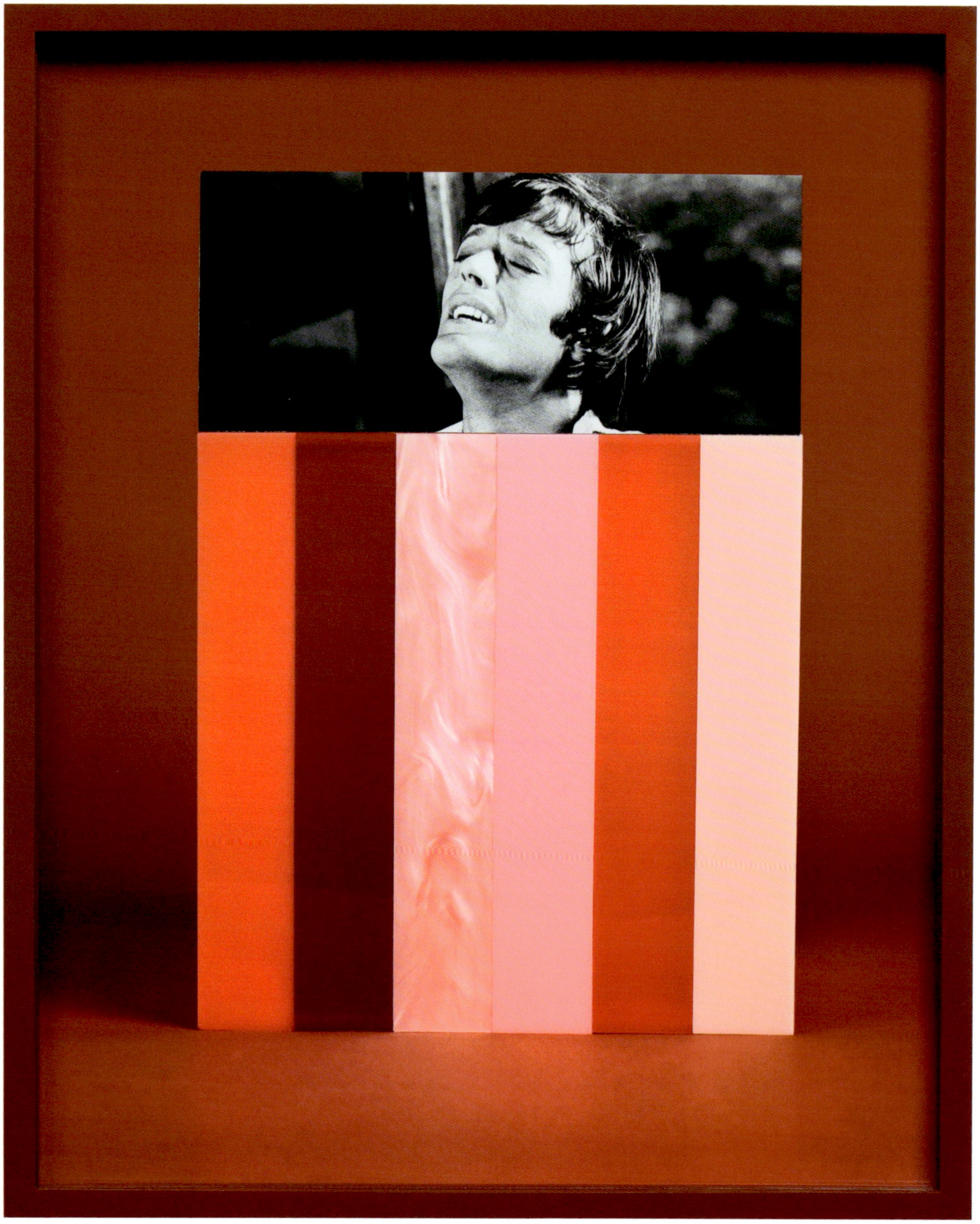

*Laminated Structure (For Him)*, 2009

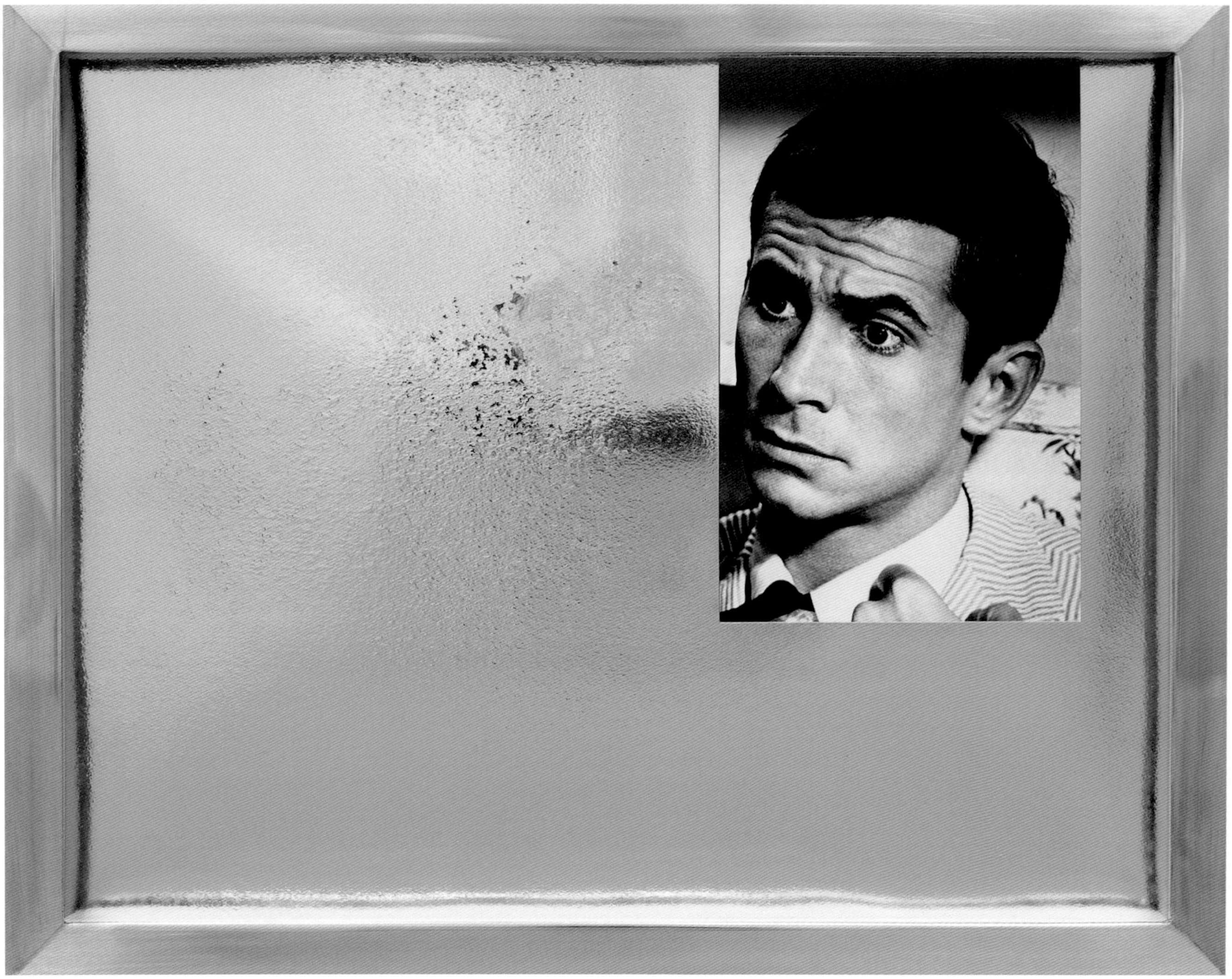

*Portrait 2 (Silver)*, 2009

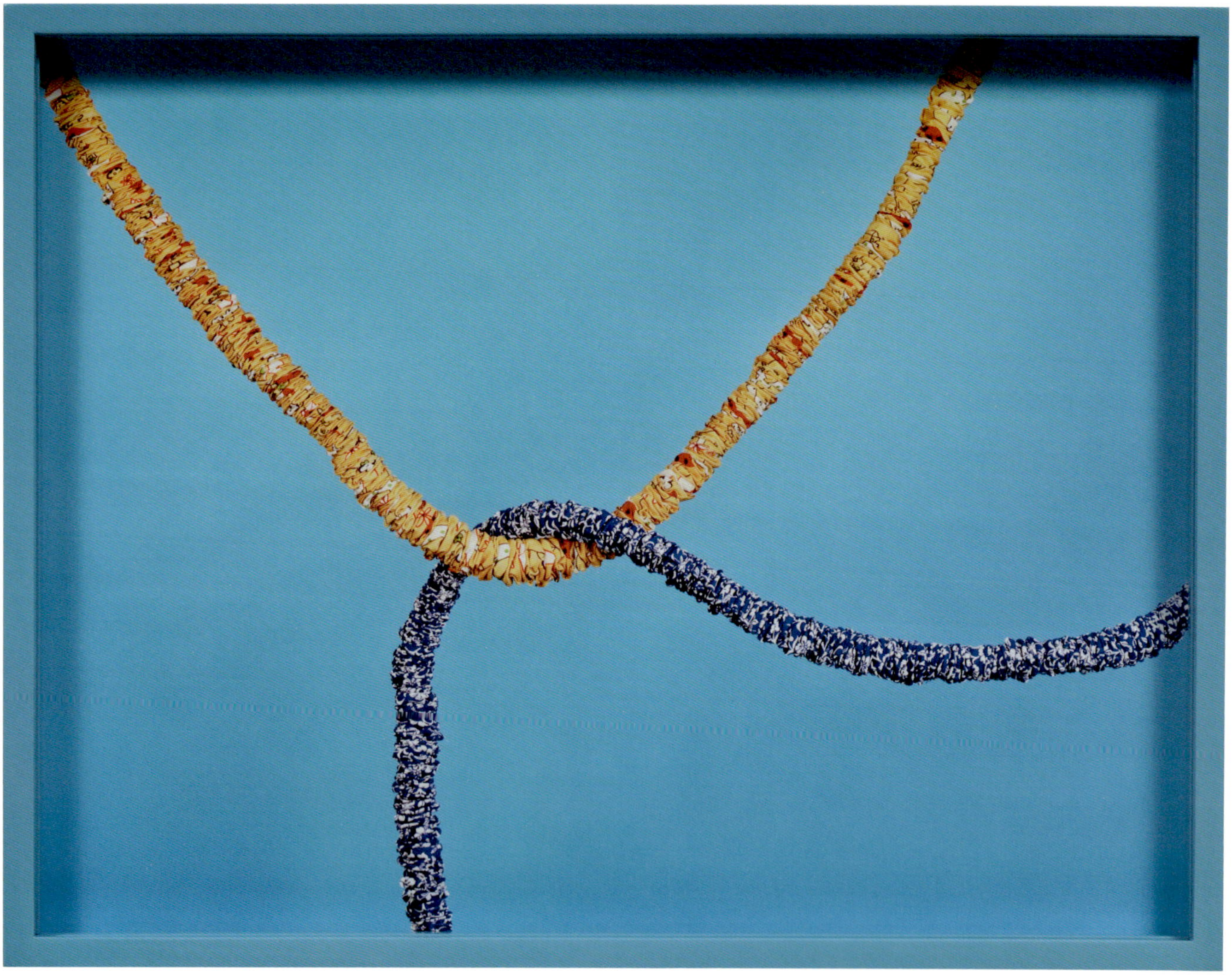

*Ropes*, 2009

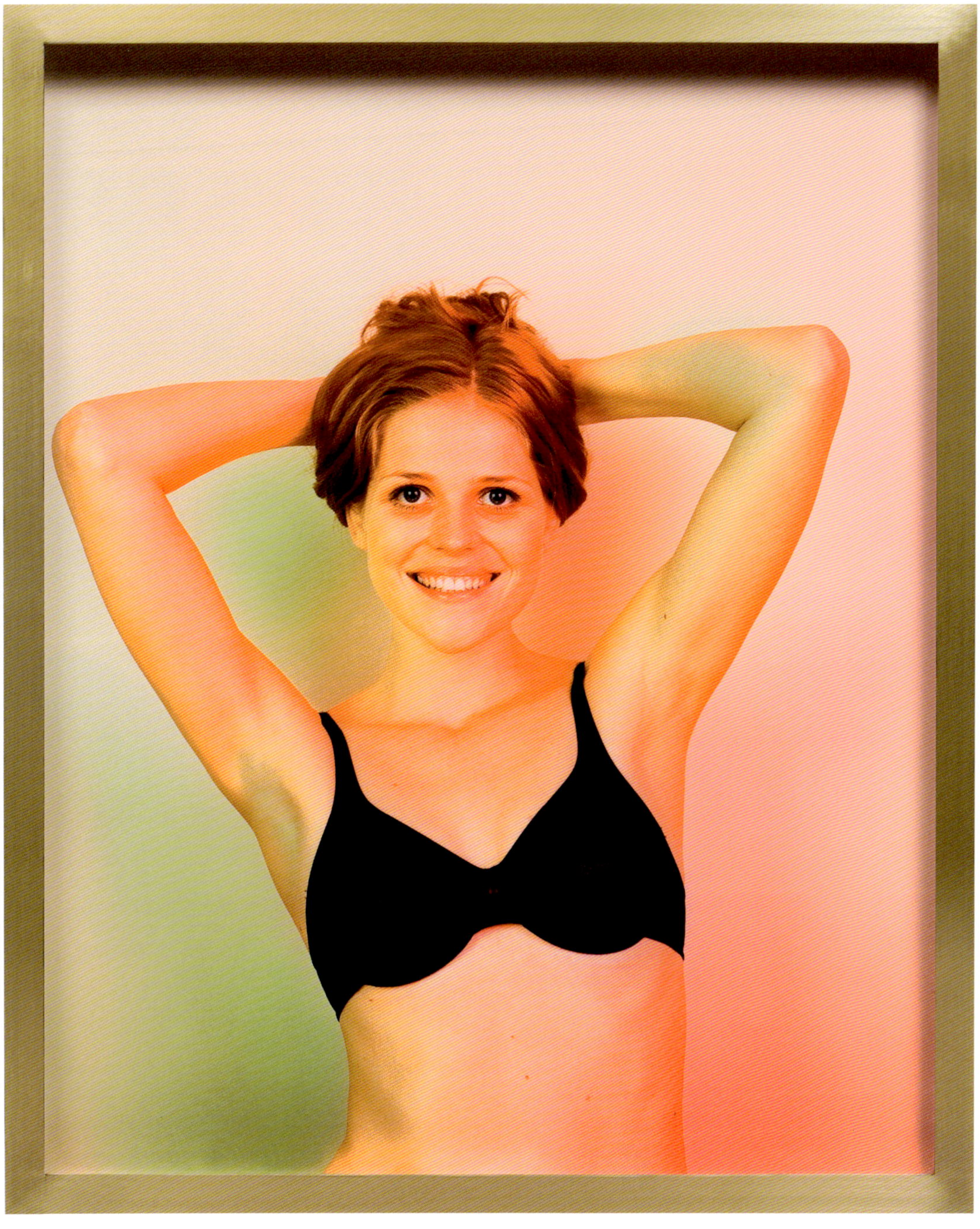

*Czech Girl*, 2009

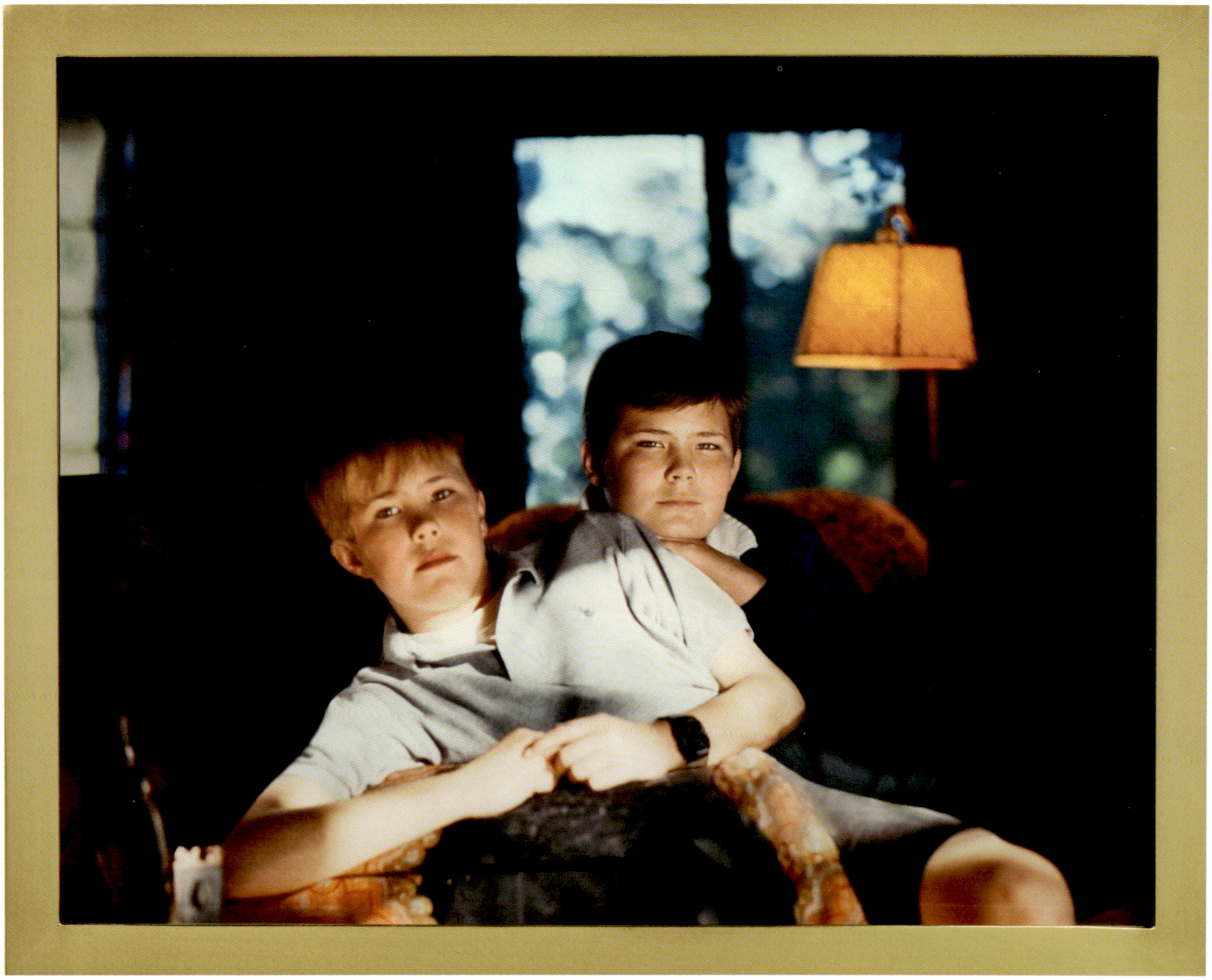

*Boys*, 2009

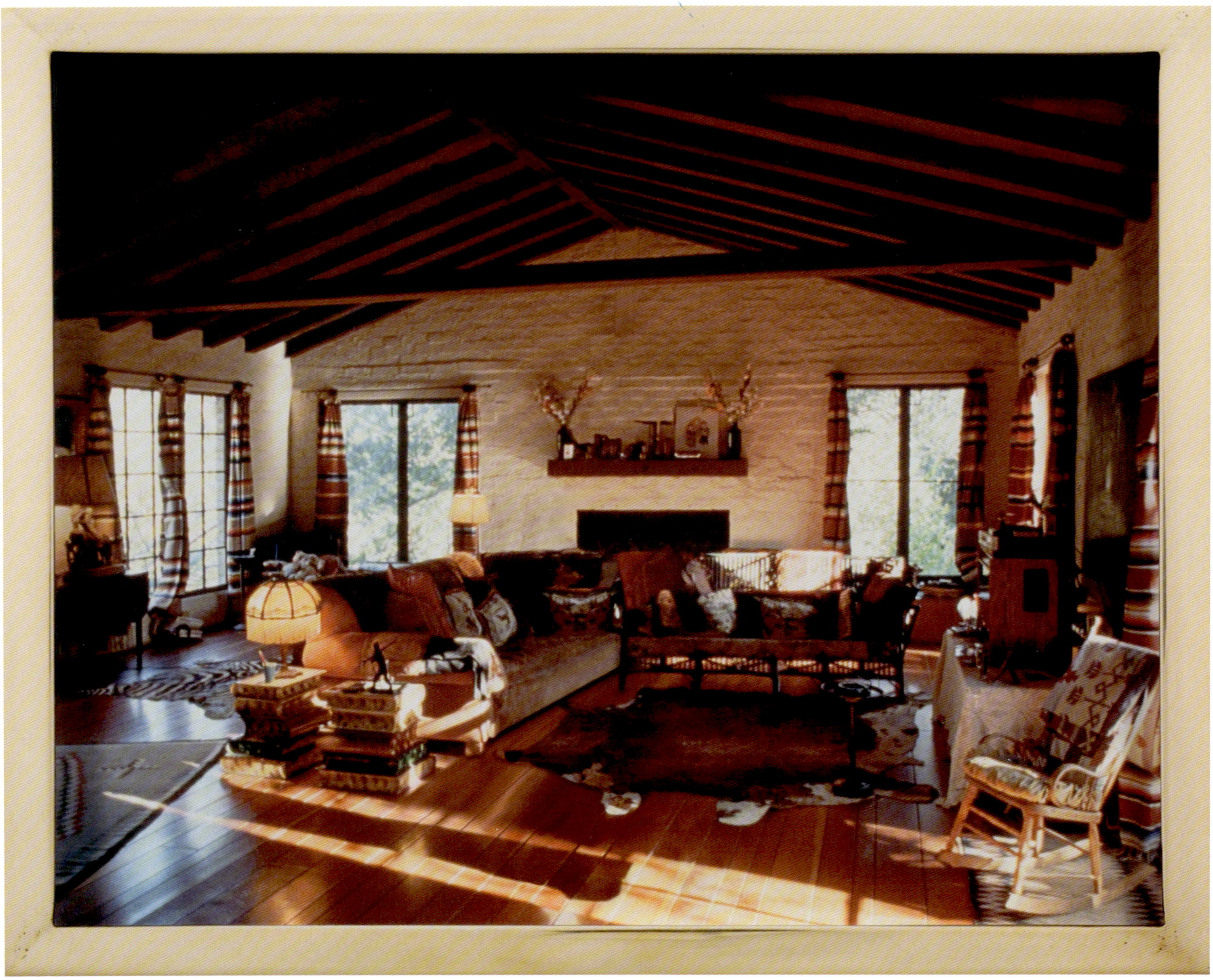

*Living Room*, 2010

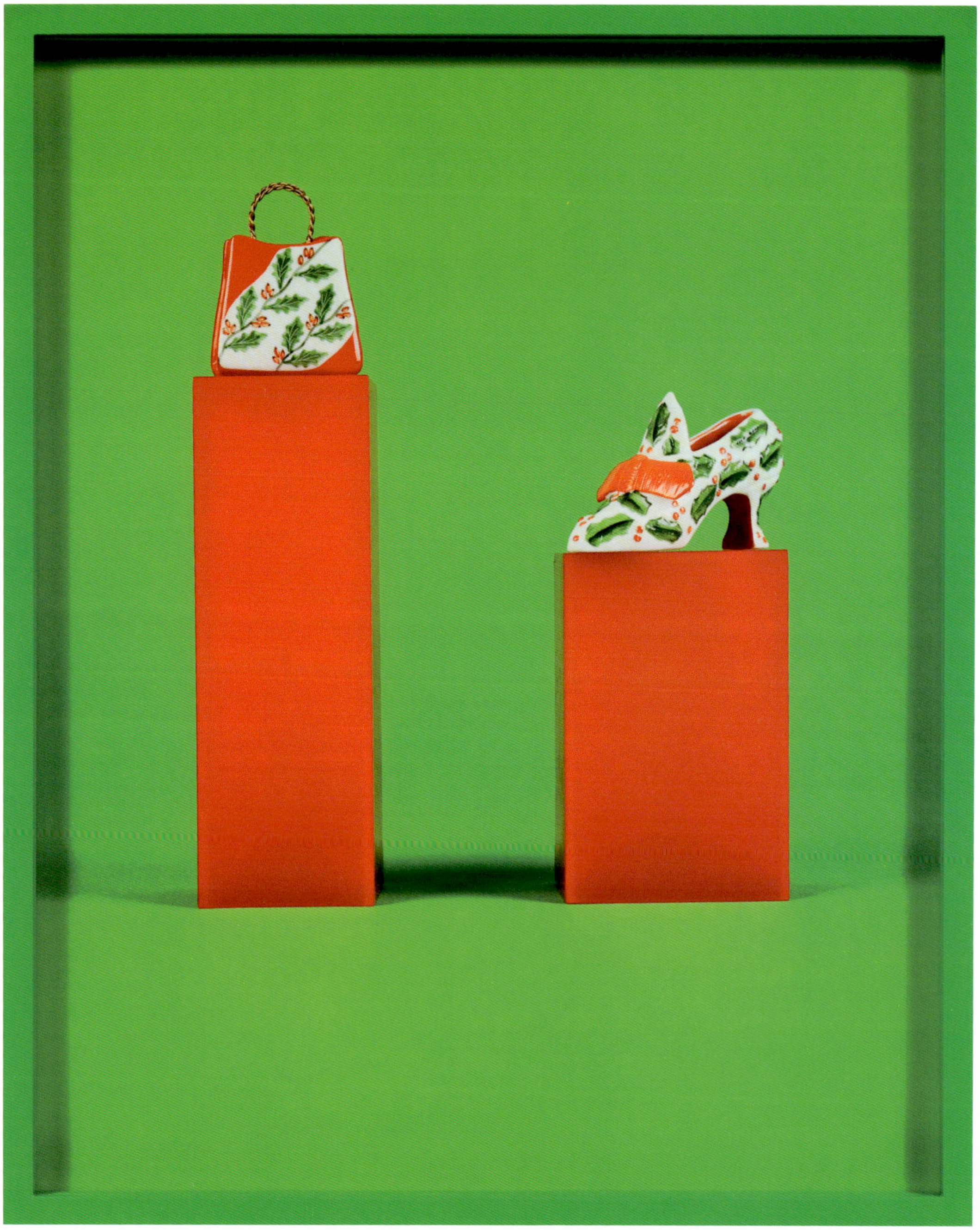

*High Heel, Purse*, 2009

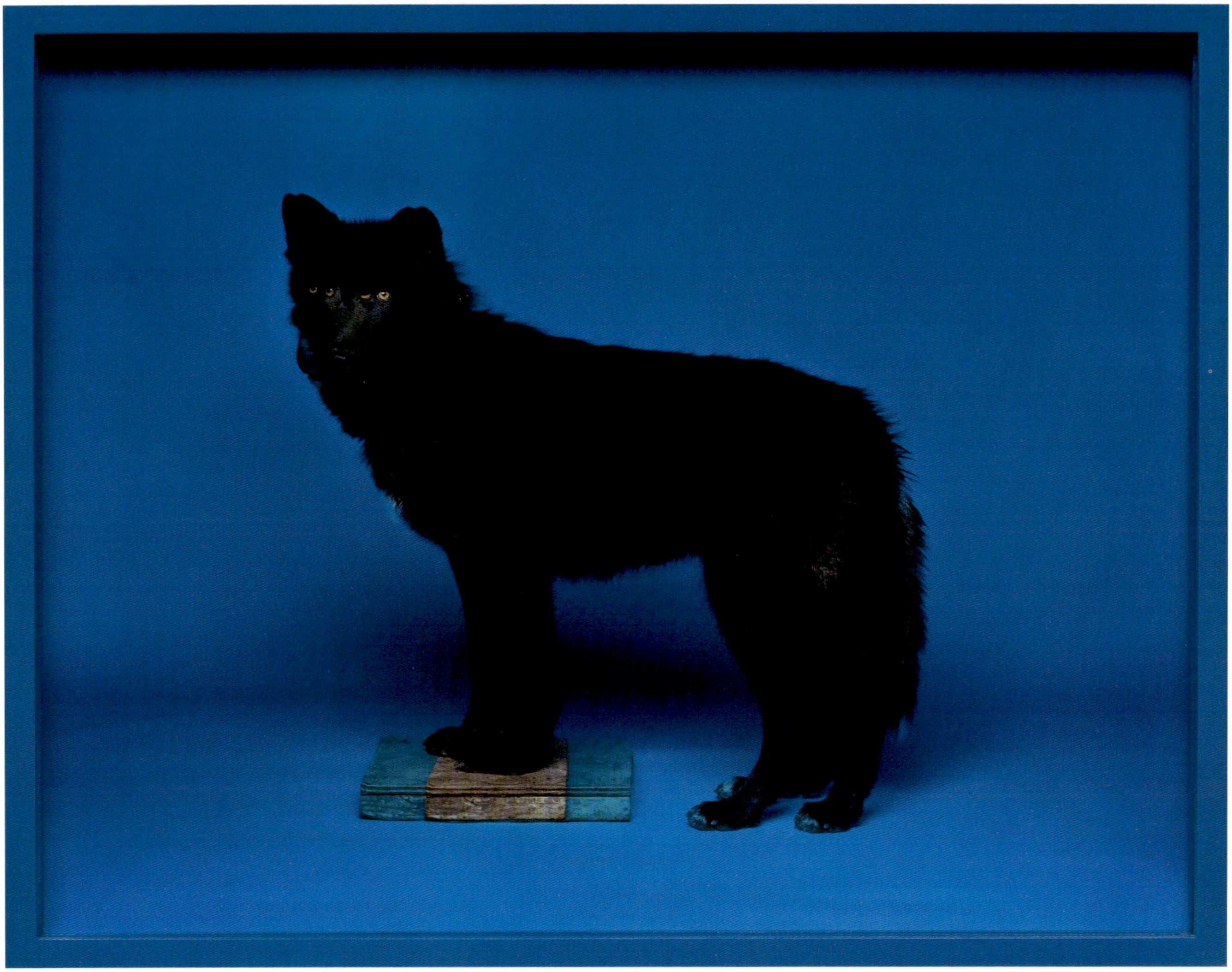

*Wolf (Blue)*, 2008

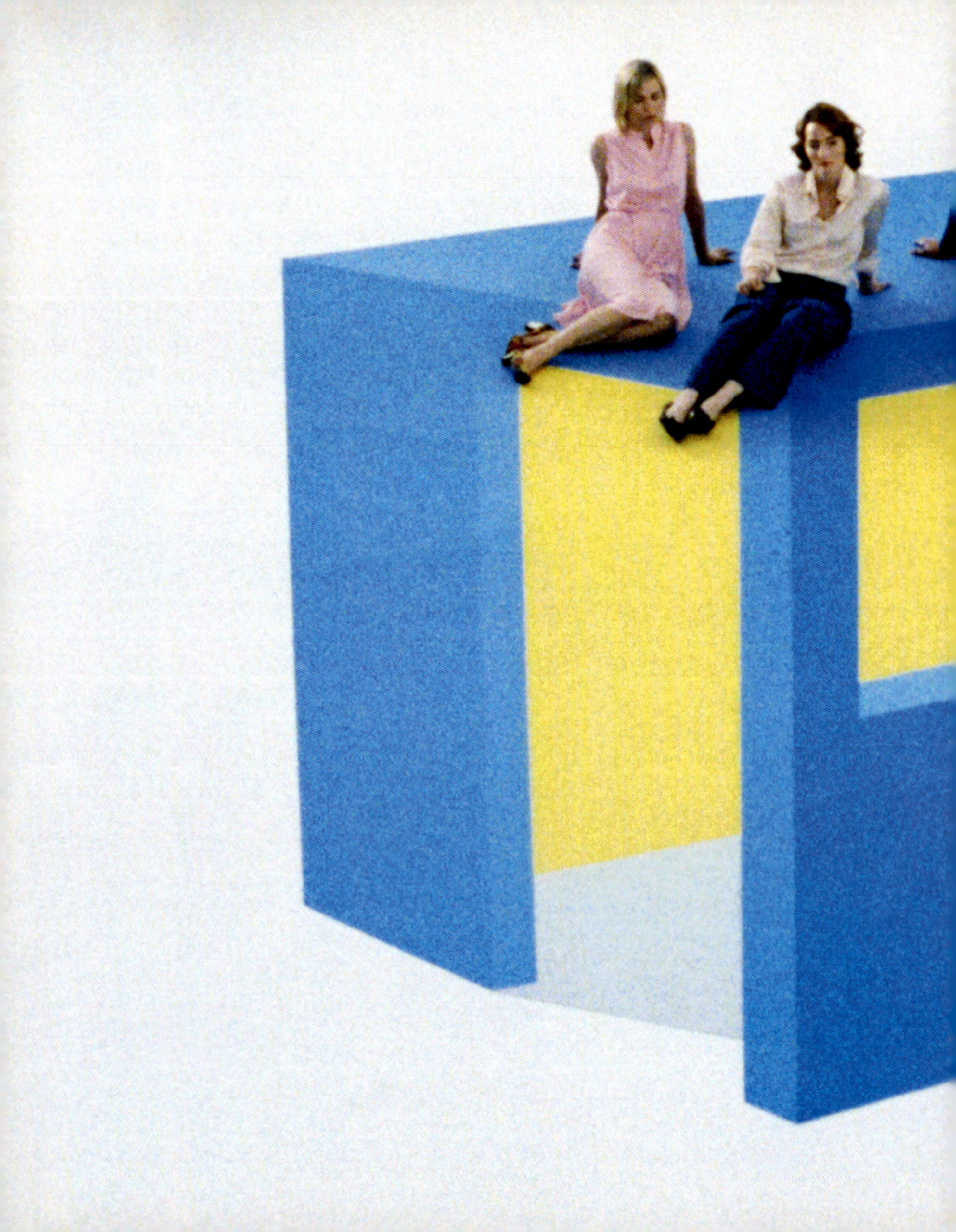

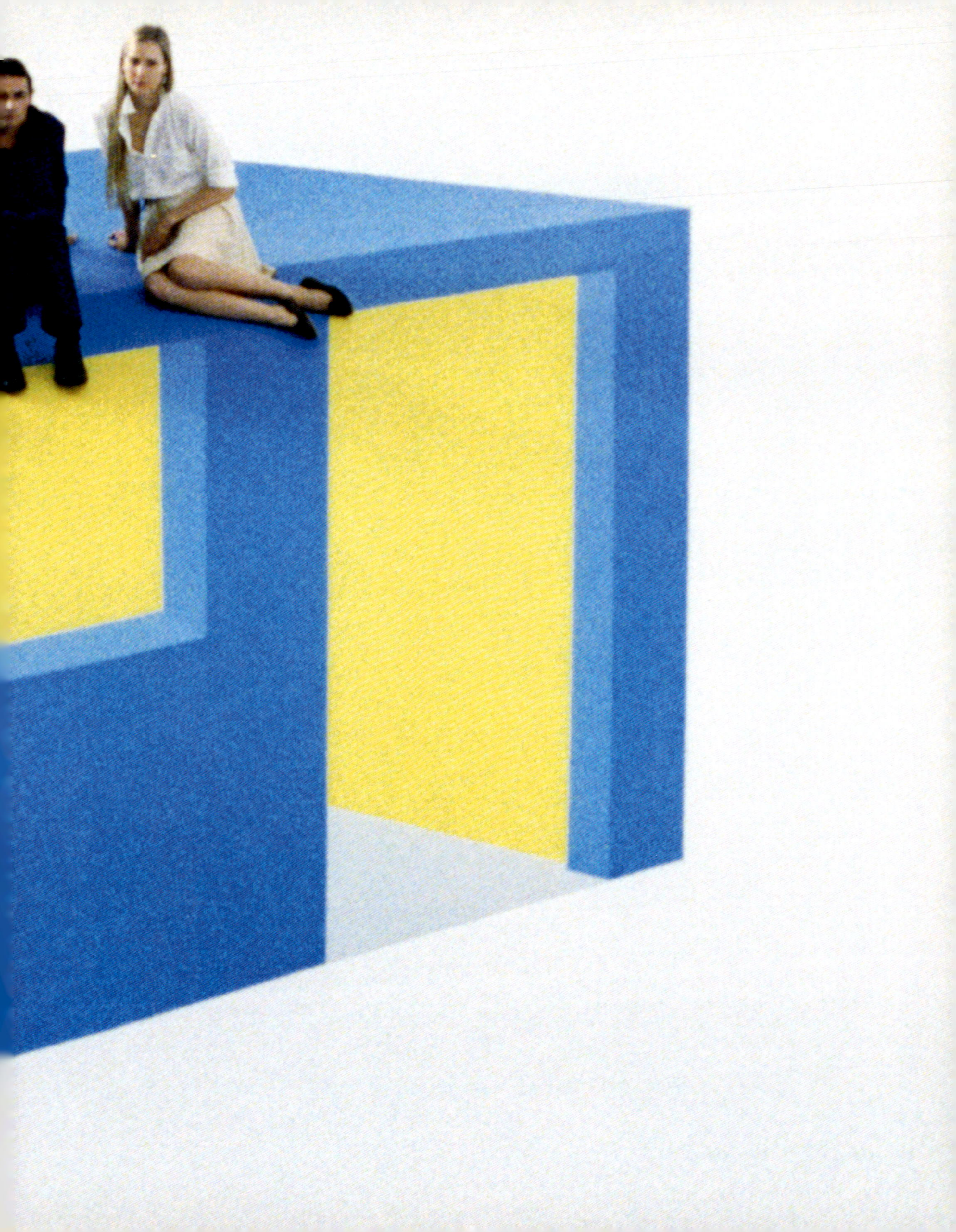

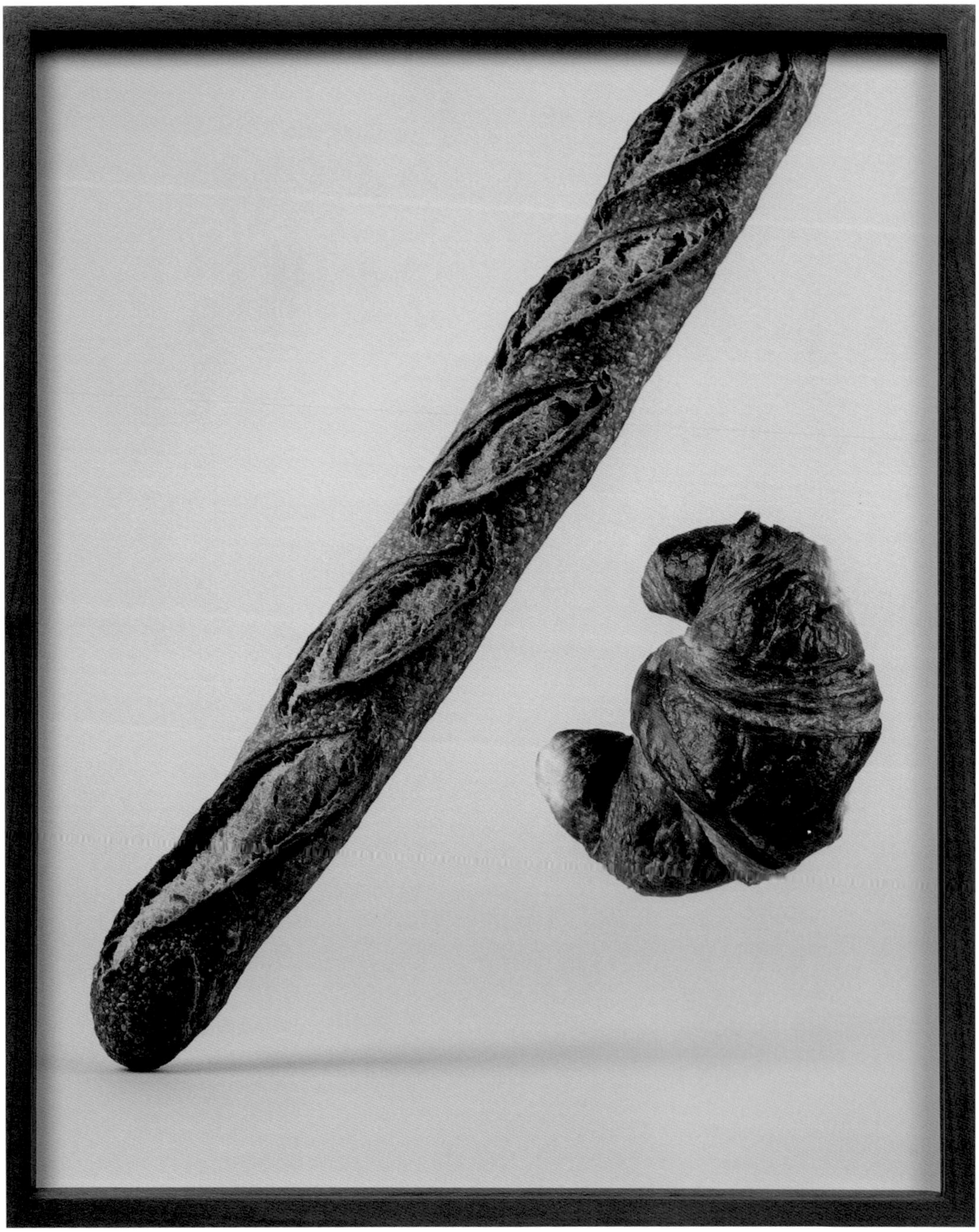

← *Untitled*, 2008

*Baguette, Croissant*, 2008

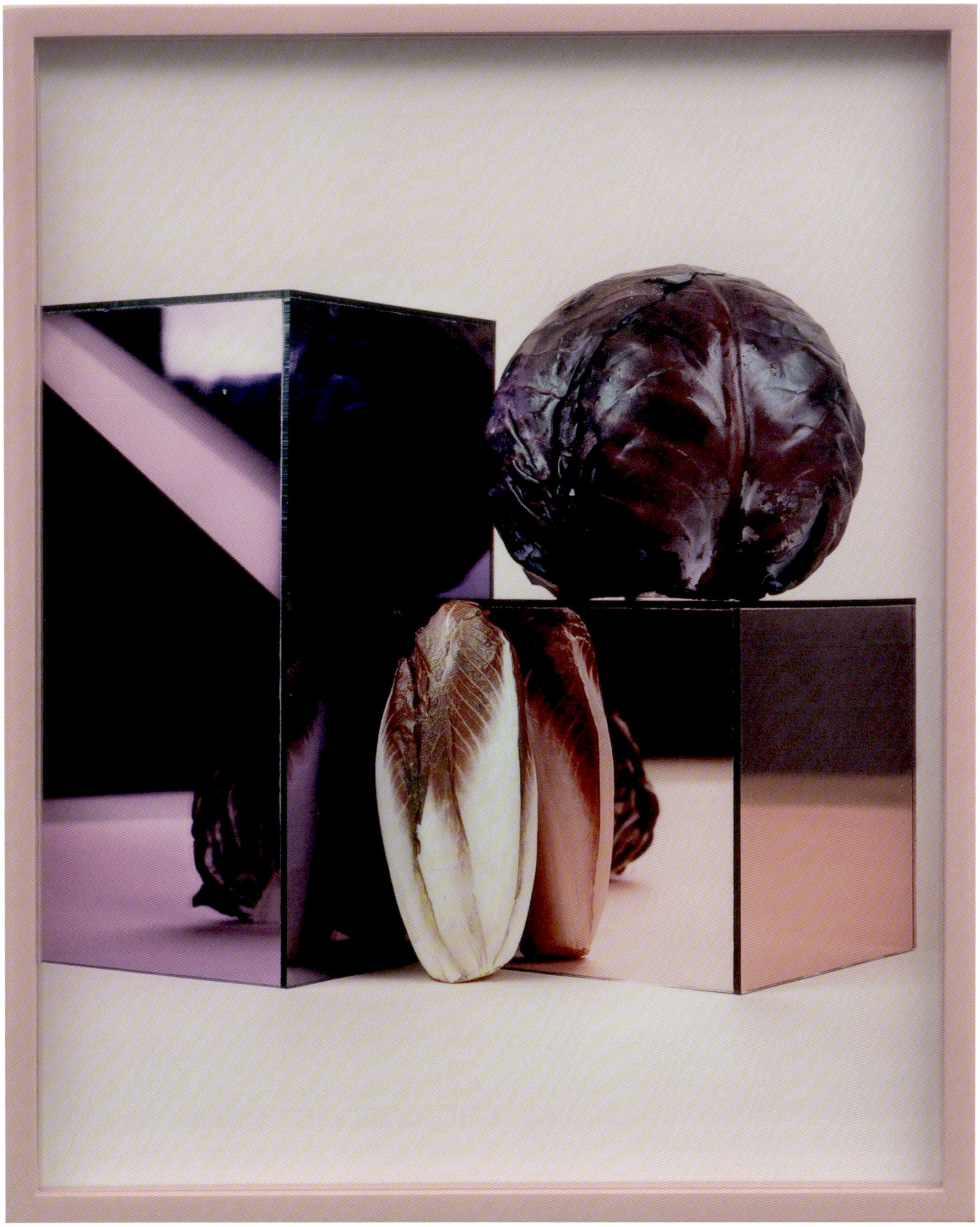

*Untitled (Red Cabbage 1)*, 2008

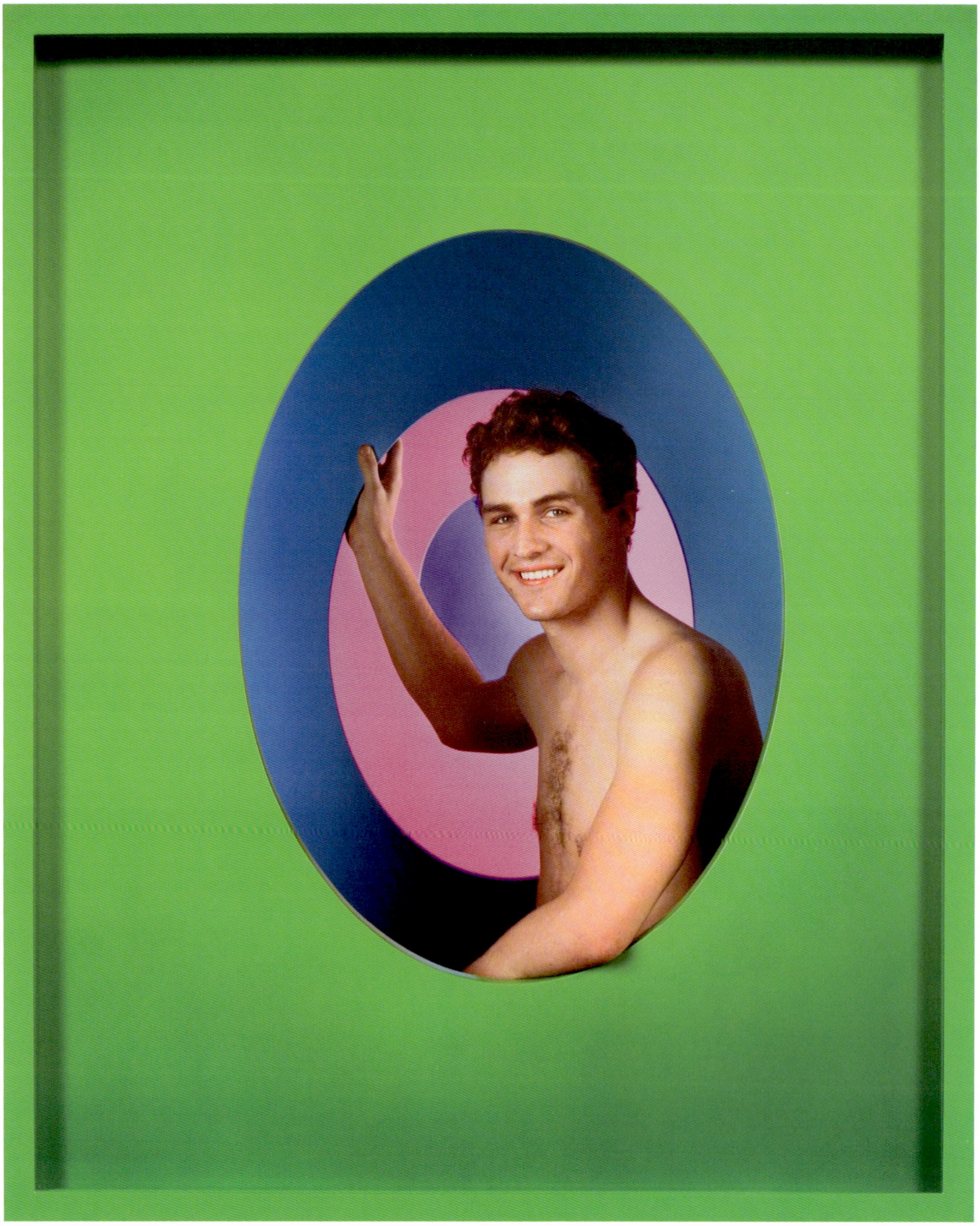

*Dustin Christenson*, 2010

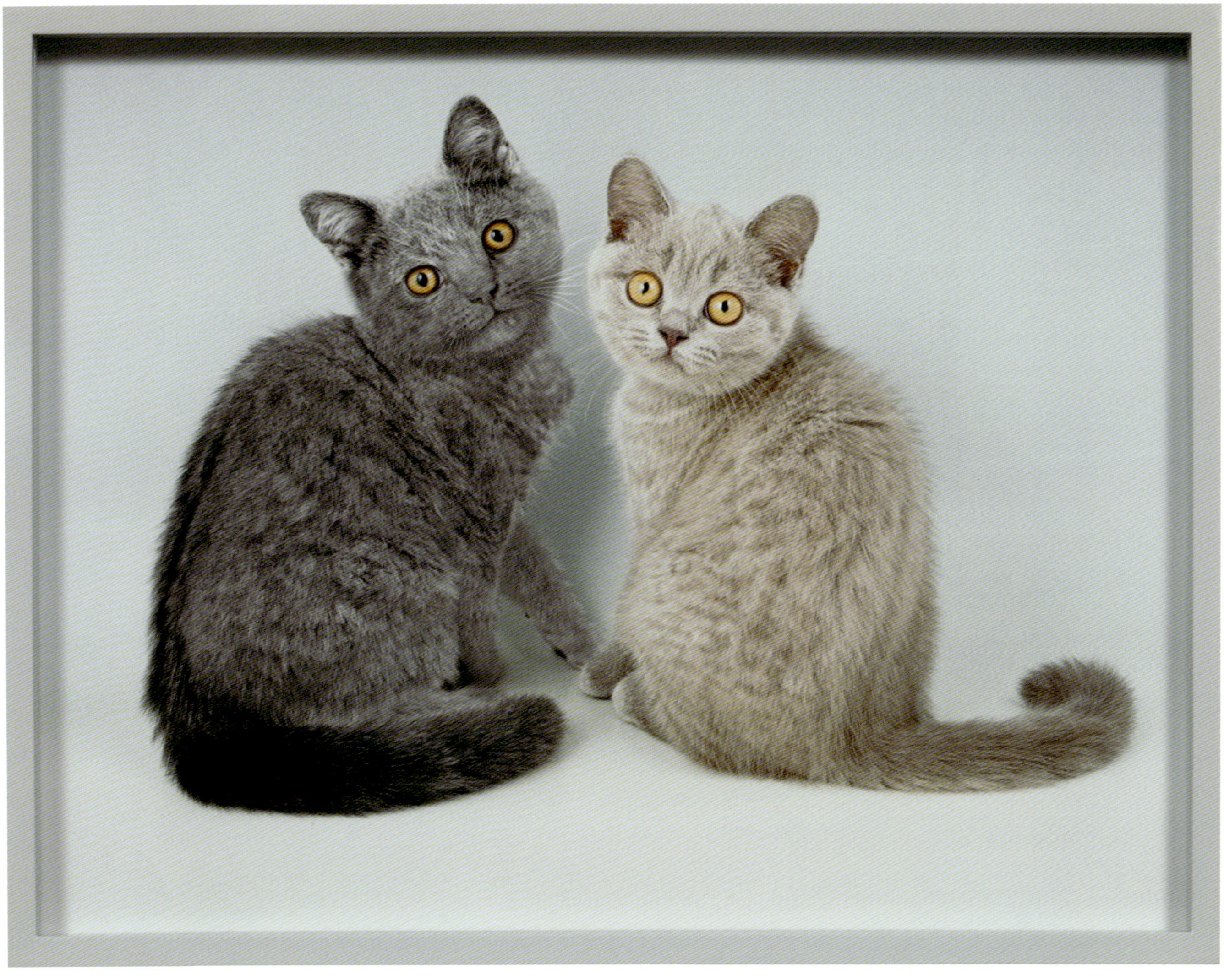

*Two British Shorthair Cats (BSH)*, 2009

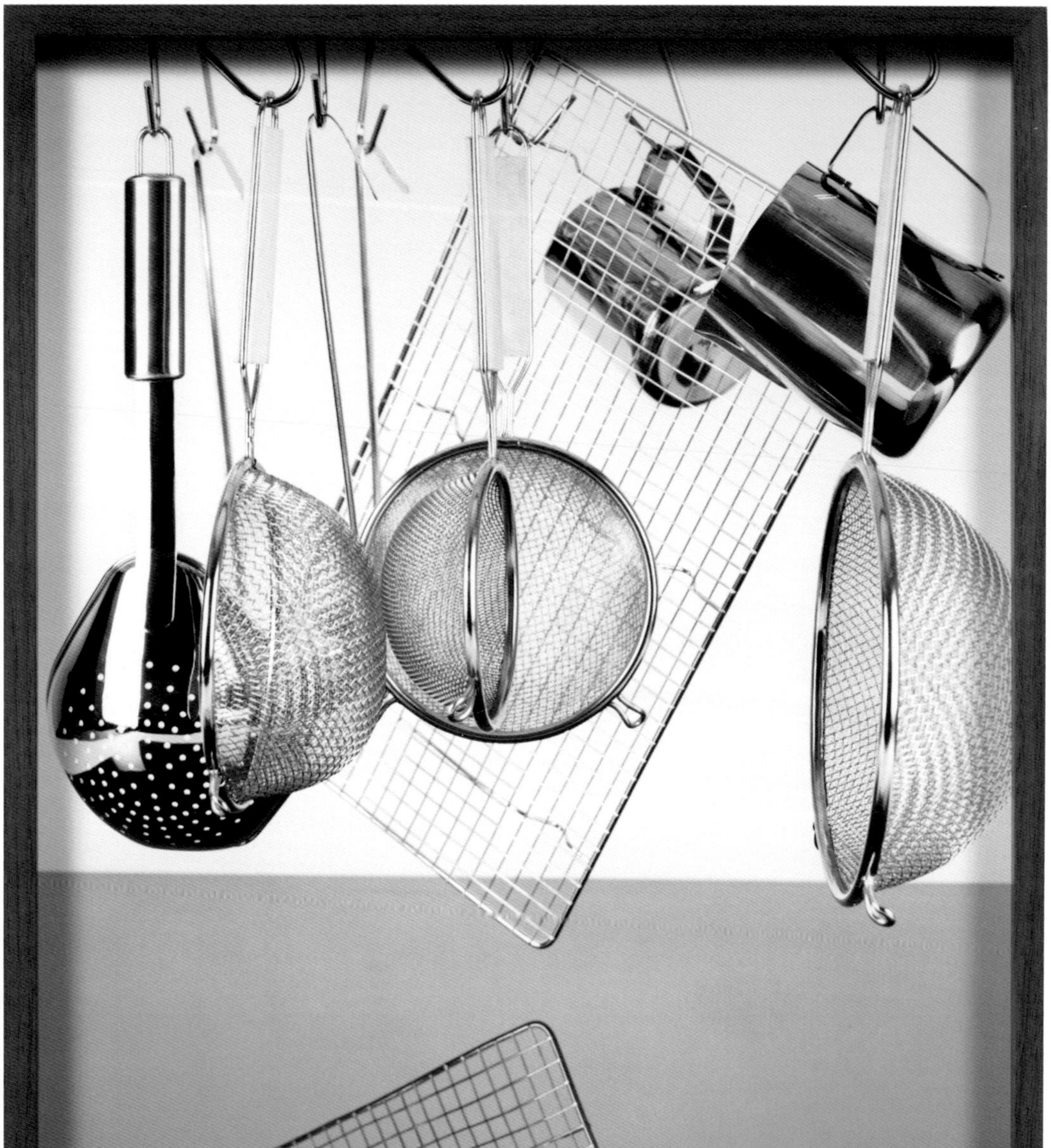

*Kitchen*, 2010

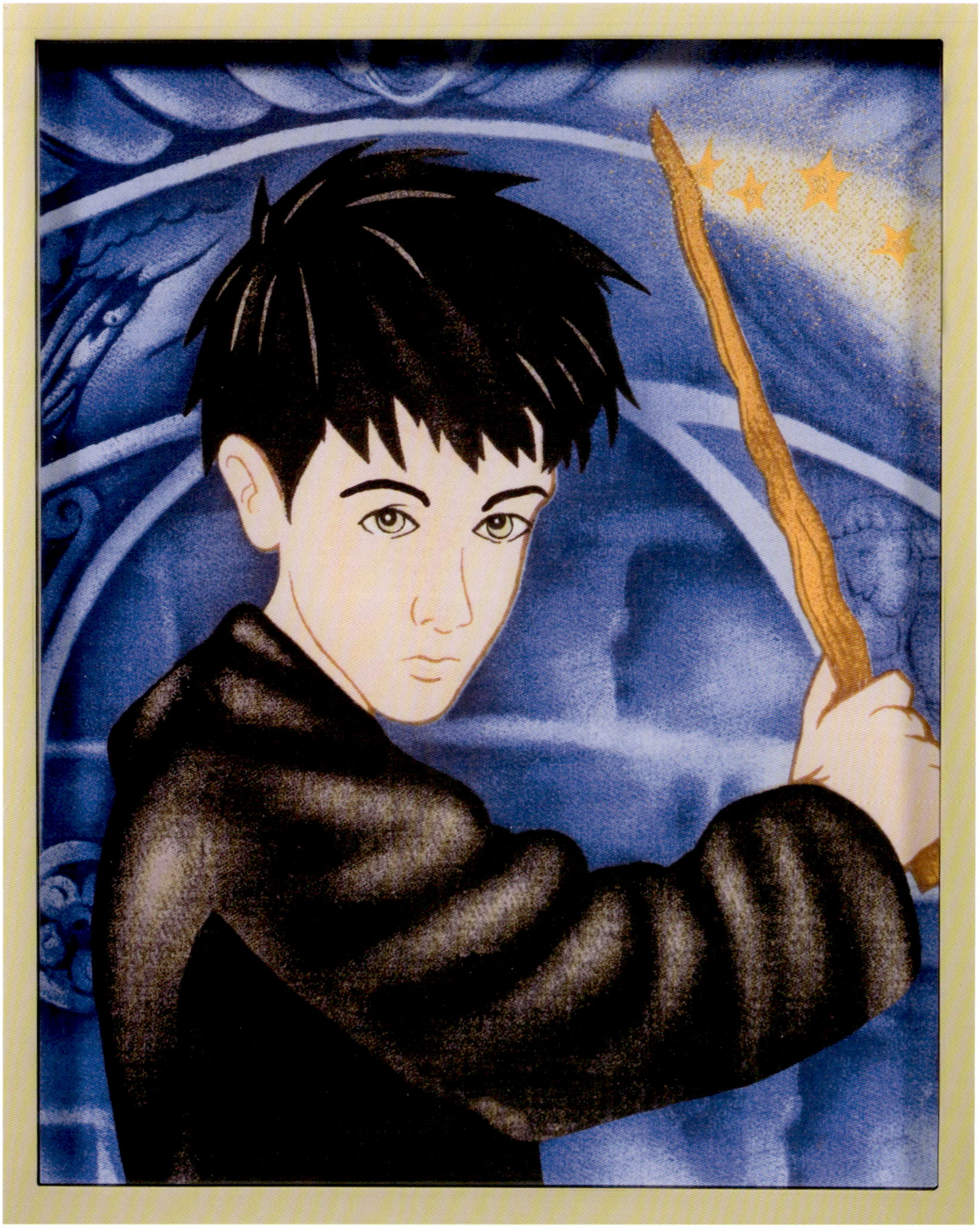

*Harry Potter*, 2010

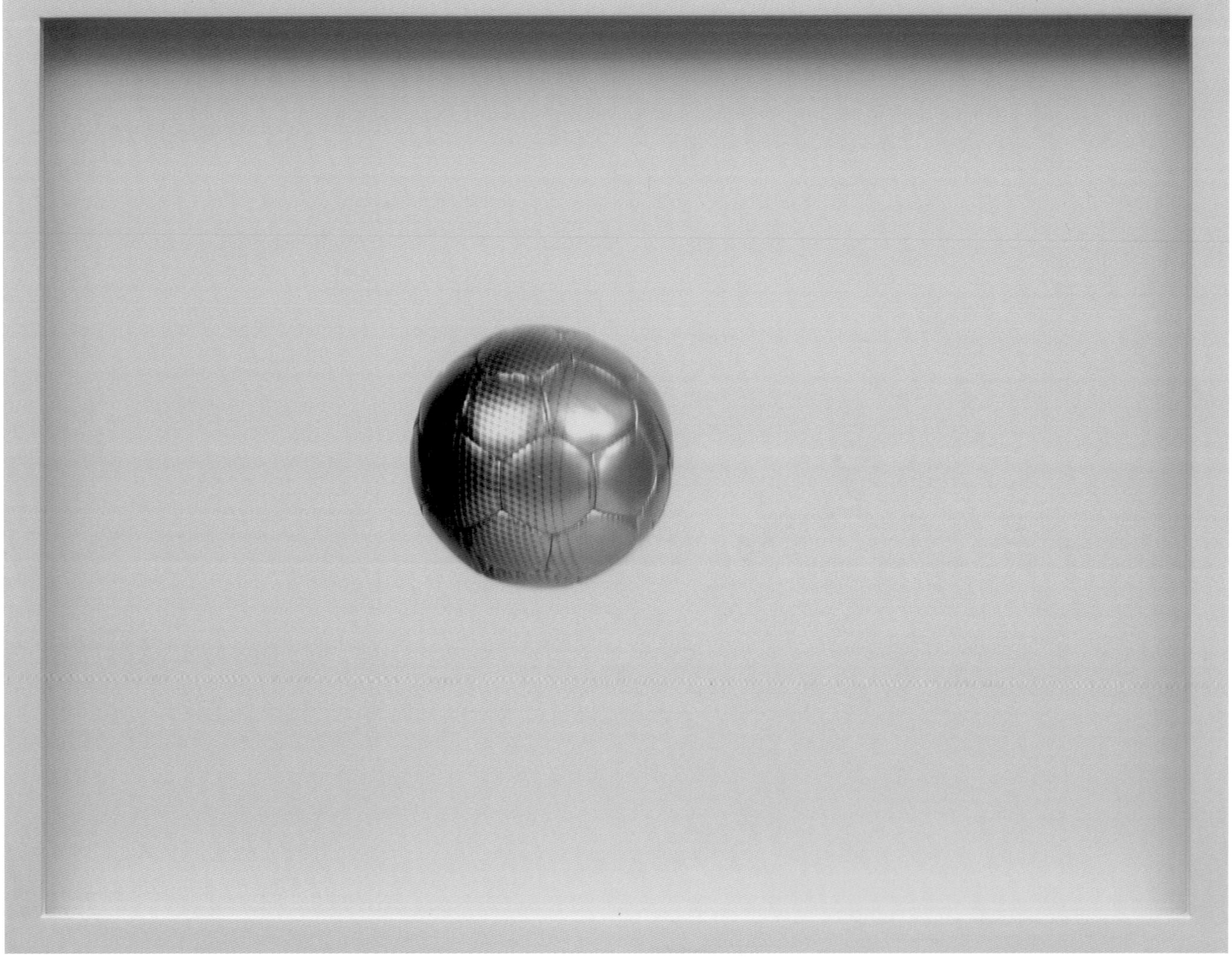

*Soccer Ball*, 2007

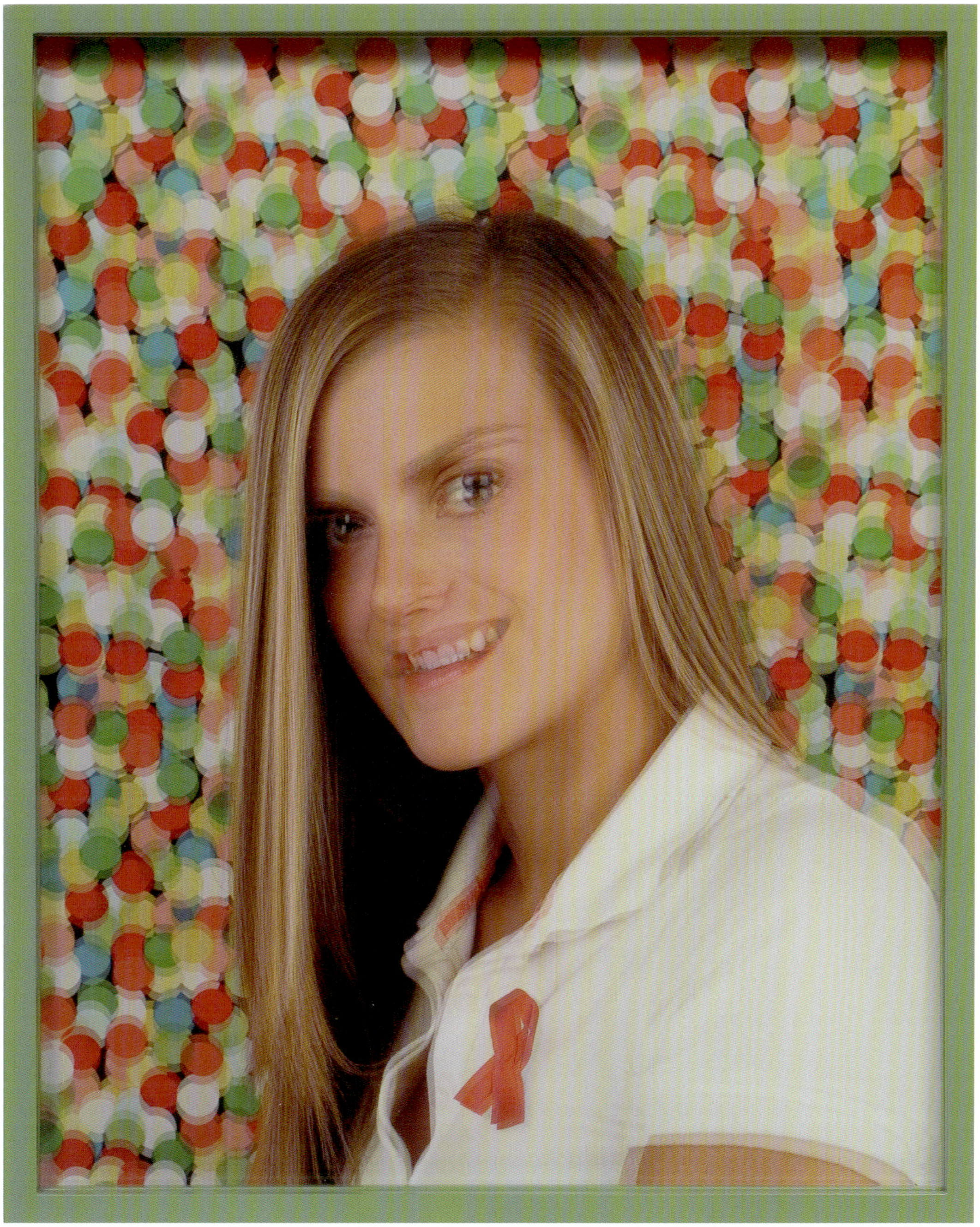

*Felicia*, 2008

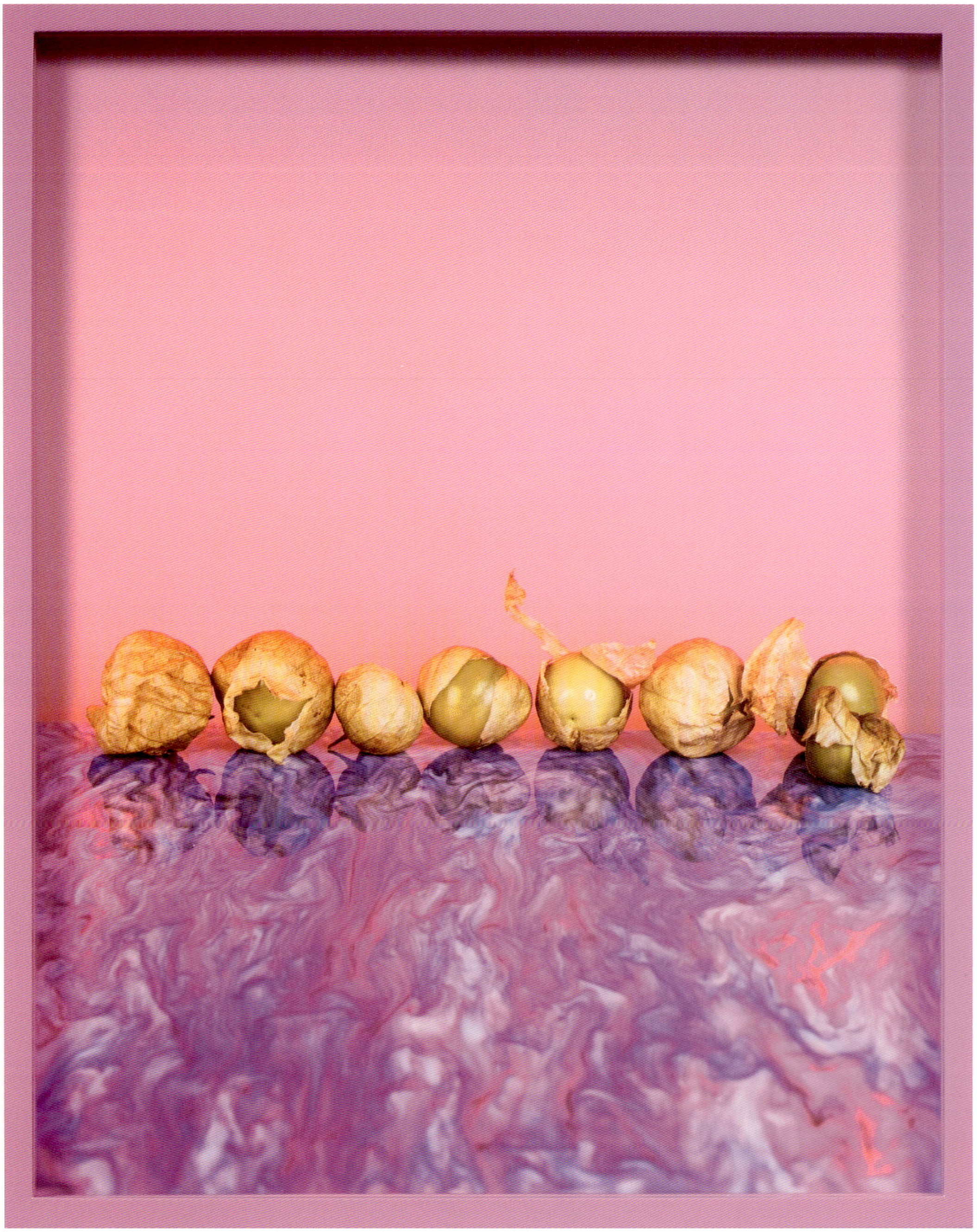

*Tomatillos*, 2010

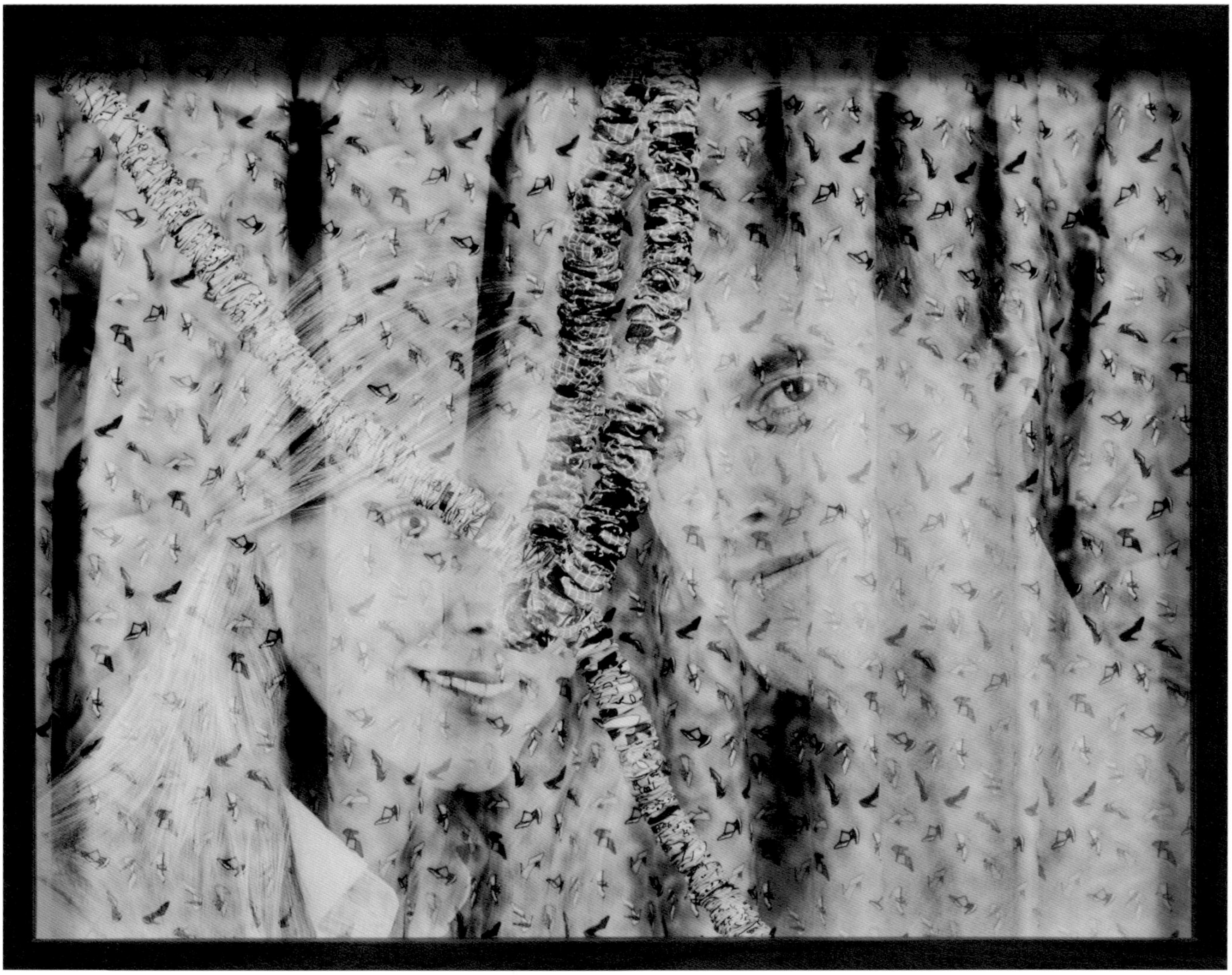

*Textile (For Him and Her)*, 2009

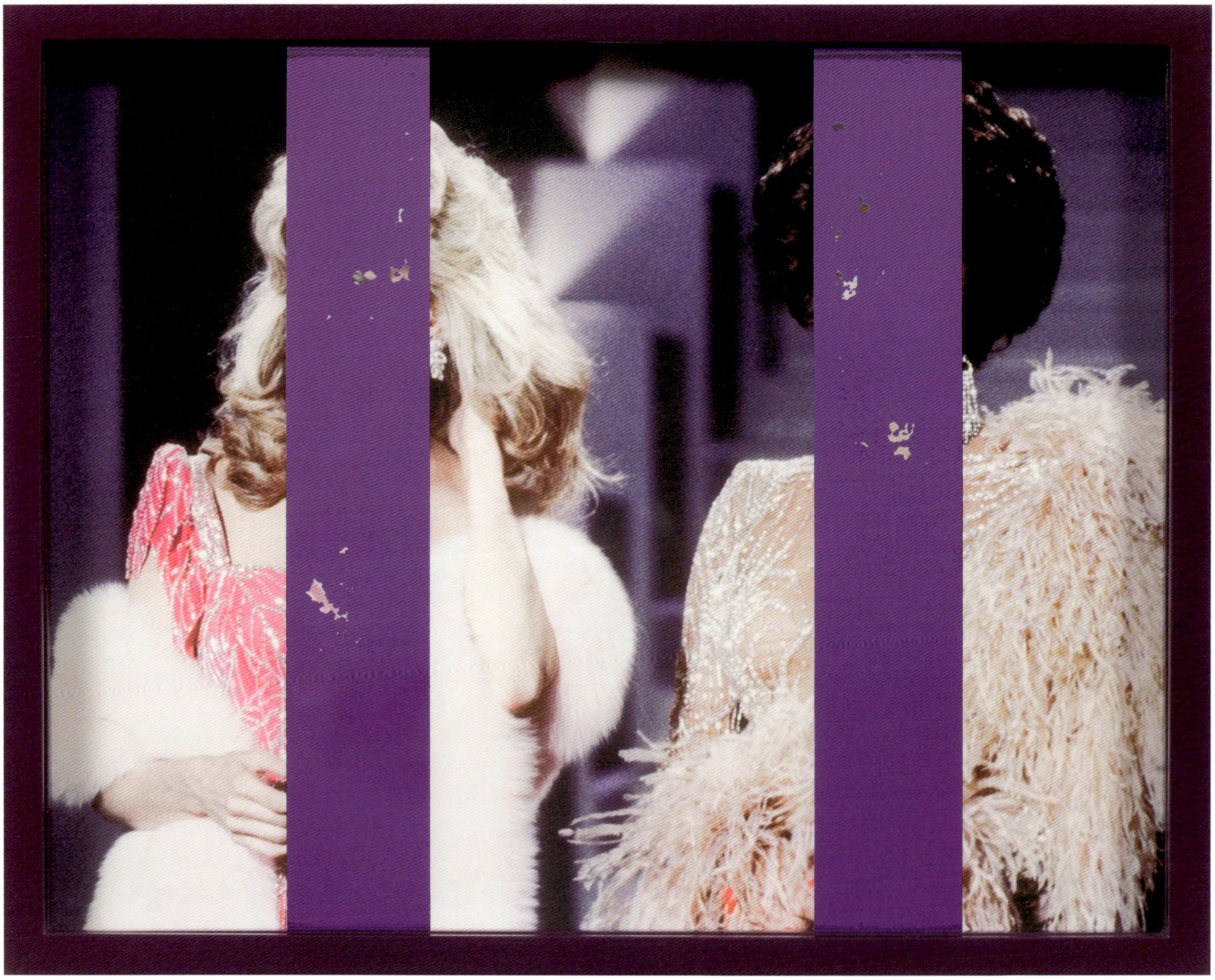

*Untitled (Two Purple Bars)*, 2010

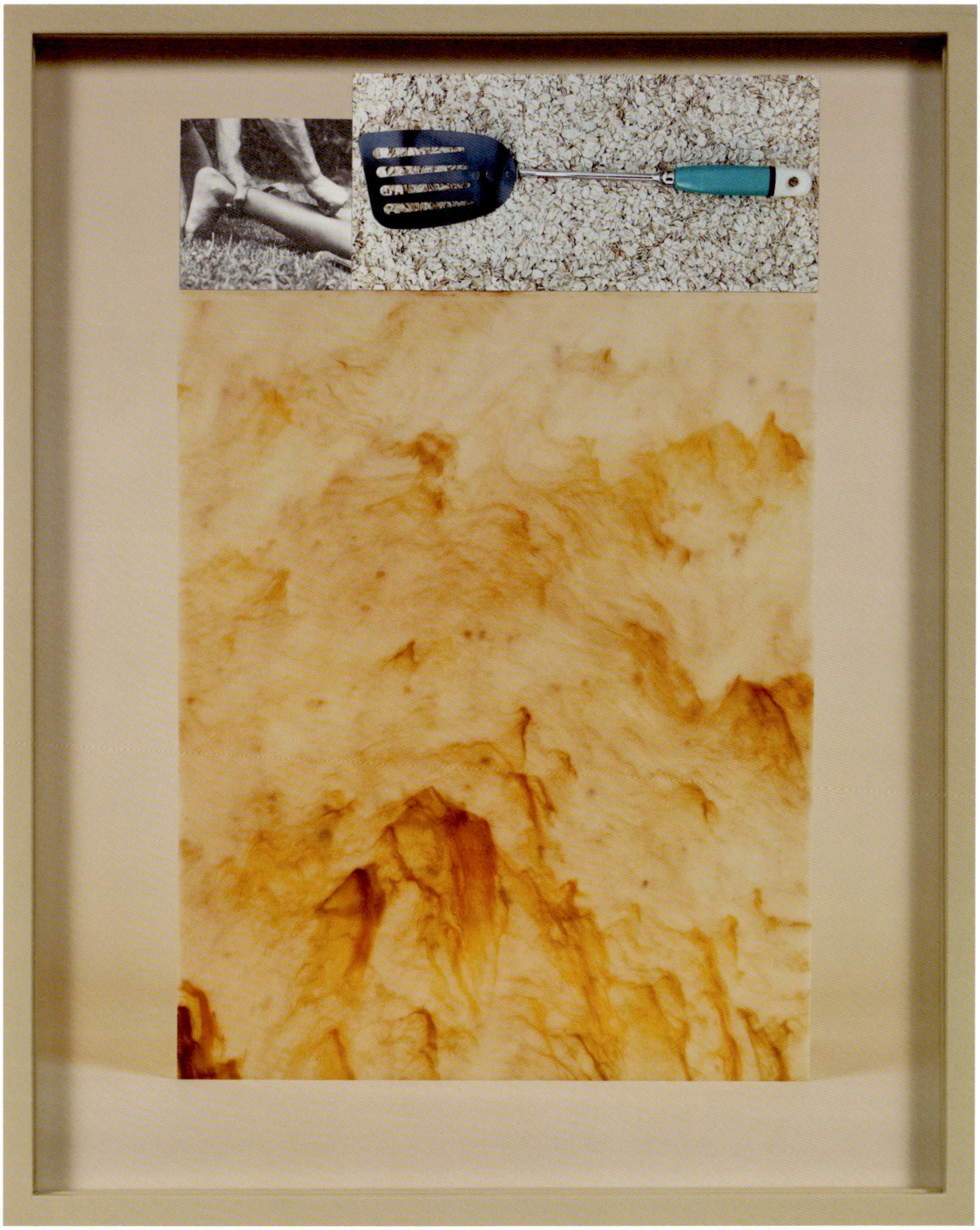

*Horn Structure (For Massage and Collectable)*, 2009

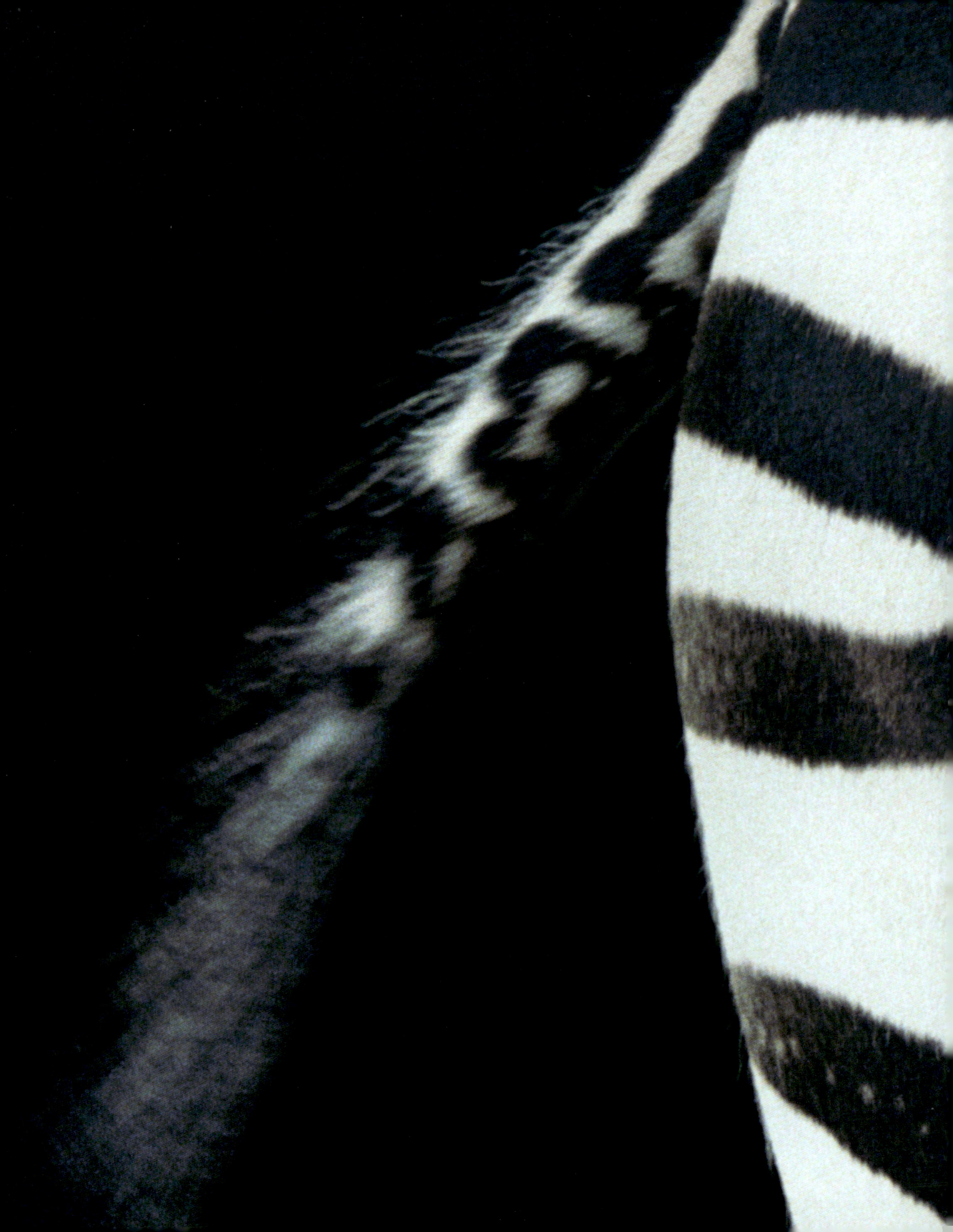

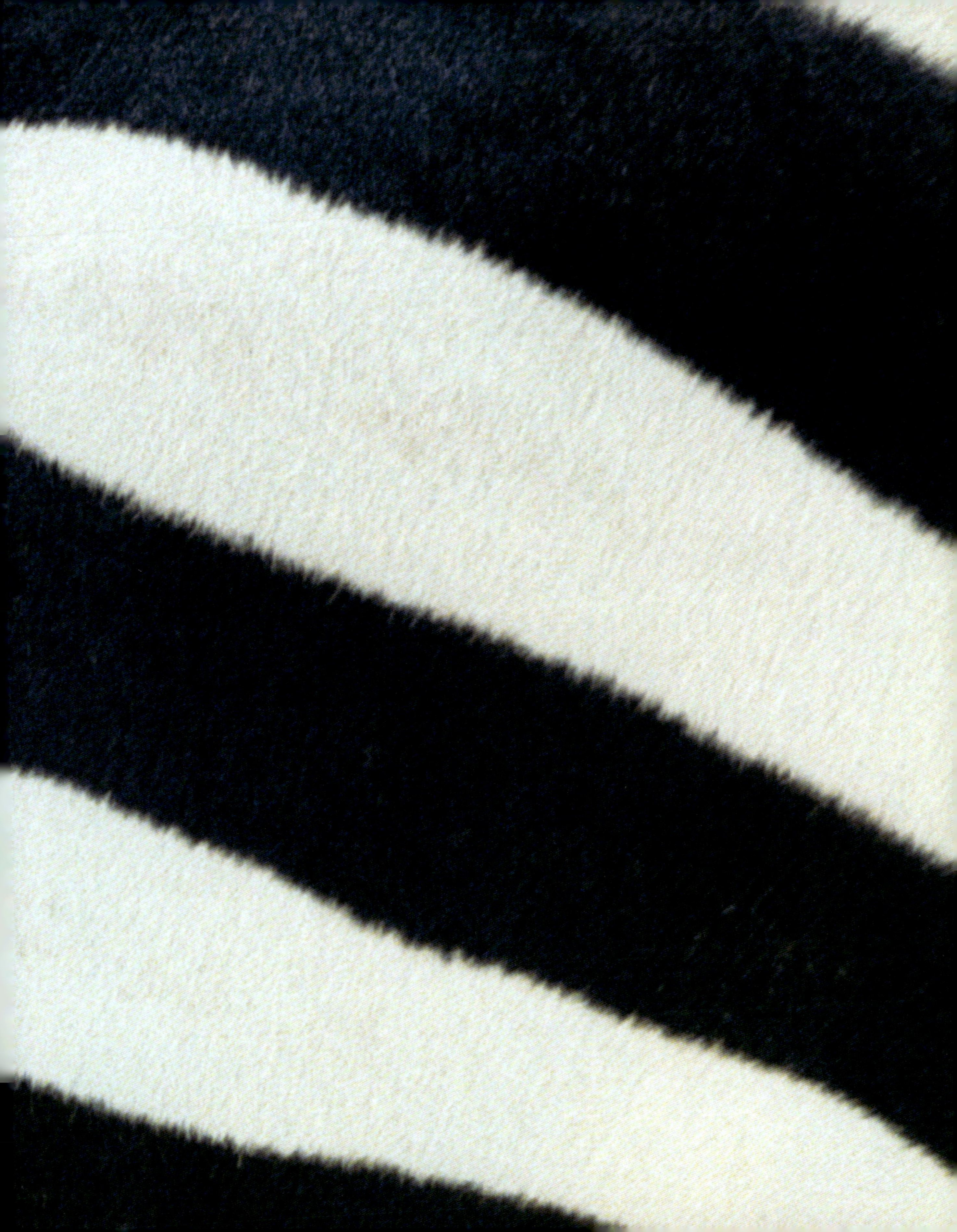

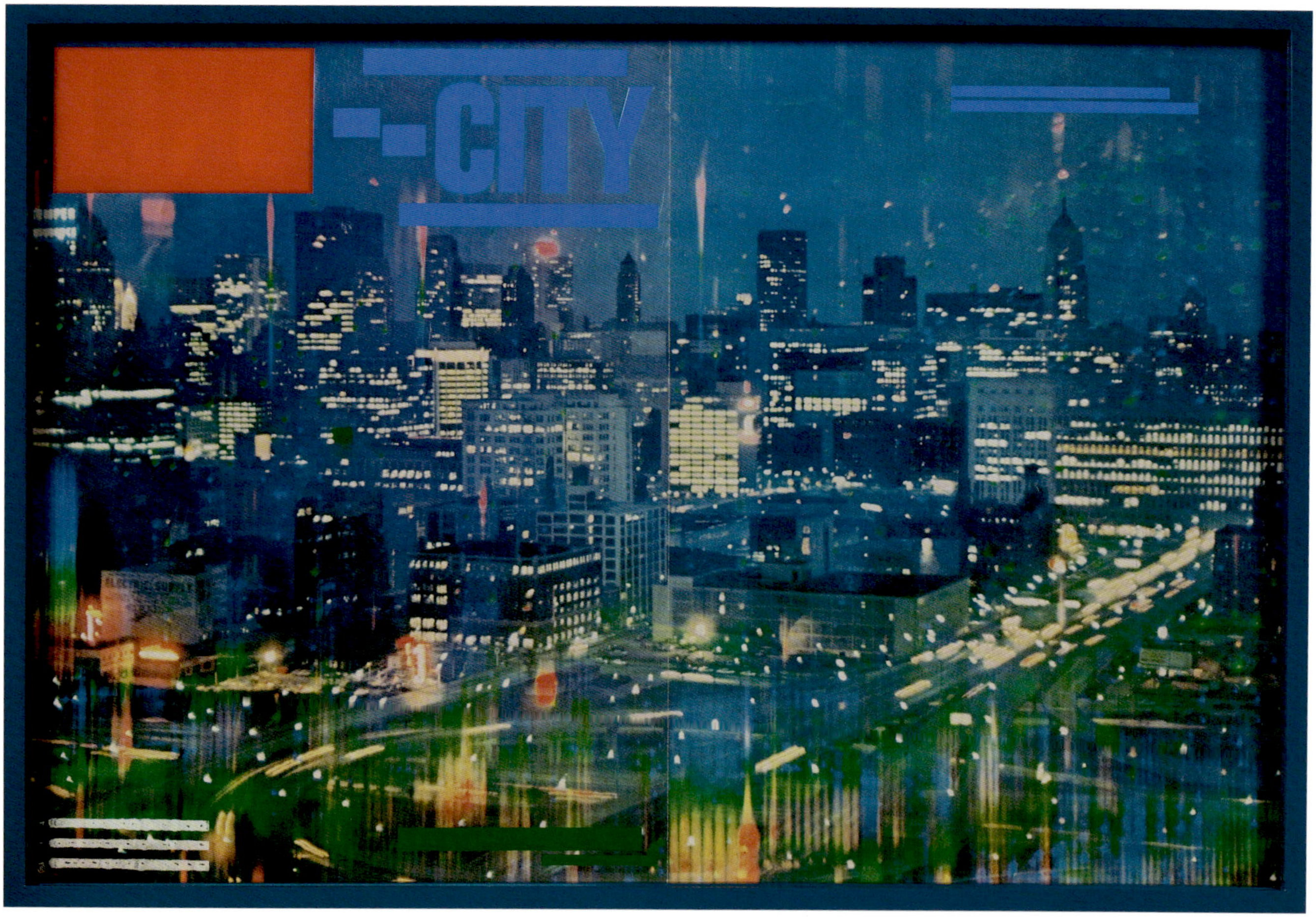


← *Zebra and Woman*, 2007

*Cityscape (Burbank)*, 2009

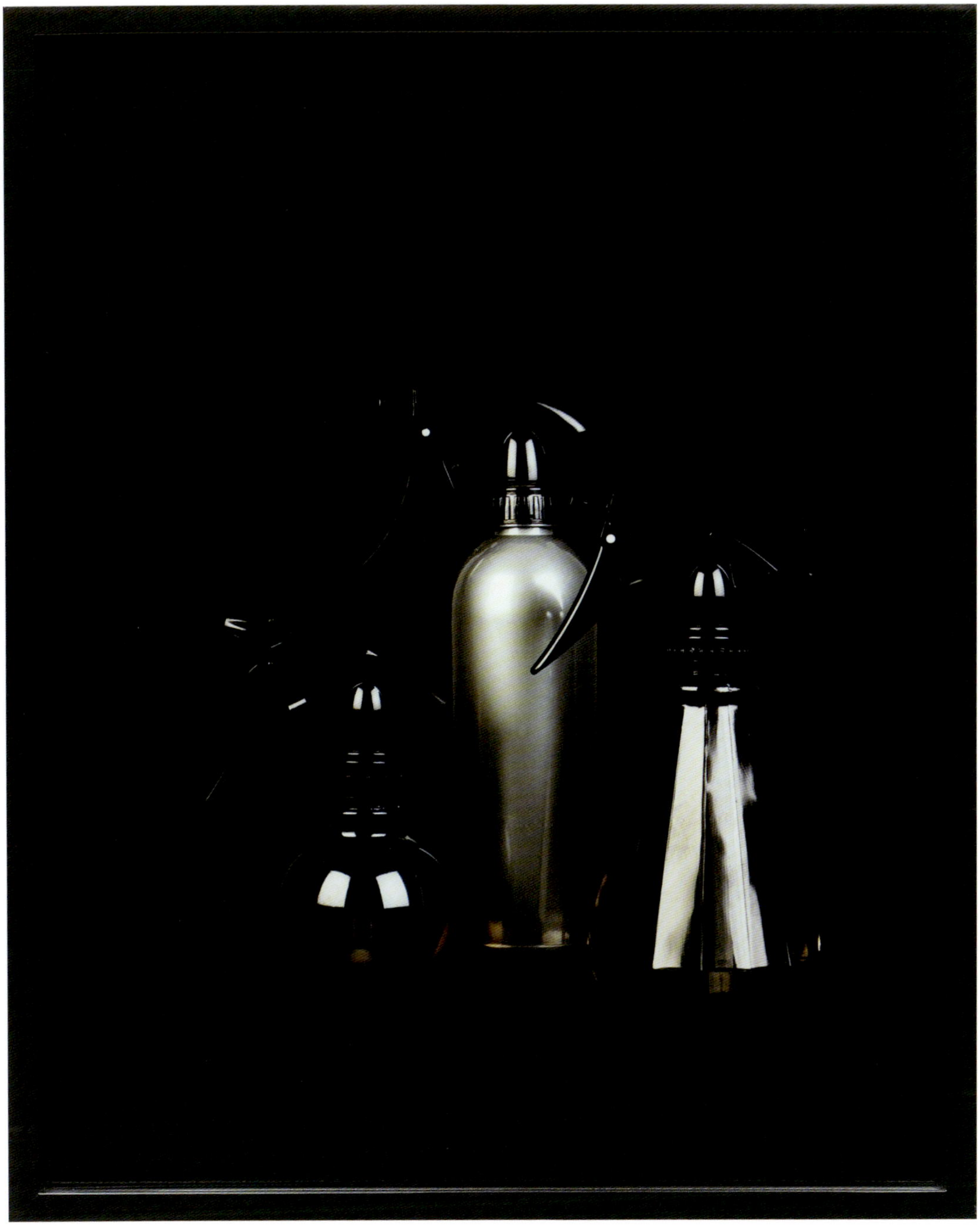

*Three Bottles*, 2009

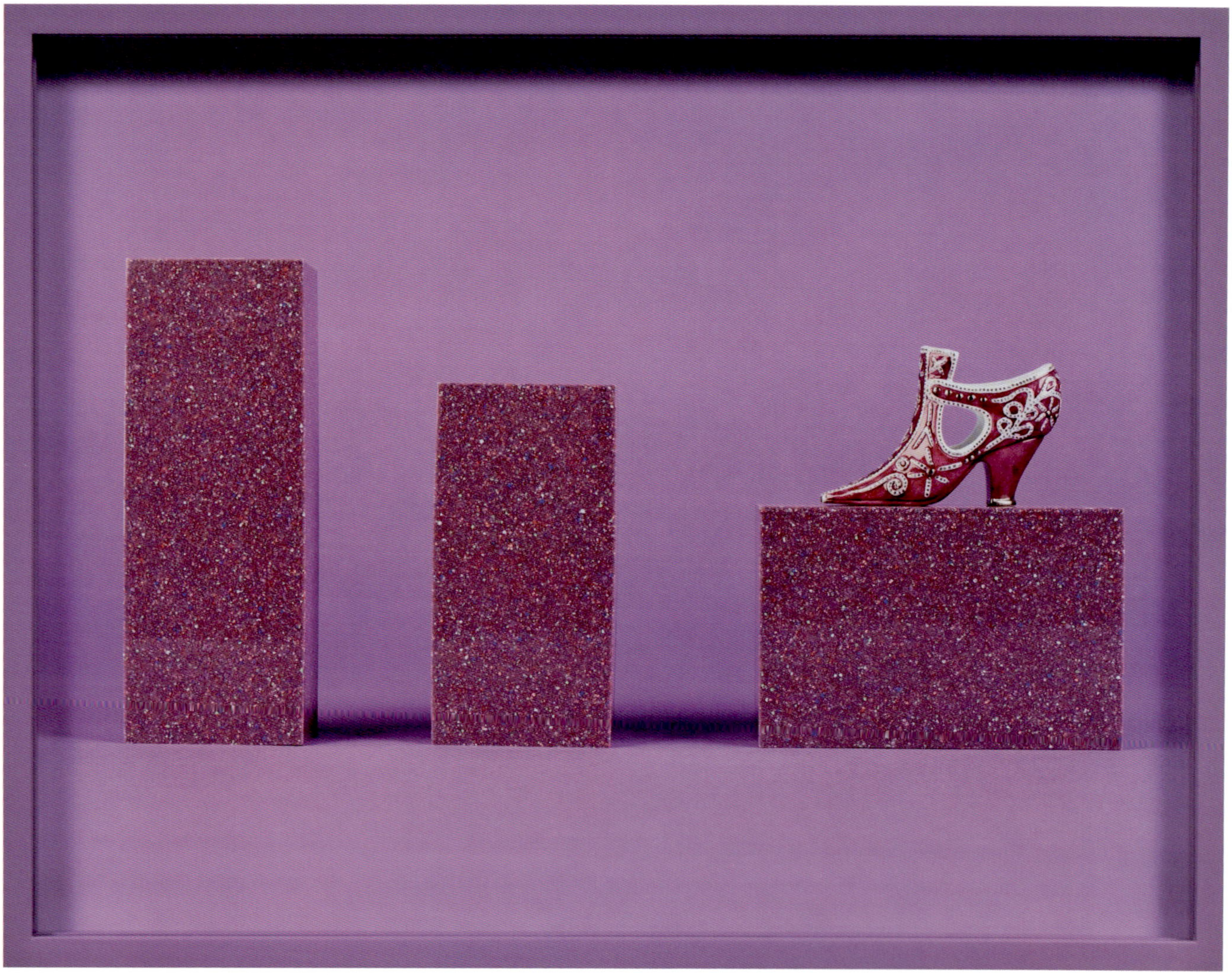

*2000*, 2009

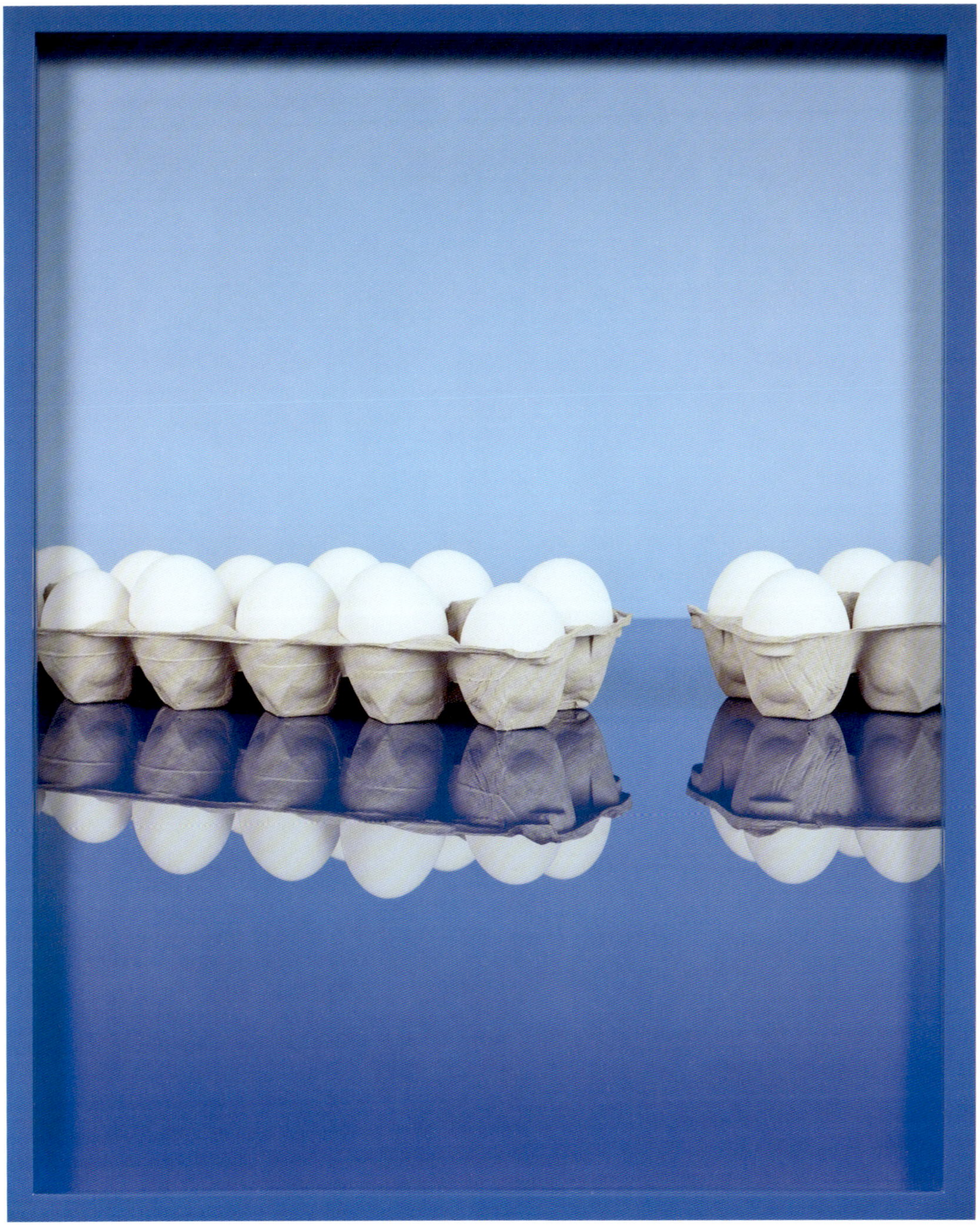

*Eggs*, 2010

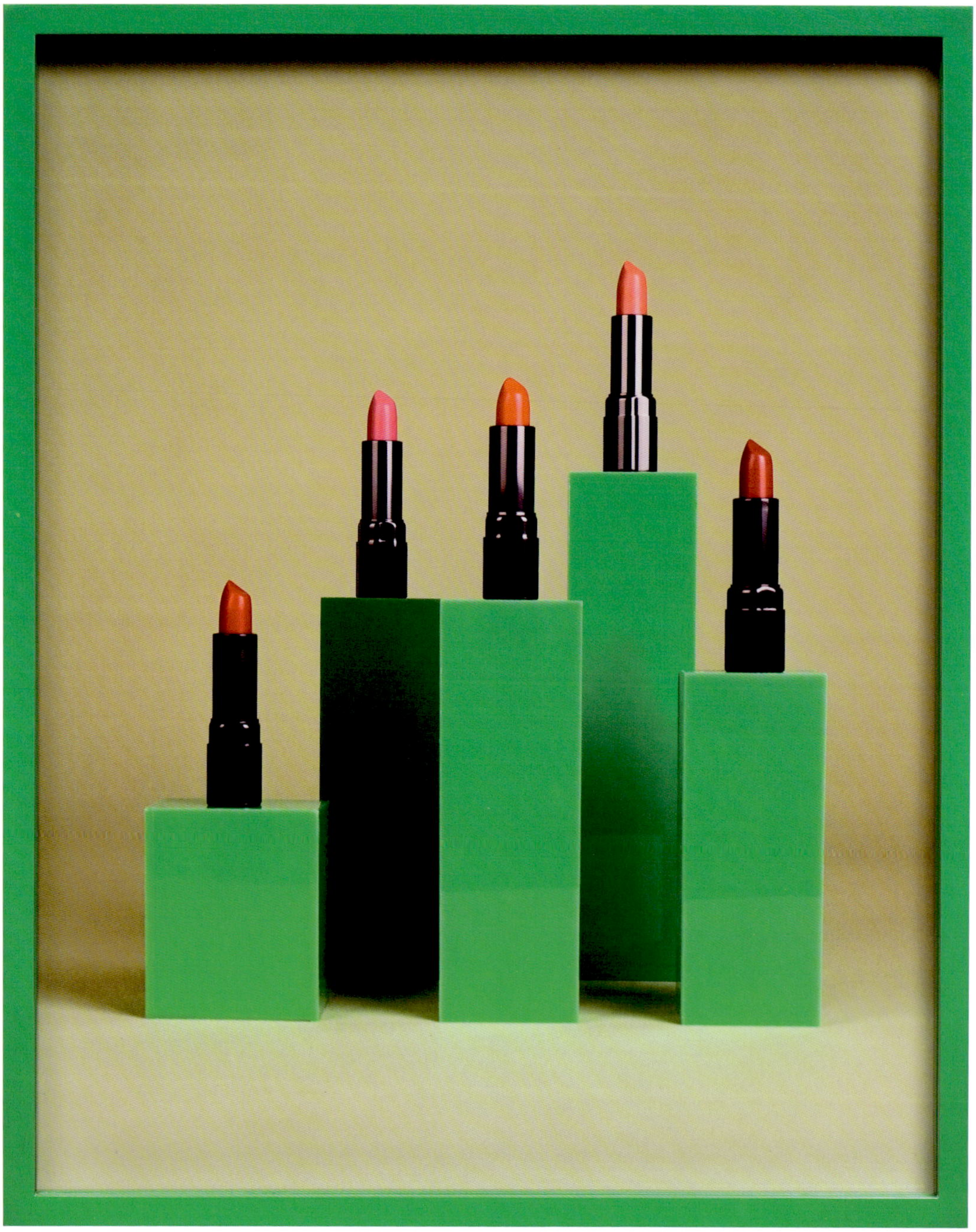

*Lipstick*, 2009

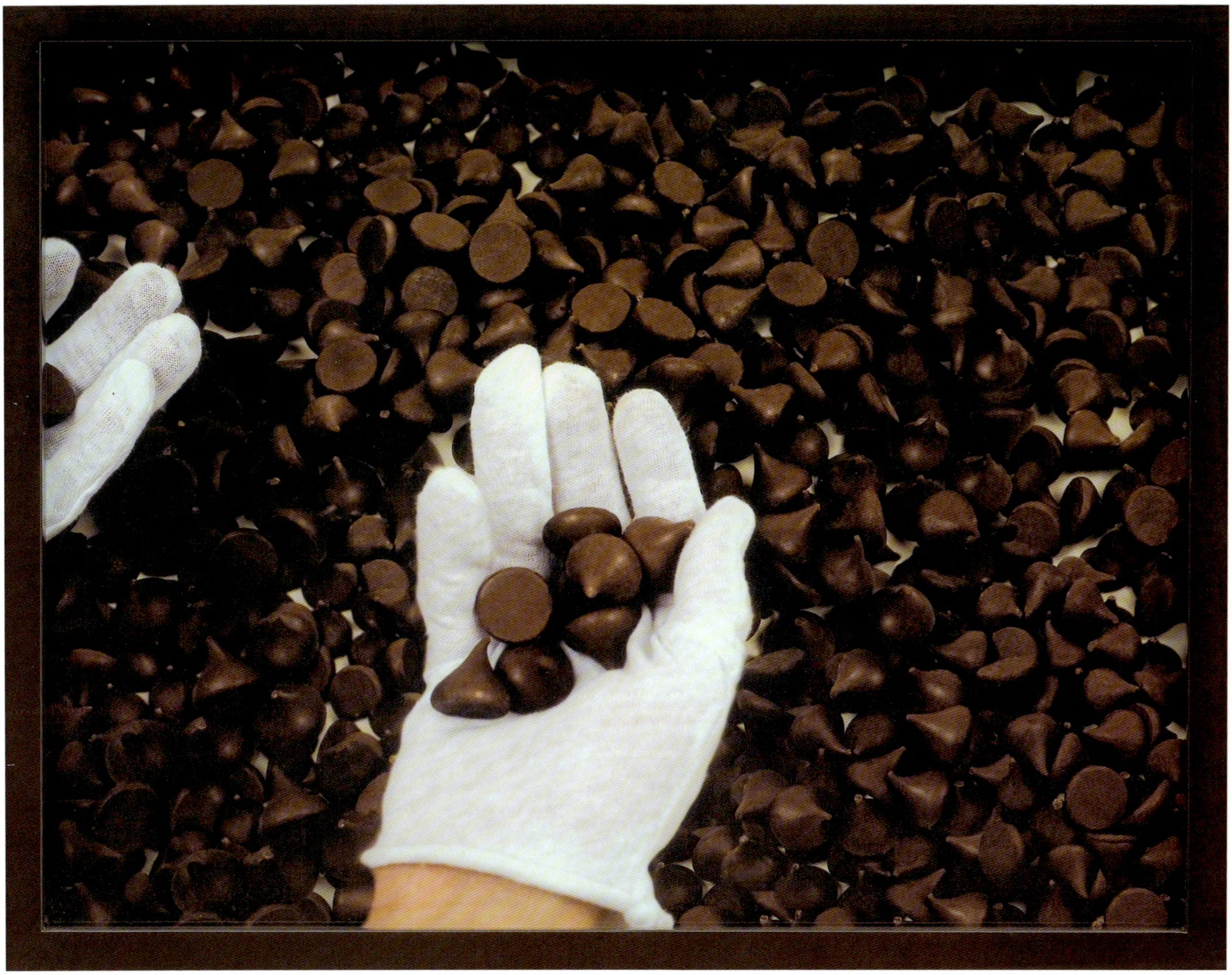

*Chocolate Factory*, 2007

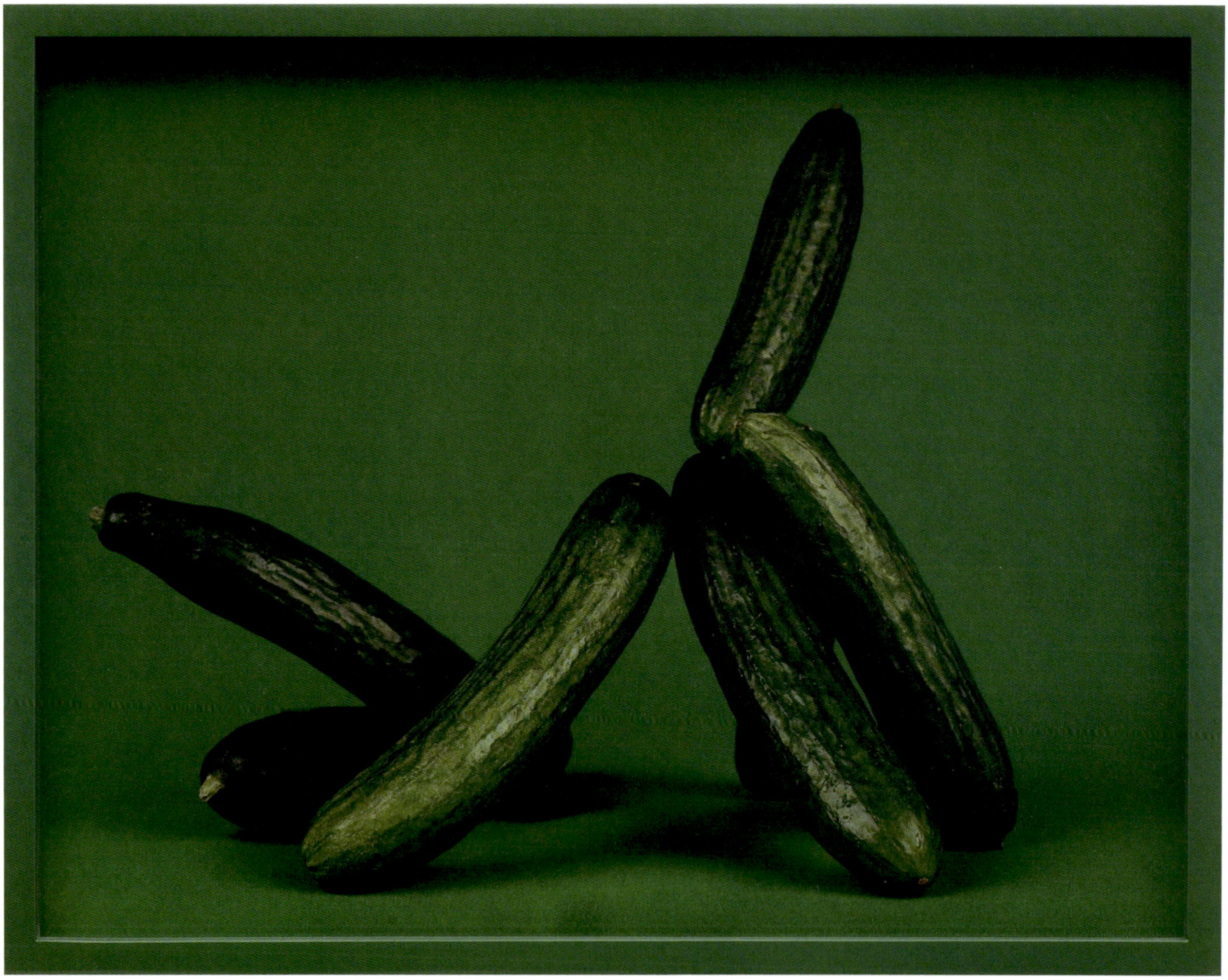

*Persian Cucumbers, Shuk Hakarmel*, 2008

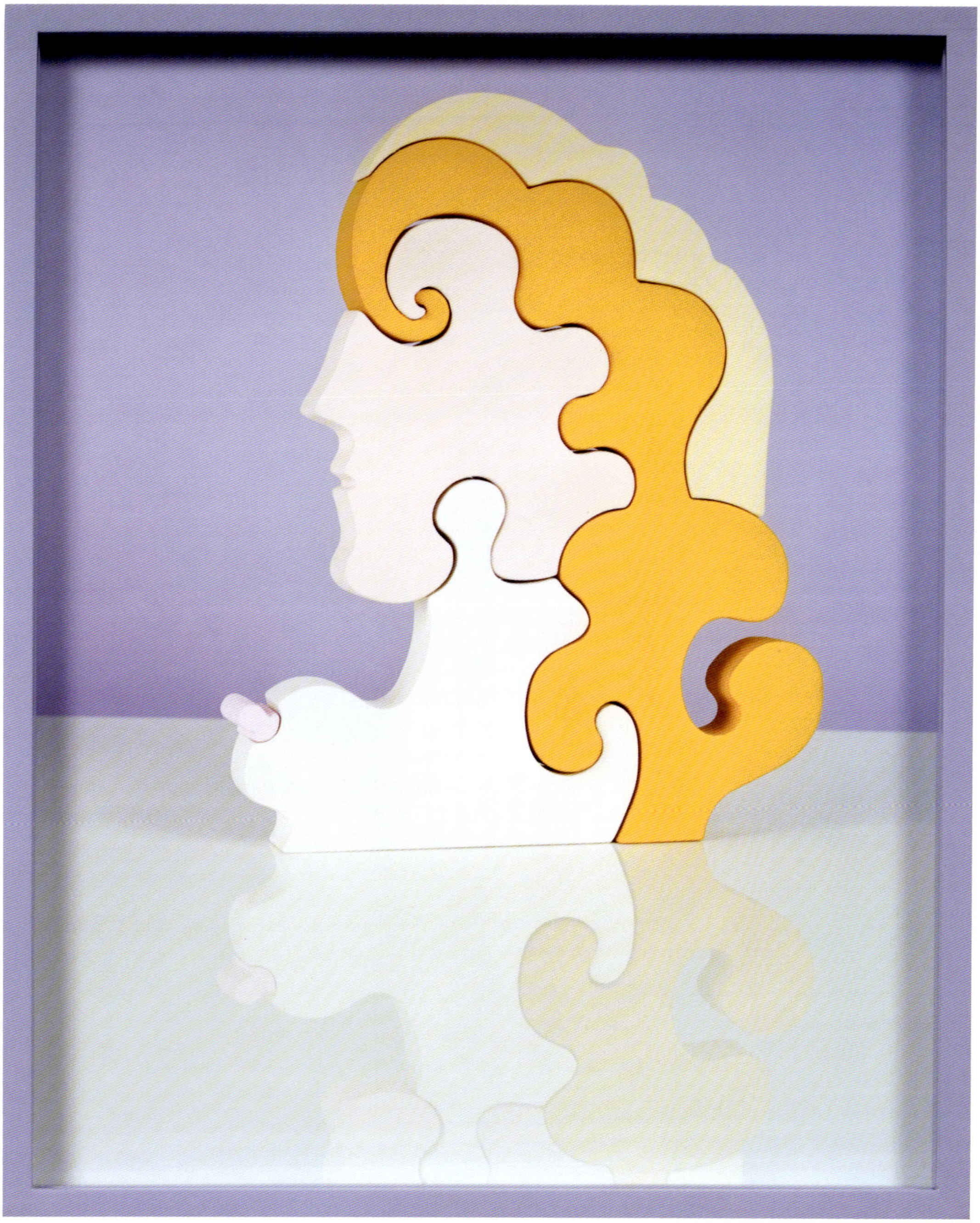

*Woman (Puzzle)*, 2010

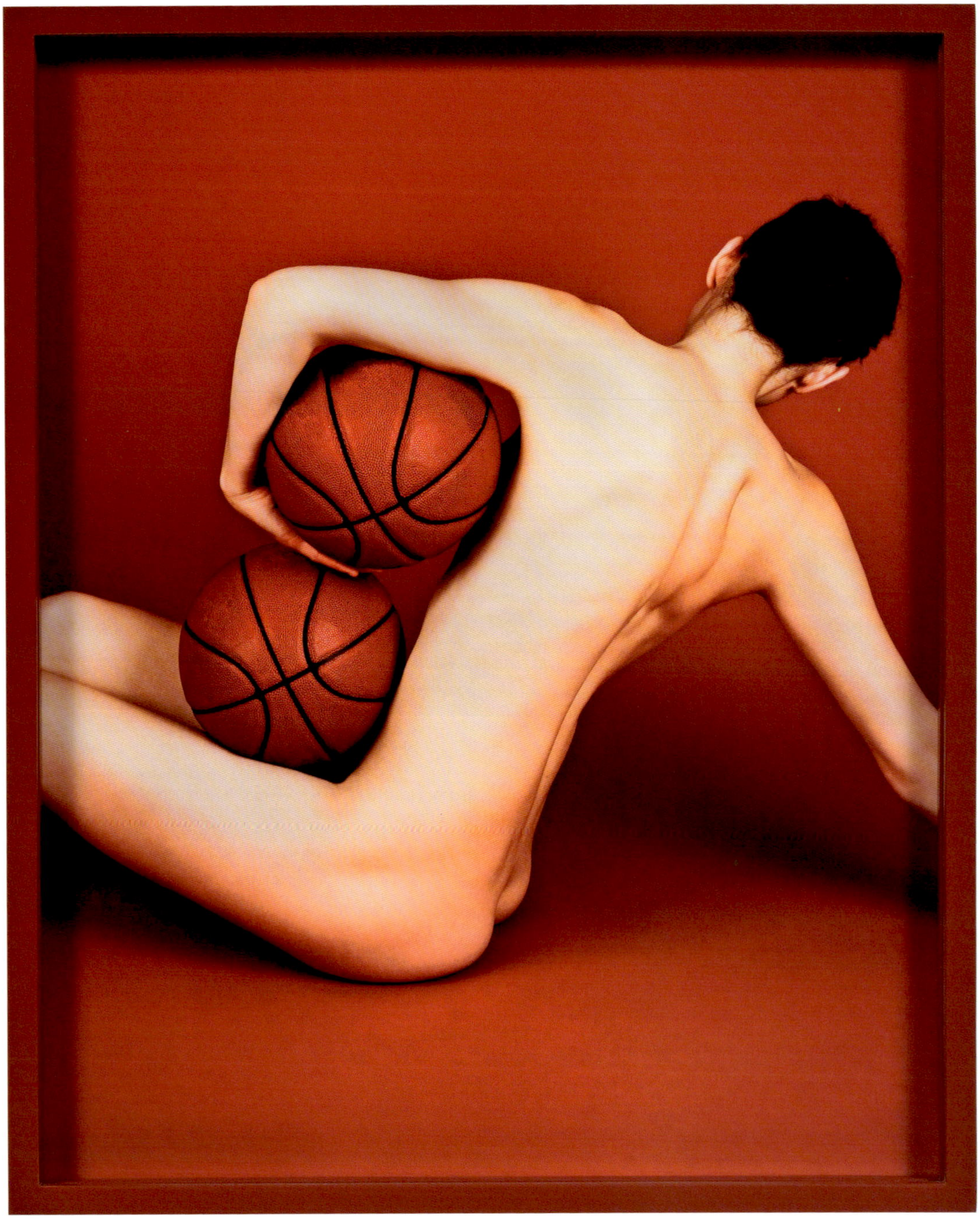

*Guinevere*, 2009

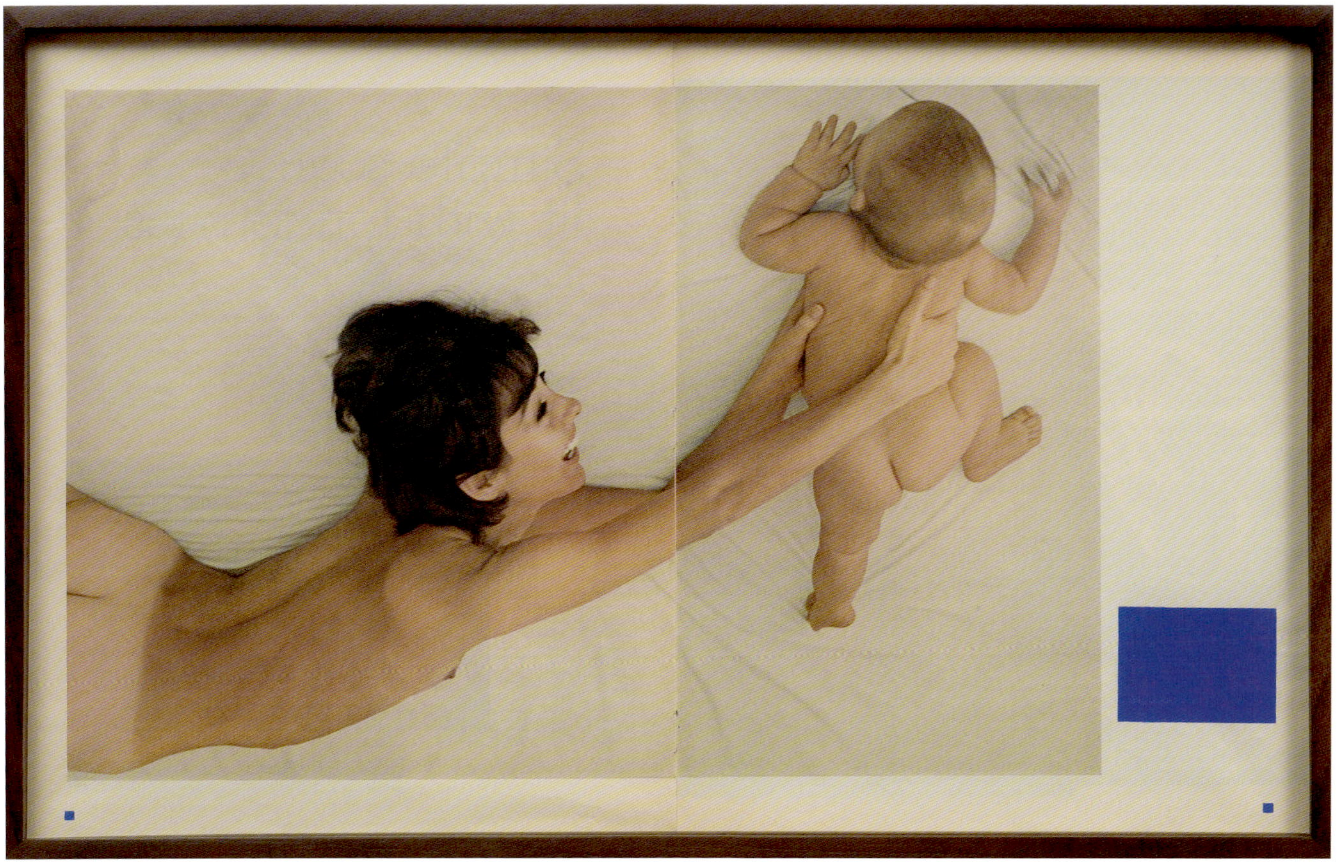

*Joanne and Trace, No Distractions*, 2007

Beatrix Ruf

# Introduction

In his both visually seductive and irritating photographic and filmic works, Elad Lassry explores canonical ideas about the use of images as influenced by various technologies and the history of the media.

His photographs—everyday and design objects, fruit and vegetable still lifes, human and animal portraits, landscapes and cityscapes—allude to visual features and image constructions that have been used in photography, advertising, magazines and illustrated books, and in films. What interests him in this context is analogue source material and duplication methods, as well as the development of different types of images in the history of the image before they were incorporated into the digital flood of the now omnipresent archive of available images.

Elad Lassry's photographic works, which do not usually exceed the format of a magazine or other printed material, comprise either collages of acquired printed matter or newly composed photographs.

The collages consist of found, illustrated, single pages and double-page spreads from magazines, which the artist either reworks by heightening their design elements or reuses several times for individual works as duplicated printed products. In terms of their visual appearance, they differ through the nature of their use and have already undergone, so to speak, additional anonymous and temporal "applied design" through the alteration of their form.

The artist contrasts these unique specimens, in which he makes direct use of products of analogue duplication methods, with his far more frequent photographs. In these he plays with the relationship between analogue and digital methods of image production and, using well-known images, questions the image itself by testing the omnipresence of images for the possibility of singularity. For example, the numerous portraits of the actor Anthony Perkins that Lassry manipulates digitally originate from analogue photographic archives. In treating them in this way he shines the spotlight on the specific nature of the individual portraits of Perkins and, at the same time, the typological nature of the film industry's publicity portrait. Other images used by Lassry are based on publicity shots, illustrated design books, and animal photographs—found images, which he restages in the studio using elaborate processes, and which initiate and implement multiple processes of the complexification of interpretation, composition, production—original and reproduction both on their way to becoming a new image.

Lassry's photographs make use of the attractiveness of the familiarity of these images. However, they are almost too intensely colored, too abstract, too staged. In addition to this process of visual emphasis, they are presented in matching colored frames, which, on yet another level, critically thematicize the relationship between the image and the "picture" as an utilitarian object, refer to the history of the presentation of objects as art and the aestheticization of perception, and prompt distortions, and, therefore, ruptures in the stereotype and the customary—in both temporal and interpretational terms—process of our perception of the images. The artist further expands these irritating presentation "pedestals" in his exhibitions by placing the photographic image beside film projections that are equivalent in terms of format and presentational form.

Lassry's films, which are always silent, also strain filmic conventions and act through the heightening of the fields of tension between realism and abstraction, narrative and abstract visual language, still photography and camera movement.

The film *Untitled (Passacaglia)* (2010) presents an exemplary combination of his complex approach to and exploration of issues concerning the circulation, reception, and media history of images, which the artist encounters on the journey to his visually striking works—works that convince by virtue of their inherent and new visual idiom.

As in all the works by this artist, the film is initiated by historical models and conventions of representation as "shaped" by the media and by taste. The "models" for the film are a TV production from 1966 of the choreography *Passacaglia* by the American dance legend Doris Humphrey; aesthetic clichés that have become part of everyday design, such as the "California drop cloth," a fabric pattern that refers to American Expressionism and trivialized visual references to, for example, the works of Jackson Pollock, and that is used for numerous interior fittings. The film also incorporates an exploration of methods for the reading of artworks for television based on insights from psychology and perception theory, and the translation of a well-known painting by Robert Delaunay from 1916, *La grande Portugaise*, into a set for the dance newly arranged by Lassry with dancers from the New York City Ballet. The short film's probing tracking shots create penetrating images and an irritating work that does not provide insight into a choreography, a painting, a stage set, or a story, but renders tangible the process of seeing, that is the complex experience that is realized in the direct relationship of the seeing subject to the seen object. This is perhaps the reason why, in the final shot the dancers, who are presented up to then as objects like the set and choreography, smile directly at us.

Elad Lassry's exhibition at the Kunsthalle Zürich, for which this book is published, was the first comprehensive presentation of his photographic and filmic oeuvre. The exhibition provided an overview of his entire activity with a selection of 53 photographic works and the five films realized to date.

Numerous people and organizations have played a crucial part in contributing to the exhibition and this publication.

First and foremost, I am deeply grateful to Elad Lassry for accepting the invitation to present his work in Zurich, and for his thoughtful and focused engagement with both the exhibition and the catalogue.

I am delighted to include texts by Bettina Funcke, Liz Kotz, and Fionn Meade, and I thank them for their thoughtful contributions.

My thanks also go to David Kordansky and the team at the David Kordansky Gallery, especially Ana Vejzovic Sharp, for their support and assistance. I am also deeply indebted to the lenders, who accept to part temporarily with their works.

Once more I would like to offer my warmest thanks to the team at Kunsthalle Zürich, whose commitment and enthusiasm are essential to realizing projects such as this.

I would like to extend my thanks for the generous contributions made by the Präsidialdepartement der Stadt Zürich and the LUMA Foundation, as well as Swiss Re for their support of our education and tour programs.

Beatrix Ruf

# Einführung

Elad Lassry thematisiert in seinen visuell verführerischen wie irritierenden Fotografien, Collagen und Filmen kanonisierte Vorstellungen über die Verwendung von Bildern, wie sie sowohl von den Techniken als auch der Geschichte der Medien geprägt worden sind.

Seine Bilder – sie zeigen Alltagsgegenstände, Designobjekte, Stilleben mit Früchten und Gemüse, Porträts von Menschen und Tieren, Landschaften und Stadtansichten – greifen visuelle Erkennungszeichen und Bildkonstruktionen auf, die in der Fotografie, der Werbung, in Magazinen und Bildbänden, aber auch im Film verwendet werden. Lassrys Interesse richtet sich dabei auf analoge Vorlagen und Vervielfältigungsmethoden sowie die Prägung von Bildtypen in der Geschichte des Bildes, bevor diese in die digitale Flut eines allgegenwärtig gewordenen Bildarchivs eingehen.

Elad Lassrys meist das Format einer Zeitschrift oder eines Druckerzeugnisses nicht überschreitenden Arbeiten sind entweder Collagen aus angeeigneten Druckerzeugnissen oder neu inszenierte Fotografien.

Die Collagen entstehen aus gefundenen Bild- und Doppelbildseiten von Magazinen, die der Künstler mit einer Überzeichnung ihrer Designelemente überarbeitet oder als Reproduktion gleich mehrmals für Einzelarbeiten benutzt. Sie unterscheiden sich durch Gebrauchsart oder Versandinsignien in ihrer visuellen Erscheinung und haben bereits ein zusätzliches anonymes und zeitliches „Gebrauchsdesign" als Veränderung ihrer Gestaltung erfahren. Diesen Unikaten, in denen der Künstler Produkte analoger Vervielfältigungsmethoden direkt verwendet, setzt er seine viel häufigeren Fotografien entgegen.

Hier spielt der Künstler mit dem Verhältnis von analogen und digitalen Methoden der Bildproduktion und stellt mit bekannten Bildern wiederum in Bildern die Frage an das Bild, indem er die Allgegenwärtigkeit von Bildern auf ihre Möglichkeit zur Singularität hin austestet. Aus analogen Bildarchiven etwa stammen die zahlreichen Porträts des Schauspielers Anthony Perkins, die Lassry digital bearbeitet. Er rückt damit das Spezifische des einzelnen Porträts Perkins' und zugleich das Typologische der Werbeporträts der Filmindustrie ins Zentrum. Andere Bilder basieren auf Werbeaufnahmen, Designbildbänden, Tierfotografien, auf gefundenen Bildern, die vom Künstler in aufwendigen Verfahren im Studio neu inszeniert werden und vielfältige Prozesse der Komplizierung von Interpretation, Komposition, Produktion, Original und Reproduktion initiieren, und die so zu „neuen" Bildern werden.

Lassrys Fotografien benutzen die Attraktivität der Bekanntheit dieser Bilder, aber sie sind beinahe zu farbintensiv, zu abstrahiert, zu inszeniert und bekommen zusätzlich zu diesen visuellen Überzeichnungen jeweils farblich abgestimmte Rahmen verpasst. Diese thematisieren das Verhältnis von Bild und Gebrauchsobjekt „Bild" auf einer weiteren Ebene kritisch: Sie sprechen über die Geschichte der Präsentation von Objekten als Kunst und der Ästhetisierung von Wahrnehmung und führen zu Störungen und damit auch zu Brüchen in der Stereotypie und dem üblichen – sowohl zeitlichen als auch interpretatorischen – Prozess unserer Wahrnehmung der Bilder. Diese irritierenden „Sockel" der Präsentation erweitert der Künstler in seinen Ausstellungen noch, indem er das fotografische Bild neben Filmprojektionen platziert, die in Format und Präsentationsform gleichwertig sind.

Lassrys immer tonlose Filme strapazieren darüber hinaus Konventionen des Filmischen und agieren mit einer Intensivierung der Spannungsfelder zwischen Realismus und Abstraktion, erzählerischer und abstrahierender Bildsprache, Standbild und Kamerabewegung.

Der Film *Untitled (Passacaglia)* (2010) verbindet exemplarisch die komplexe Vorgehensweise und Auseinandersetzung mit Fragen nach der Verbreitung, Rezeption und medialen Geschichte von Bildern, die der Künstler auf dem Weg zu seinen visuell frappierenden und durch eine eigene und neue Bildsprache überzeugenden Arbeiten beschreitet.

Wie bei allen Arbeiten des Künstlers ist der Film initiiert von historischen Vorlagen und Konventionen der durch Medien und Geschmack „gestalteten“ Repräsentation. Vorlagen für den hier realisierten Film ist eine 1966 für das Fernsehen produzierte Dokumentation der Choreographie *Passacaglia* der amerikanischen Tanzlegende Doris Humphrey; des weiteren ins Alltagsdesign eingegangene ästhetische Klischees wie der „California Drop Cloth“, ein Stoffmuster, das auf dem Amerikanischen Expressionismus und auf banalisierten Erkennungszeichen zum Beispiel der Arbeiten von Jackson Pollock beruht und für zahlreiche Innenausstattungen herhalten musste. Ebenso integriert ist eine Auseinandersetzung mit Methoden für das Lesen von Kunstwerken am Fernseher, basierend auf psychologischen und wahrnehmungstheoretischen Erkenntnissen sowie die Übersetzung des bekannten Gemäldes *La grande Portugaise* (1916) von Robert Delaunay in ein Bühnenbild für den von Lassry neu arrangierten Tanz mit Tänzerinnen und Tänzern des New York City Ballet. Die tastenden Kamerafahrten des kurzen Filmes schaffen eindringliche Bilder und ein irritierendes Werk, das keinen Aufschluss über eine Choreographie, ein Gemälde, ein Bühnenbild oder eine Geschichte gibt, sondern den Prozess des Sehens als komplexe Erfahrung erlebbar macht, die sich in der direkten Beziehung des Sehenden zum gesehenen Objekt realisiert. Und vielleicht deshalb lächeln uns die bis anhin als Objekte wie Gemälde, Teil von einem Set und der Choreographie erfassten Tänzerinnen in der Endeinstellung des Filmes direkt ins Gesicht.

Elad Lassrys Ausstellung in der Kunsthalle Zürich, zu der diese Publikation erscheint, war die erste umfassende Zusammenschau seines fotografischen und filmischen Werkes. Die Ausstellung umfasste einen Überblick über das gesamte Schaffen Elad Lassrys mit einer Auswahl von 53 Fotoarbeiten und den bis anhin realisierten fünf Filmarbeiten.

Zahlreiche Einzelpersonen und Organisationen haben entscheidend dazu beigetragen, dass die Ausstellung und diese Publikation realisiert werden konnten.

Zuallererst möchte ich Elad Lassry dafür danken, dass er die Einladung, seine Arbeiten in Zürich zu zeigen, angenommen und die Ausstellung sowie den Katalog enthusiastisch und engagiert begleitet hat.

Wir freuen uns sehr, dass Texte von Bettina Funcke, Liz Kotz und Fionn Meade in diese Publikation aufgenommen werden konnten, und danken ihnen für ihre bereichernden und anregenden Beiträge.

David Kordansky und das Team der David Kordansky Gallery, insbesondere Ana Vejzovic Sharp, haben sich unermüdlich für die Realisierung des Projektes eingesetzt und zahlreiche, grosszügige Leihgeber haben sich bereit erklärt, sich zeitweise von ihren Werken zu trennen. Dafür möchten wir uns herzlich bedanken.

Mein grosser Dank gilt erneut dem Team der Kunsthalle Zürich, das die Ausstellung wie immer mit grossem Einsatz vorbereitet hat und dessen Engagement und Enthusiasmus wesentlich dazu beiträgt, dass Projekte wie diese realisiert werden können.

Für kontinuierliche Unterstützung danken wir dem Präsidialdepartement der Stadt Zürich und der LUMA Stiftung sowie der Swiss Re für die Förderung unseres Vermittlungsprogramms.

Liz Kotz

# "This Is to Be Looked At"

It is a short, simple film of movement and stillness. A zebra's tail rhythmically moves next to its still and massive rump as the camera slowly pans, more or less horizontally, forward across the zebra's body. The angled stripes create a bold painterly composition, a flat abstract pattern filling a rectangular frame. It is startling when this graphic field suddenly moves, as the zebra twitches its muscles, and the pan, which briefly reverses, reaches the neck and the much narrower stripes of the head. Suddenly the eye blinks rapidly as the animal turns to briefly face us. Half animal and half Op art: is this what a zebra looks like?

After cutting to black, the pan slowly arrives at the theatrically-lit face of a blonde woman in three-quarter view, gazing intently in what seems to be the direction of the zebra. She is lit both from front and from behind, her glowing blond hair sharply isolated against the dimensionless black backdrop, creating an overtly artificial scene. Her eyes blink and she purses her lips, then briefly looks down, before she too disappears. Shot in Super-16mm, *Zebra and Woman* (2007) is silent and a little over five minutes long, but its oddness does not decrease with multiple viewings. A curious combination of cropping and movement allows the film to oscillate between painterly abstraction and three-dimensional reality. As Lisa Dorin notes, Elad Lassry "transforms his literal subjects—the zebra and the woman—into a means of presenting a space that is both cinematic and painterly."[1]

Animate and inanimate, human and animal, moving and still, two-dimensional and three-dimensional: these are some of the core elements that structure Elad Lassry's work. They recur differently among his several short films, and in his many C-print photographs and collages, an ensemble of works that share a curious and unstable visual language that somehow collects together a diverse and idiosyncratic set of subjects. Lassry's work since 2007 essentially combines three different types of materials: short films shot on either 16mm or Super-16mm, unique silkscreened magazine pages, and C-prints produced as small editions. The two-dimensional works are all fairly compact in size, roughly 36 × 28 cm, about the size of a large-format magazine page or coffee-table book. The films, which are projected alongside the photographs rather than in a separate darkened space, are shown quite small, at about the same scale and height as the images. This close-up projection allows them to retain their sharpness and luminosity even in a fairly well-lit space, and emphasizes the intermingling and interpenetration of the three formats. Lassry's choice of an intimate and modest scale is clearly posed against the massive size and technical mastery of 1990s art photography modeled on large-scale history paintings. And in a similar counter-move, Lassry's use of modest painted frames color-keyed to the dominant tone of each image reinforces photography's keepsake quality and its existence as a framed object to be handled and displayed.

Much has been made of Lassry's combination of the altered magazine pages, which are vaguely Constructivist-looking collages, and the carefully toned C-prints, which include both studio-shot and altered photographs.[2] Other hallmarks of Lassry's practice are his broad range of visual styles (combining 1970s product photography, film stills, portraiture, and modernist tropes like double-exposures), his constant moving back and forth between "original" and found or altered materials, and the fact that he clearly doesn't differentiate between these genres and formats. This shifting between proper photography and collage, between art and vernacular styles, and between found and originally-shot images is not uncommon among younger artists working with photography. Yet in Lassry's project this strange disparity has acquired a surprising unity and coherence, even if its organizing principles remain elusive.

In one of his earliest exhibited images, *Los Angeles at Night* (2006) (ill. 1), a Xeroxed two-page spread from a book or magazine depicts a nighttime view of the city's bright lights shot from above the Hollywood Bowl. The gutter cuts vertically across the image, and we see the telltale sheen along the inner edge of one page; the caption, recounting the making of the image, is retained, but half the left-hand page has been cropped out. It is one of relatively few magazine page works in which the text has not been blocked out; another is *The Family Dog* (2007), a slightly off-kilter image of three white Spaniel puppies posed on a floral surface, with one incongruously sitting in a wicker bowl. These are completely generic images, taken from American magazines of perhaps the 1960s or 1970s, and yet they are also very personal—we can sense without knowing, for instance, that the artist has long lived in Hollywood, and is an avid animal lover. All images are images of desire, of course, substitutes for things near at hand, out of reach, and completely impossible. And Lassry's images alternately suggest scenes of cheerful and wholesome postwar Americana, and its stranger more ominous undertows.

In one C-print that particularly recalls *Zebra and Woman*, a man's two hands, cropped midway up the forearm, awkwardly hold a boldly striped black and white snake that seems to intertwine around his wrists (*California King Snake, CKS*, 2007). Shot in acutely sharp focus, the hands and snake are suspended in a dimensionless black field we recognize as a studio backdrop: that empty neutral space that is nowhere, that serves to isolate and dramatize whatever is placed in front of it. Whether they feature people or inanimate objects, the subjects of Lassry's pictures appear posed and self-consciously on display—even the strange double-exposed wolves standing before a studio backdrop (*Two Wolves*, 2008) are clearly actors, hired animals that have been trained to hold poses for the camera. Across all kinds of subject matter, Lassry investigates conventions of presentation and display: in *Chocolate Factory* (2007), two white-gloved hands pick up unwrapped Hershey's chocolate kisses against a flattened field of oddly-luminous chocolates. In *Circles and Squares* (2007), a double-exposed still life of melons lying on reflective boxes places fruit in a glossy display setting we might expect for shoes or cosmetics; the doubling of reflections and of the double-exposure renders the field spatially dense and confusing. In *Hollywood Bowl, Fog* (2007), we look down from a wooded hill toward a freeway and cityscape shrouded in fog, as the picture's receding horizon is obstructed by the gray haze (looking closely, we can recognize nearly the same scene and vantage point as that in the earlier *Los Angeles at Night*).

One could go on, describing example after example, because it is difficult to provide any overview or apparent rationale that defines or describes these images as a set. Some subjects—wigs, melons, particular models, the actor Anthony Perkins—reappear in different images. And in a frequent device, consumer objects like lipsticks or shoes are placed on rectangular or square display pedestals that are oriented frontally toward the picture plane, so that their three-dimensionality is only revealed by shadows; in other works, two-dimensional pictures are placed on top of these stands, rendering the relation between flatness and depth even more puzzle-like and undecidable. Based on real things, the compositions continually fracture into pattern and abstraction. Yet it is an abstraction arrived at through representation, or, as Lassry terms it, "abstraction through the subject": "I start from a place where I don't see much difference between the backdrop and the subject [ … ] It is abstraction in the sense that the subject almost disappears."[3]

To elucidate what Elad Lassry is doing, it may help to clarify what he is *not* doing, what paths he seems to be breaking from. If his static studio-shot photographs share a surface resemblance to some of the equally stagey color-saturated photographs of Christopher Williams, Lassry presents his pictures severed from the kinds of textual anchoring and analysis provided by Williams' extravagantly detailed titles. The sumptuous color image is not a lure into a larger game of reference and signification, in which apparently diverse subjects—an ear of corn, a camera, a woman in curlers—are integrated into a larger historical narrative. There is nothing to know, or to learn, in Lassry's strangely blank and seductive images. If there is a logic that links, for instance, photographs of a skunk, scattered vegetables, and a female nude holding a basketball (to recall the artist's most recent show in Los Angeles), it can only be found through formal, pictorial, or psychological associations.

For some time, many of the more vigorous strains of "critical" photography (and wider art practice) have pursued what we might still understand as a project of "demystification"—aspiring to break down and analyze the image and its larger apparatus, to strip these of mystery and seduction, and lay them bare as sets of strategies, codes, and conventions. From Stephen Prina and Christopher Williams to countless younger practitioners, contemporary artists informed by Conceptual art and its legacies have sought to investigate media and institutional archives, trace otherwise invisible historical connections among images, and reveal their production processes and institutional underpinnings, often by employing strategies of displacement, disjunction, alienation effects, and layered commentaries. Of course, part of the fascination of this project lies in the absurdity of its drives to reason, clarity, and system, and in the perverse ironies of using neo-conceptual strategies that are, by now, as nuanced and mannered as, say, gestural abstraction.

Sliding off this pedagogical impulse, Lassry tends to talk about the occult, about the persistent ghosting or haunting of an image by its absent context. Lassry likewise sidesteps familiar tropes of conceptual photography, avoiding text or commentary, and rarely working in series, to instead focus, yet again, on the singular image, and on the strange singularity of images. He speaks of this as a regression, a circling back to certain almost 19th-century attitudes toward the image. And he quite consciously turns his photographs into objects, in which tightly composed compositions feel trapped in vitrines, or, as Sarah Lehrer-Graiwer described them, "sealed in their tidy frames."[4]

"THIS IS NOT TO BE LOOKED AT" (ill. 2) reads a celebrated 1968 painting by the Los Angels-based artist John Baldessari. Some 40 years later, much work done in the wake of Baldessari, Douglas Huebler, et al, could be captioned something like "I know very well, but"—as disavowals of different types organize present-day photographic practice. We know very well that the classic moves of conceptual photography have long since been exhausted, codified, and recuperated by the art market—yet generations of art students continue to plumb them for some mix of easily-recognizable "criticality" and savvy marketability. Another set of practitioners simply proceeds as if conceptual art or postmodern photography never happened, and we can continue to take cool-looking photographs of everything around us as if it were 1950 and arty photo-journalism was still young. And yet others aspire to retool modernist photography and its self-reflexive explorations of the photographic medium for a digital age.[5]

Animated for decades by the powerful intellectual and aesthetic experiments of early 20th century modernism, Conceptual art, and postmodern photography, present-day photographic practice often finds itself at a standstill, where a rich experimental history seems to have arrived at countless dead ends. Lassry tries to find aesthetic and psychological charge precisely through this pervasive sense of exhaustion and over-familiarity. In so doing, he perhaps plumbs a side of the "Pictures" project sidelined in its dominant reception, which fixates on crucial but well-trod questions of authorship, originality, and institutional context. Indeed, his persistent references to "haunting" and ghosts recall language used early on by key Pictures Generation figures. In his 1977 essay "Pictures" (expanded and republished in 1979), Douglas Crimp was at pains to elucidate how an art context organized around duration and performance underpinned the making of pictures, describing how "An art whose strategies are thus grounded in the literal temporality and presence of theater has been the crucial formulating experience for a group of artists currently beginning to exhibit in New York."[6] In discussing the work of Jack Goldstein—an artist important to Lassry as well—Crimp notes that, "The psychological resonance of this work is not that of the subject matter of his pictures, however, but of the way those pictures are presented, staged; that is, it is a function of their structure."[7] For Crimp, the curious temporality of a work like Goldstein's 1978 film *The Jump* (ill. 3) comes from how the technique of rotoscopy renders it both a drawing and an erasure, a making and an effacing—a temporality that he sees not as tied to a specific medium but as possible in both still and moving images.

In a 2009 roundtable on the legacy of the Pictures Generation, Lassry singled out Goldstein's *The Jump* as a work that needs to be freed from "the overwhelming emphasis on the act of appropriation. When you revisit the works themselves, and you let go of this framework, there is actually so much more that can arise [ ... ] Neither the fact that the film originates from stock footage nor its rotoscope special effects eliminate the possibilities of engaging with another kind of experience or another meaning in the work."[8] Protesting that the term "appropriation" has become so reductive that "it doesn't allow one to move toward a new set of questions," Lassry suggests that Goldstein's films using appropriated materials nonetheless "become autonomous gestures," and that "there are other things happening, within the work, like the negation of cinematic agency and the diffusion of cinematic experience."[9] Lassry's debt to Goldstein's short films like *Some Butterflies* (1974) and *Shane* (1974) is clear, in that they offer a cryptic way forward beyond questions of authorship and context by shifting back onto the very curious things happening within the frame.

In a 1985 interview in *Arts Magazine*, Sherrie Levine protested how critics tended to neglect the actual pictorial content of her work and, in effect, ignored what was going on inside the frame. Recounting a conversation with the writer Howard Singerman, who proposed that "people tend to look at the work as if it starts at the frame and goes out, as opposed to looking at the picture from the frame in," Levine notes how "we've become so sensitive to context that we sometimes just see the picture as a hole in the wall. In fact they are pictures. They're very complicated pictures, but they can be read iconographically. The images in the *1917* show are crosses and people masturbating. Most people who have written about this work have either ignored or repressed the iconographic content."[10]

Levine also frequently makes recourse to a language of ghosting in discussions of her work, particularly to describe the relation between "original" and "copy": "The pictures I make are really ghosts of ghosts; their relationship to their original images is tertiary, i.e. three or four times removed [ ... ] When I started doing this work, I wanted to make a picture which contradicted itself. I wanted to put a picture on top of a picture so that there are times when both pictures disappear and other times when they're both manifest; that vibration is basically what the work's about for me—that space in the middle where there's no picture."[11] This absence is, of course, relative, as Levine proceeds to insist: "I think a lot of the people seem to get lost in the gap, and think that there's no picture there, when in fact there are two pictures there."[12]

Like much early "Pictures" work, Lassry investigates the photograph as it exists in print media. Yet his interest lies in where this economy of circulation and reproduction stops, where it condenses into a single complex image, to explore a kind of circulation that is more mental and interior. For Lassry, the mediation involved in reworking and reanimating a found image, in severing it from its source and thereby "orphaning" it, is intimately related to the relations between working with still and moving images.[13] In a recent interview, he suggests that "Something about trying to print on photographs or magazine paper, or dealing with the physicality of how photographs register on another surface (while in the process erasing something that was preexisting) marks the transition from collage to film."[14] Yet the very filmmaking he is most interested in hovers on the boundary of the pre-cinematic, and on the historically old and yet still disconcerting shock of pictures that move, admitting that, "There's something regressive about the idea of film being no more than a sequence of photographs."[15]

For Lassry, film becomes a key tool for exploring the possibilities and impossibilities of rendering subjects in a two-dimensional field. Drawing on an illustration in a 1971 science textbook, *Untitled* (2008) (ill. 4) places a series of young people on top of a brightly colored diagram of a house. Although we know the diagram is two-dimensional, the actors struggle to present it as if it occupied real space—sitting on the roof, posing as if to stand in the doorway. As Anat Edgi notes, the brightly colored scene echoes a "1970s-era PBS educational television style in which primary colors, bold shapes, forced perspectives [and] visual games [ ... ] get compared and contrasted."[16] And yet more than a visual lesson in perception, the film takes on psychological associations about the family and the deeply odd relationship of human figures to such an artificially constructed set of spaces—and to one another.

These perceptual games are intensified in *Untitled* (2009), a 16mm film loosely based on restaging production stills from Jerome Robbins' 1955 made-for-television version of *Peter Pan* (ill. 5). Lassry has long understood his work as informed by both appropriation art and structural film, an idiosyncratic pairing that becomes forcefully evident in this work, which segments and recombines highly-abstracted fragments of an already warped children's classic (in which the childlike Peter Pan is played by an adult female actress). Yet the actual cultural antecedents nearly disappear in Lassry's restaging, which pushes the materials toward series of abstract compositions that just happen to be made with human bodies. As the film starts, a female dancer's cropped torso, sealed in an intensely bright red leotard, fills the frame. She bends over and begins to move, and slowly the camera moves with her, through what appear to be series of gray and black columns that divide the frame into vertical stripes. Intercut with other materials, including a blue-eyed man gesticulating against a light blue background and walking amid a series of brightly colored polished columns, the dancer's red body becomes a graphic emblem used to explore space and motion in a two-dimensional medium. Just as the leotard itself functions to abstract the body, to simultaneously reveal and conceal, Lassry's persistent close-ups and pans play with this figure on the boundary of human and objects.

Across his body of films, Lassry uses a series of simple devices—the close-up, the slow pan, the superimposition of pictorial perspective—to explore how filming "real space" can complicate the spatial surface in strange ways. We can understand his films as a kind of primer for how to look at the photographs, as they explore the inherent problematics of representing space with a camera, producing a constantly changing sense of depth and surface, and repeatedly returning experience to flatness. In so doing, they pose a series of questions about film that then double back on pictorial media like photographs. What is the texture of depth on the screen, and how is it or isn't it related to other pictorialized space? Can cinematic or pictorial space arrive at a point where it surpasses imitative depth, and achieves some other uncanny depth? What does it mean to have a continuous glimpse of screen space that moves, rather than to move through a discontinuous series of still glimpses? In Lassry's work, flat planes of color that border on the monochrome become reanimated as inhabitable by objects or figures, yet in ways that continually undercut any sense of these as coherent or rational spaces. In the end, Lassry's pictures—both still and moving—work to erode distinctions between subject and backdrop, between figure and ground, using intensely fabricated surfaces to move photography and cinema toward perceptual concerns more often associated with painting. "There's this moment," he described in conversation, "where the picture you thought you knew starts moving."[17]

1. Lisa Dorin, *Film, Video, New Media: At the Art Institute of Chicago*, Yale University Press, London & New Haven 2009, p. 104.
2. Sarah Lehrer-Graiwer describes the relation between the found and original images as a kind of rhythmic interplay: "Inserted into groups of his studio-shot photographs, they serve as a kind of punctuation, imparting an aura of mystery to the other works." In Sarah Lehrer-Graiwer, "Openings: Elad Lassry," *Artforum*, New York, vol. 48, no. 2, October 2009, p. 219.
3. Walead Beshty, Elad Lassry, Carter Mull, and Erika Vogt, "After Materiality and Style," *Art in America*, New York, April 2009, p. 134.
4. Lehrer-Graiwer, "Openings: Elad Lassry," p. 221.
5. After all, as Abigail Solomon-Godeau was at pains to point out nearly 30 years ago, the formalist appropriation of once-radical modernist techniques formed the backbone of post-WWII American art photography; see "The Armed Vision Disarmed—Radical Formalism from Weapon to Style," *Afterimage*, Rochester, January 1983.
6. Douglas Crimp, "Pictures," *October. MIT Press Journals*, Cambridge, Massachusetts, no. 8, Spring 1979, p. 77.
7. Ibid., p. 79–80.
8. Beshty, Lassry, Mull, and Vogt, "After Materiality and Style," p. 131–132.
9. Ibid., p. 132.
10. Sherrie Levine, in Jeanne Siegel, "After Sherrie Levine" (1985), reprinted in Siegel (ed.), *Art Talk: the Early 80s*, Da Capo Press, New York 1988, p. 253.
11. Ibid., p. 247.
12. Ibid., p. 253.
13. In a 2008 interview, Lassry describes the remnants of a picture's original context as "a ghost that remains. The history of it persists, haunting the picture, always [ … ] I am sort of kidnapping this picture and removing it from its story, with the acknowledgment that the story has never been stable." In Sarah Lehrer-Graiwer, "Studio Visit," *FlashArtonline.com*, November 18, 2008, http://www.flashartonline.com/interno.php?pagina=studio_det&id_art=210&det=ok&title=Elad-Lassry (last accessed: June 17, 2010).
14. Elad Lassry, "Hijacked in a Winter Garden Moment: Cay Sophie Rabinowitz with Erin Tao in Conversation with Elad Lassry," *Fantom Photographic Quarterly*, no. 3, 2010, www.fantomeditions.com/issues/issue-03/ (last accessed: June 29, 2010).
15. Ibid.
16. Anat Ebgi, "Elad Lassry" *artisrael.org*, June 2009, http://www.artisrael.org/feature/press/elad-lassry-june-2009 (last accessed: June 17, 2010).
17. Conversation with the artist, April 1, 2010.

Liz Kotz

# „Das ist zum Anschauen“

Es ist ein kurzer schlichter Film über Statik und Dynamik. Der Schwanz eines Zebras schlägt rhythmisch gegen seinen reglosen massigen Rumpf, während die Kamera langsam, mehr oder weniger horizontal, dem Körper des Tieres entlang nach vorn wandert. Die ineinander verwinkelten Streifen bilden eine kühne, malerisch wirkende Komposition, ein flaches abstraktes Muster, das den rechteckigen Bildausschnitt ganz ausfüllt. Man ist überrascht, wenn diese grafische Fläche sich plötzlich bewegt, weil das Zebra mit den Muskeln zuckt, und wenn die Kamera, die kurz rückwärts schwenkt, schliesslich den Hals und die wesentlich schmaleren Streifen am Kopf erreicht. Plötzlich ein rascher Wimpernschlag, als das Tier sich umdreht und uns kurz frontal gegenübersteht. Halb Tier, halb Op-Art: Sieht ein Zebra wirklich so aus?

Schnitt, alles schwarz, dann erreicht der Kameraschwenk das theatralisch beleuchtete Gesicht einer blonden Frau im Dreiviertelprofil, die allem Anschein nach konzentriert Richtung Zebra blickt. Sie ist von vorn und hinten beleuchtet, ihr leuchtend blondes Haar hebt sich scharf vor dem dimensionslosen schwarzen Hintergrund ab – offensichtlich eine künstliche Inszenierung.

Sie blinzelt, schürzt die Lippen und senkt dann den Blick kurz, bevor sie ebenfalls verschwindet. *Zebra and Woman* (2007) ist ein gut fünf Minuten langer Stummfilm, der auch nach mehrfachem Anschauen nicht weniger befremdend wirkt. Eine seltsame Mischung von Schnitten und Bewegungen lässt den Film zwischen abstrakter Malerei und dreidimensionaler Realität oszillieren. Wie Lisa Dorin bemerkt, nutzt Elad Lassry „seine eigentlichen Sujets – das Zebra und die Frau – als Werkzeuge, um einen Raum zu erschaffen, der sowohl filmischen als auch malerischen Charakter hat.“[1]

Lebendig und unbelebt, Mensch und Tier, bewegt und stillstehend, zweidimensional und dreidimensional: Das sind einige der Grundelemente, auf denen Elad Lassrys Arbeit basiert. Sie wiederholen sich in unterschiedlicher Form in seinen Kurzfilmen und seinen vielen Farbfotografien und Collagen, ein Werkkomplex, der sich durch eine seltsame und unstete Bildsprache auszeichnet, der es jedoch gelingt, eine vielfältige und eigenwillige Reihe von Themen irgendwie zu bündeln. Lassrys Werk nach 2007 besteht im Wesentlichen aus drei verschiedenen Arten von Materialien: Aus Kurzfilmen im 16-mm- oder Super-16-mm-Format, aus Unikaten von mit Siebdruck bearbeiteten Zeitschriftenseiten und aus C-Prints als Editionen in kleiner Auflage. Die zweidimensionalen Arbeiten sind alle ziemlich kompakt in der Grösse, rund 28 × 36 cm, also etwa so gross wie die Seite einer grossformatigen Zeitschrift oder eines Bildbandes. Die Filme, die in der Regel im gleichen Raum wie die Fotografien gezeigt werden und nicht in einem separaten verdunkelten Kabinett, werden ziemlich kleinformatig projiziert, etwa gleich gross und gleich hoch wie die Bilder an den Wänden. Dank dieser Projektion aus geringer Distanz bewahren sie ihre Schärfe und Leuchtkraft selbst in einem relativ hellen Raum; zudem wird die Vermischung und gegenseitige Durchdringung der drei Formate dadurch noch deutlicher. Lassrys Wahl dieses intimen und bescheidenen Massstabs setzt sich deutlich ab von den Riesenformaten und der technischen Raffinesse der Kunstfotografie der 1990er Jahre, die grossformatigen Historienbildern nachempfunden war. Und in einer ähnlich gegenläufigen Bewegung unterstreicht Lassrys Verwendung von einfachen, passend zum dominanten Bildfarbton bemalten Rahmen die Erinnerungsqualität der Fotografie und ihren Charakter als gerahmtes Objekt zum In-die-Hand-Nehmen, Aufhängen und Präsentieren.

Über Lassrys Kompositionen aus bearbeiteten Zeitschriftenseiten – vage konstruktivistisch anmutende Collagen –, und die farblich sorgfältig abgestimmten C-Prints, die sowohl Studioaufnahmen als auch bearbeitete Fotografien umfassen, ist schon viel geschrieben und gesagt worden.[2] Weitere Merkmale von Lassrys Arbeit sind sein breites Spektrum visueller Techniken (eine Mischung aus Produktfotos der 1970er Jahre, Filmstills, Porträts und gängigen Techniken der Moderne, etwa Doppelbelichtungen), sein fortwährendes Hin und Her zwischen „Originalbildern" und vorgefundenem oder verfremdetem Material sowie die Tatsache, dass er zwischen diesen Gattungen und Formaten überhaupt keinen Unterschied macht. Dieser ständige Wechsel – zwischen Fotografie im eigentlichen Sinn und Collage, zwischen Kunst und alltäglichen Ausdrucksmitteln, zwischen vorgefundenen Bildern und Originalaufnahmen – ist nicht ungewöhnlich für jüngere Künstler, die fotografisch arbeiten. Doch in Lassrys Arbeit hat diese seltsame Disparität eine erstaunliche Einheit und Kohärenz erreicht, obwohl ihre Organisationsprinzipien schwer fassbar sind.

*Los Angeles at Night* (2006) (Abb. 1), eines der ersten Bilder, die Lassry ausstellte, zeigt eine fotokopierte Doppelseite aus einem Bildband oder einer Zeitschrift, eine Nachtaufnahme der hell erleuchteten Stadt von irgendwo oberhalb des Hollywood-Bowl-Geländes. Im Falz blitzt der weisse Bildrand auf dem Druckbogen hervor und zerschneidet das Bild senkrecht, parallel zum Falz ist auf der einen Seite ein Lichtreflex zu erkennen; die Bildlegende ist intakt geblieben und beschreibt die Entstehung der Aufnahme, doch die linke Buchseite ist in der Hälfte beschnitten. Es ist eine von relativ wenigen Arbeiten mit Zeitschriftenseiten, in denen der Text nicht abgedeckt ist; eine weitere ist *The Family Dog* (2007), ein leicht schräges Bild von drei weissen Spanielwelpen auf einer geblümten Decke, eines davon unpassenderweise in einer Korbschale sitzend. Es handelt sich um Allerweltsbilder aus amerikanischen Zeitschriften der 1960er oder 1970er Jahre, dennoch sind sie auch sehr persönlich – man spürt das, ohne zu wissen, dass der Künstler beispielsweise lange in Hollywood gelebt hat und ein begeisterter Tierfreund ist. Alle Bilder sind natürlich Sehnsuchtsbilder, ein Ersatz für naheliegende, nicht erreichbare oder ganz und gar unmögliche Dinge. Lassrys Bilder erinnern abwechslungsweise an ein fröhliches und gesundes Nachkriegs-Amerika und an dessen befremdlichere und bedrohlichere Untertöne.

In einem C-Print, der besonders stark an *Zebra and Woman* erinnert, halten die bis Mitte Unterarm sichtbaren Hände eines Mannes etwas unbeholfen eine breit gestreifte schwarz-weisse Schlange, die sich anschickt seine Handgelenke zu umschlingen (*California King Snake, CKS*, 2007). In äusserst scharfer Bildeinstellung schweben Hände und Schlange vor einer dimensionslosen schwarzen Fläche, offenbar eine normale schwarze Studiokulisse: Dieser leere neutrale Raum ist ein Nirgendwo, das alles, was sich vor ihm abspielt, isoliert und dramatisiert. Ob es sich um Menschen oder unbelebte Objekte handelt, die Sujets in Lassrys Bildern wirken immer gestellt und wie auf dem Präsentationsteller serviert – sogar die seltsamen, doppelt belichteten, vor einem Studiohintergrund stehenden Wölfe (*Two Wolves*, 2008) sind offensichtlich „Schauspieler", gemietete Tiere, die darauf abgerichtet sind, vor der Kamera zu posieren. Quer durch alle möglichen Themenbereiche untersucht Lassry die bestehenden Präsentations- und Ausstellungskonventionen: In *Chocolate Factory* (2007) halten zwei Hände in weissen Handschuhen unverpackte Hershey's Chocolate Kisses, den Hintergrund bilden unzählige weitere seltsam leuchtende Schokoküsse, die dicht an dicht auf einer Fläche verteilt liegen. In *Circles and Squares* (2007), einem doppelt belichteten Stillleben, in dem Melonen auf und vor Spiegelkuben platziert sind, werden diese Früchte in einem Hochglanzmodus präsentiert, den man eher bei Schuhen oder Kosmetik erwarten würde; der Doppeleffekt von Reflexionen und Doppelbelichtung verdichtet das Blickfeld enorm und wirkt verwirrend. In *Hollywood Bowl, Fog* (2007) schauen wir von einem bewaldeten Hügel auf eine Schnellstrasse und eine Stadtlandschaft, beides nebelverschleiert, während der fernere Horizont im grauen Dunst verschwindet. (Bei näherem Hinsehen ist es fast dieselbe Szenerie und derselbe Blickwinkel wie in dem früher entstandenen Bild *Los Angeles at Night*.)

Man könnte fortfahren, Beispiel um Beispiel zu beschreiben, denn es ist schwierig, einen Überblick zu geben oder ein klares Prinzip zu benennen, das diese Bilder in ihrer Gesamtheit definieren oder erfassen würde. Einige Motive – Perücken, Melonen, einzelne Modelle, der Schauspieler Anthony Perkins – tauchen in mehreren Bildern auf. Ein häufig auftretendes Muster sind auch Konsumobjekte, wie Lippenstifte oder Schuhe, die auf rechtwinkligen oder quadratischen Sockeln präsentiert werden, die frontal zur Bildfläche stehen, sodass ihre Dreidimensionalität nur anhand der Schatten zu erkennen ist. Bei anderen Arbeiten sind auf diesen Sockeln zweidimensionale Bilder platziert, sodass das Verhältnis zwischen Zweidimensionalität und Tiefe noch rätselhafter und unbestimmbarer wird. Zwar beruhen diese Kompositionen auf wirklichen Dingen, lösen sich aber zusehends in Muster und abstrakte Formen auf. Die Abstraktion entsteht jedoch durch die Darstellung, oder ist, wie Lassry es nennt, „eine Abstraktion durch das Motiv": „Ich beginne an einem Punkt, wo ich keinen grossen Unterschied zwischen Hintergrund und Motiv erkenne. [...] Es ist abstrakt in dem Sinn, dass das Motiv fast verschwindet."[3]

Um zu erhellen, was Elad Lassry eigentlich tut, könnte es hilfreich sein, zu klären, was er *nicht* tut, welche Wege er nicht beschreitet. Obwohl seine statischen Studioaufnahmen auf den ersten Blick Ähnlichkeiten mit den nicht minder gestellten farbsatten Fotografien von Christopher Williams aufweisen, präsentiert Lassry seine Bilder völlig frei von der textuellen Verankerung und Analyse, die Williams in seinen ungewöhnlich detaillierten Titeln mitliefert. Das üppige Farbbild ist kein Lockvogel, um uns in ein komplexes Spiel der Referenzen und Bedeutungen zu verstricken, in dessen Verlauf auf den ersten Blick voneinander unabhängige Sujets – eine Kornähre, eine Kamera, eine Frau mit Lockenwicklern – in den umfassenderen zeitlichen Zusammenhang einer Geschichte eingebettet werden. In Lassrys seltsam leeren, verführerischen Bildern gibt es nichts zu wissen oder zu erfahren. Wenn es eine übergreifende Logik gibt, die beispielsweise die Fotografien von einem Stinktier, verstreutem Gemüse und einem weiblichen Akt mit Basketball (um die jüngste Ausstellung des Künstlers in Los Angeles anzusprechen) verbindet, so wäre sie allenfalls in formalen, bildlichen oder psychologischen Assoziationen zu finden.

Eine Zeit lang haben viele der stärkeren Zweige der „kritischen" Fotografie (und der Kunst im Allgemeinen) einen Weg verfolgt, den man nach wie vor als „Demystifikations"-Projekt verstehen kann – mit dem Ziel, das Bild und seine Mechanismen aufzubrechen und zu analysieren, sie von ihrem Geheimnis und ihrer Verführungskraft zu befreien und das Ganze als Kombination von Strategien, Codes und Konventionen zu entlarven. Von Stephen Prina und Christopher Williams bis zu zahllosen jüngeren Fotografen, waren zeitgenössische, von der Konzeptkunst und ihren Folgen geprägte Künstlerinnen und Künstler bestrebt, Medien und institutionelle Archive zu untersuchen, um verborgene historische Verbindungen zwischen Bildern aufzuspüren und deren Produktionsprozesse und institutionelle Hintergründe offenzulegen; dabei arbeiteten sie häufig mit den Mitteln der Verlagerung, des Aus-dem-Kontext-Reissens und der Verfremdung sowie mit vielschichtigen Kommentaren. Natürlich liegt ein Teil der Faszination dieses Vorhabens in der Absurdität seines Strebens nach Vernunft, Klarheit und System sowie in der perversen Ironie, auf neokonzeptuelle Strategien zu setzen, die mittlerweile etwa so nuanciert und manieriert sind wie, sagen wir, die gestische Abstraktion.

Lassry weicht von diesem pädagogischen Impetus ab und spricht gerne über das Okkulte, das anhaltend Gespenstische oder das Heimgesucht-Sein eines Bildes durch seinen abwesenden Kontext. Desgleichen umschifft Lassry die vertrauten Gemeinplätze der Konzeptfotografie, indem er Texte oder Kommentare vermeidet und selten in Serien arbeitet; stattdessen konzentriert er sich einmal mehr auf das einzelne Bild und die seltsame Singularität von Bildern. Er bezeichnet dies als Regression, als Rückkehr zu einer eher dem 19. Jahrhundert entliehenen Einstellung zum Bild. Und er verwandelt seine Fotografien ganz bewusst in Objekte, sodass streng komponierte Kompositionen in Vitrinen sitzen wie in einer Falle, oder wie Sarah Lehrer-Graiwer schrieb: „in ihren makellosen Rahmen versiegelt".[4]

„THIS IS NOT TO BE LOOKED AT" (Abb. 2) heisst es auf einem berühmten Gemälde des in Los Angeles lebenden Künstlers John Baldessari aus dem Jahr 1968. Rund vierzig Jahre später könnte man viele in der Nachfolge Baldessaris entstandene Werke – etwa von Douglas Huebler und anderen – mit „Ich weiss natürlich, aber" umschreiben – entsprechend den diversen „Lossagungen", welche die heutige Fotokunst kennzeichnen. Wir wissen natürlich, dass die klassischen Schachzüge der Konzeptfotografie sich längst erschöpft haben, zur Chiffre erstarrt sind und vom Markt künstlich am Leben erhalten werden – dennoch werden sie von Generationen von Kunststudenten weiterhin genutzt, um eine leicht durchschaubare Mischung aus „kritischer Haltung" und gewiefter Vermarktbarkeit zu erzielen. Einige Kunstschaffende tun einfach so, als ob es die Konzeptkunst und postmoderne Fotografie nie gegeben hätte und wir weiterhin cool aussehende Fotos von allem und jedem um uns herum knipsen könnten, als schrieben wir das Jahr 1950 und der künstlerisch ambitionierte Fotojournalismus steckte noch in den Kinderschuhen. Doch es gibt andere, welche die Fotografie der Moderne und deren selbstreflexive Erforschung des Mediums für das digitale Zeitalter aufzurüsten versuchen.[5]

Nachdem sie jahrzehntelang durch die intellektuell und ästhetisch starken Experimente des frühen 20. Jahrhunderts am Leben erhalten wurden, sind Konzeptkunst, postmoderne Fotografie und aktuelle Fotokunst heute an einen toten Punkt gelangt, an dem eine Geschichte vielfältiger Experimente in zahllosen Sackgassen endet. Genau mit diesem alles durchdringenden Gefühl des Zu-Tode-geritten- und Nur-zu-vertraut-Seins versucht Lassry eine ästhetische und psychologische Spannung aufzubauen. Indem er dies tut, knüpft er vielleicht an einen Aspekt des „Pictures"-Projekts an, der von der damals vorherrschenden – auf die zentralen, aber altbekannten Fragen von Urheberschaft, Originalität und institutionellem Kontext fixierten – Rezeption in den Hintergrund gedrängt wurde. Tatsächlich erinnern Lassrys hartnäckige Anspielungen auf „Heimsuchung" und Gespenster an eine Sprache, die schon früh von Schlüsselfiguren der „Pictures"-Generation verwendet wurde. In seinem Essay „Pictures" aus dem Jahr 1977 (1979 in erweiterter Form erneut veröffentlicht) bemühte sich Douglas Crimp zu erläutern, wie ein auf zeitliche Dauer und Bühnenpräsenz ausgerichtetes künstlerisches Umfeld die Herstellung von Bildern unterschwellig beeinflusste; er schrieb: „Eine Kunst, deren Strategien auf der konkreten Zeitlichkeit und Realität des Theaters beruhten, war für eine ganze Gruppe von Kunstschaffenden, die nun in New York auszustellen beginnen, die prägende Erfahrung schlechthin."[6] In seinem Kommentar zum Werk von Jack Goldstein – ein Künstler, der Lassry ebenfalls viel bedeutet – bemerkt Crimp: „Die psychologische Resonanz seines Werks rührt nicht von der Thematik seiner Bilder her, sondern von der Art, wie diese Bilder präsentiert, inszeniert werden; das heisst, sie ist eine Funktion ihrer Struktur."[7] Für Crimp hängt die seltsame Zeitlichkeit eines Werks wie Goldsteins Film *The Jump* (1978) (Abb. 3) mit dem Rotoskopieverfahren zusammen, bei dem etwas zugleich gezeichnet und getilgt, erschaffen und gelöscht wird. Dabei glaubt er nicht, dass diese Zeitlichkeit an ein spezifisches Medium gebunden, sondern dass sie sowohl bei statischen wie bei bewegten Bildern möglich ist.

Im Rahmen einer Diskussionsrunde über das Vermächtnis der „Pictures"-Generation im Jahr 2009 bezeichnet Lassry Goldsteins *The Jump* als besonderes Werk, das endlich von der „übermässigen Betonung seines appropriativen Charakters" befreit werden müsse. „Wenn man sich die Werke selbst wieder anschaut und auf diese Begrifflichkeit verzichtet, wird so unendlich viel mehr sichtbar [...] Weder die Tatsache, dass der Film auf bestehendem Material basiert, noch seine dem Rotoskop zu verdankenden Spezialeffekte schliessen die Möglichkeit aus, sich mit anderen Formen der Erfahrung oder anderen Bedeutungsebenen dieses Werks zu befassen." Lassry bemängelt, dass der Begriff „Appropriation" mittlerweile so einschränkend gebraucht werde, dass er „gar nicht mehr zulässt, sich neuen Fragen zuzuwenden."[8] Er weist darauf hin, dass Goldsteins Filme sich zwar bestehendes Material aneignen, aber nichtsdestoweniger „zu autonomen Gesten werden", und dass „innerhalb des Werks noch anderes geschieht, etwa die Negation der filmischen Wirkung und eine Störung des Filmerlebnisses."[9] Es ist klar, dass Lassry den Kurzfilmen Goldsteins – etwa *Some Butterflies* (1974) und *Shane* (1974) – insofern viel verdankt, als sie einen verborgenen Pfad aufzeigen, der über die Fragen von Urheberschaft und Kontext hinausführt, sobald man sich wieder den äusserst seltsamen Dingen zuwendet, die sich in den Filmbildern selbst abspielen.

In einem Interview von 1985 im *Arts Magazine* beklagte Sherrie Levine, dass die Kritiker gern den eigentlichen Bildinhalt ihrer Arbeit vernachlässigten und letztlich ignorierten, was sich im Bild selbst ereigne. Levine erzählt von einem Gespräch mit dem Schriftsteller Howard Singerman, der meinte, „die Leute betrachten ein Werk gerne so, als beginne es mit dem Rahmen und reiche von da nach aussen, statt vom Rahmen her nach innen", und bemerkt dazu: „Wir sind so kontextbewusst geworden, dass wir das Bild manchmal nur noch als Loch in der Wand wahrnehmen. Es handelt sich aber um Bilder. Es sind zwar sehr komplexe Bilder, aber sie sind ikonografisch entzifferbar. Die Bilder der *1917*-Ausstellung zeigen Kreuze und masturbierende Menschen. Die meisten Leute, die über diese Arbeit schrieben, haben den ikonografischen Bildinhalt entweder ignoriert oder verdrängt."[10]

Auch Levine greift häufig auf das Vokabular der Gespenstergeschichte zurück, wenn sie über ihr Werk spricht, besonders, um das Verhältnis zwischen „Original" und „Kopie" zu beschreiben: „Die Bilder, die ich schaffe, sind eigentlich Gespenster von Gespenstern; ihr Verhältnis zu den Originalvorlagen ist tertiär, das heisst es liegen drei oder vier Stufen dazwischen [...] Als ich mit dieser Arbeit begann, wollte ich ein Bild machen, das sich selbst widersprach. Ich wollte ein Bild über ein anderes legen, sodass manchmal beide Bilder verschwinden und dann wieder beide hervortreten; diese Vibration ist im Grunde das, worum es für mich in dem Werk geht – dieser Zwischenraum, wo kein Bild ist."[11] Diese Absenz ist natürlich relativ, wie Levine sogleich anfügt: „Ich denke, viele Leute verlieren sich in dieser Lücke und glauben, es sei gar kein Bild vorhanden, obwohl es tatsächlich zwei Bilder sind."[12]

Wie viele frühe „Pictures"-Arbeiten erkundet auch Lassry die Fotografie der Printmedien. Dabei interessiert er sich jedoch dafür, wo diese Ökonomie der Verbreitung und Reproduktion aufhört, wo sie sich zu einem einzigen komplexen Bild verdichtet, um eine Form der Verbreitung zu untersuchen, die eher geistig und innerlich ist. Für Lassry ist die Vermittlungsarbeit, die mit dem Bearbeiten und Wiederbeleben eines bestehenden Bildes einhergeht, wenn man es aus seinem ursprünglichen Kontext reisst und dadurch „verwaist", eng verwandt mit dem Verhältnis zwischen der Arbeit mit statischen und der mit bewegten Bildern.[13] In einem neueren Interview vermutet er: „Irgendetwas an dem Versuch, Fotografien oder Zeitschriftenseiten zu bedrucken oder sich konkret damit zu befassen, wie Fotografien auf einer anderen Oberfläche wirken (wodurch zugleich etwas vorher dort Befindliches gelöscht wird), markiert den Übergang von der Collage zum Film."[14] Und dennoch bewegt sich das Filmemachen, das ihn am brennendsten interessiert, an der Grenze zum Vor-Filmischen und zu dem zwar historisch lange zurückliegenden, aber nach wie vor verstörenden Schock, den bewegte Bilder auszulösen vermögen. Und er gesteht ein: „Der Gedanke, dass Film nichts weiter ist als eine Abfolge von Fotografien, hat etwas Regressives."[15]

Für Lassry wird der Film zu einem Schlüsselinstrument der Erkundung der Möglichkeiten und Unmöglichkeiten der Wiedergabe von Gegenständen auf einer zweidimensionalen Fläche. Anhand einer Illustration in einem wissenschaftlichen Lehrbuch platziert er in *Untitled* (2008) (Abb. 4) eine Reihe junger Leute auf der leuchtend bunten Grafik eines Hauses. Obwohl wir wissen, dass die Grafik zweidimensional ist, bemühen sich die Darsteller darum, es so zu präsentieren, als befände es sich im realen Raum – indem sie sich aufs Dach setzen oder so tun, als stünden sie in der Tür. Wie Anat Ebgi bemerkt, erinnert die bunte Szene an den „pädagogischen Stil des Fernsehsenders PBS in den 1970er Jahren, der Grundfarben, kühne Formen, extreme Blickwinkel [und] optische Spielereien [...] in vergleichender und kontrastierender Weise präsentierte."[16] Dennoch ist der Film mehr als eine Lektion in optischer Wahrnehmung und weckt psychische Assoziationen zur Familie und der zutiefst schrägen Beziehung menschlicher Gestalten zu derart künstlich konstruierten Räumen – und zueinander.

Noch weiter getrieben werden diese Spiele mit der Wahrnehmung in *Untitled* (2009), einem 16-mm-Film, der sich lose an Standaufnahmen von Jerome Robbins anlehnt, die dieser 1955 bei der Reinszenierung von *Peter Pan* fürs Fernsehen machte (Abb. 5). Seit Langem begreift Lassry sein Werk als gleichermassen von der Appropriationskunst wie vom konstruktiven Film geprägt, eine eigenwillige Kombination, die in dieser Arbeit besonders heftig zutage tritt, da sie höchst abstrakte Fragmente eines bereits verfremdeten Kinderbuchklassikers (der kindliche Peter Pan wird im Film von einer erwachsenen Schauspielerin verkörpert) noch einmal zerschneidet und wieder neu zusammensetzt. Doch die tatsächlichen kulturellen Vorlagen gehen beinahe unter in Lassrys Reinszenierung, die das Material zu einer Reihe abstrakter Kompositionen verarbeitet, die nur noch zufällig aus menschlichen Körpern bestehen. Als der Film beginnt, füllt der abgetrennte, in ein leuchtend rotes Trikot gehüllte Torso einer Tänzerin die gesamte Bildfläche. Sie beugt sich vornüber und beginnt sich zu bewegen und die Kamera bewegt sich langsam mit ihr durch etwas hindurch, was wie eine Reihe grauer und schwarzer Säulen aussieht, die das Bild in vertikale Streifen unterteilen. Mit anderen Materialfragmenten zusammengeschnitten – darunter ein blauäugiger Mann, der vor einem hellblauen Hintergrund gestikuliert und zwischen bunten, glänzend polierten Säulen umherspaziert – mutiert der rote Körper der Tänzerin zum grafischen Symbol, das dazu dient, Raum und Bewegung in einem zweidimensionalen Medium zu untersuchen. Genauso wie das Trikot selbst dazu dient, vom Körper zu abstrahieren, ihn gleichzeitig zu enthüllen und zu verbergen, spielen Lassrys ständige Nahaufnahmen und Schwenks mit dieser Figur an der Grenze zwischen Mensch und Objekt.

In all seinen Filmen verwendet Lassry eine Reihe einfacher technischer Elemente – die Nahaufnahme, den langsamen Schwenk, das Überlagern verschiedener Blickwinkel –, um zu untersuchen, wie das Filmen des „realen Raums“ die räumliche Fläche seltsam komplizieren kann. Man kann seine Filme als eine Art erste Einführung in die Betrachtung seiner Fotografien verstehen, welche die Probleme erforschen, die der Raumdarstellung mit der Kamera innewohnen, und dabei eine ständig wechselnde Empfindung von Tiefe und Fläche erzeugen und unsere Erfahrung immer wieder auf die Fläche zurückführen. Dabei werfen sie eine Reihe von Fragen zum Film auf, die dann wiederum auf Bildmedien wie Fotografien zurückfallen. Wie sieht die Textur der Tiefe auf einer Leinwand aus? Und wie hängt sie – oder hängt sie nicht – mit anderen Bildräumen zusammen? Kann der Film- oder Bildraum einen Punkt erreichen, an dem er die blosse Nachahmung von Tiefe überwindet und eine andere unheimliche Tiefe erlangt? Was heisst es, einen kontinuierlichen Blick auf einen bewegten Bildschirmraum zu haben, im Unterschied zur Bewegung durch eine unzusammenhängende Folge von statischen Bildern? In Lassrys Werk werden flache Farbebenen, die fast monochrom wirken, als von Objekten oder Figuren bewohnbare Flächen reanimiert, aber so, dass der Eindruck, es handle sich um kohärente oder rationale Räume, laufend untergraben wird. Am Ende zersetzen Lassrys – bewegte und statische – Bilder die Unterschiede zwischen Motiv und Hintergrund, Figur und Boden, indem sie extrem verfremdete Flächen einsetzen, um Fotografie und Film in Wahrnehmungsprobleme zu verstricken, die man sonst eher mit der Malerei in Verbindung bringt. „Es gibt einen Moment“, meinte er im Gespräch, „in dem sich das Bild, das man zu kennen glaubte, zu bewegen beginnt.“[17]

1. Lisa Dorin, *Film, Video, New Media: At the Art Institute of Chicago*, London & New Haven 2009, S. 104. (Dieses und alle folgenden – ursprünglich englischen – Zitate wurden von der Übersetzerin des Essays ins Deutsche übertragen.)
2. Sarah Lehrer-Graiwer beschreibt das Verhältnis zwischen appropriierten und Originalbildern als eine Art rhythmische Wechselwirkung: „In Gruppen von Studioaufnahmen eingefügt, setzen sie eine Art Akzente, die den übrigen Bildern eine geheimnisvolle Aura verleihen.“ In: Sarah Lehrer-Graiwer, „Openings: Elad Lassry“, in: *Artforum*, New York, Jg. 48, Nr. 2, Oktober 2009, S. 219.
3. Walead Beshty, Elad Lassry, Carter Mull & Erika Vogt, „After Materiality and Style“, in: *Art in America*, New York, April 2009, S. 134.
4. Lehrer-Graiwer, „Openings: Elad Lassry“ (Anm. 2), S. 221.
5. Immerhin bildete – wie Abigail Solomon-Godeau schon vor fast 30 Jahren zu erklären bemüht war – die formale Appropriation einst radikal-moderner Techniken das Rückgrat der amerikanischen Nachkriegs-Kunstfotografie; siehe „The Armed Vision Disarmed – Radical Formalism from Weapon to Style“, in: *Afterimage*, Rochester, Januar 1983.
6. Douglas Crimp, „Pictures“, in: *October. MIT Press Journals*, Cambridge/ Massachusetts, Nr. 8, Frühjahr 1979, S. 77.
7. Ebd., S. 79–80.
8. Beshty, Lassry, Mull & Vogt, „After Materiality and Style“ (Anm. 3), S. 131–132.
9. Ebd., S. 132.
10. Sherrie Levine, in: Jeanne Siegel, „After Sherrie Levine“ (1985), erneut abgedruckt in: Siegel (Hg.), *Art Talk: the Early 80s*, New York 1988, S. 253.
11. Ebd., S. 247.
12. Ebd., S. 253.
13. In einem Interview von 2008 beschreibt Lassry die Überreste des ursprünglichen Bildkontextes als „ein Geist, der fortlebt. Seine Geschichte lebt weiter, sucht das Bild heim, für immer [...] Ich entführe das Bild gewissermassen, hole es aus seiner Geschichte heraus im Wissen darum, dass diese Geschichte nie definitiv feststand.“ In: Sarah Lehrer-Graiwer, „Studio Visit“, *FlashArtonline.com*, 18. November 2008, http://www.flashartonline.com/interno.php?pagina=studio_det&id_art=210&det=ok&title=Elad-Lassry (Stand: 17. Juni 2010).
14. Elad Lassry, „Hijacked in a Winter Garden Moment: Cay Sophie Rabinowitz with Erin Tao in Conversation with Elad Lassry“, *Fantom Photographic Quarterly*, Nr. 3, 2010, www.fantomeditions.com/issues/issue-03/ (Stand: 29. Juni 2010).
15. Ebd.
16. Anat Ebgi, „Elad Lassry“, *artisrael.org*, Juni 2009, http://www.artisrael.org/feature/press/elad-lassry-june-2009 (Stand: 17. Juni 2010).
17. Gespräch mit dem Künstler, 1. April 2010.

Bettina Funcke

# So While in One Sense She Shares a Space with the Animal, in Another She Doesn't

"The animals have secrets, which, unlike the secrets of caves, mountains, and seas, are specifically addressed to man and his loneliness as a species [ ... ] All the secrets are about the animal as an intercession between man and his origin."

—John Berger[1]

"My work is an investigation of both the impossibilities and possibilities that surround pictures."

—Elad Lassry[2]

We only began to separate animals from our intimate domestic lives about 150 years ago. For millennia animals had been in our midst for economic or productive use, and as spiritual messengers and oracles. One of the first pictures in human history depicts an animal, and it is likely that animal blood was among the first paints with which pictures were made. But once animals had largely lost the traditional domestic functions of use and food, the question could arise: why do we *look* at animals?

We are not linked to animals through the possession of a shared language, at least not a symbolic or spoken one; instead we move into what John Berger called "unspeaking companionship,"[3] a primarily visual or physical exchange: eyes, lips, the entire body, a response expressed through sound, scent, or touch, with which animals seem to convey emotion and expression. We look at these creatures in order to consider the mysteries of our connection with and difference from them, to meditate on their symbolic connection to our life as expressed in fables, allegories, images. How are we like them? Can they tell us something we don't have access to otherwise? What might be the advantage to lacking a common language, what might it be like without language?

In his work the artist Elad Lassry often focuses on animals: cats, wolves, zebras, flamingos, or skunks. They are taken from their natural environment and imbued with artificial stillness, posed in a controlled studio setting, frozen like inanimate objects in arrangements with props and backdrops, all photographed at a similarly close range, often with striking monochrome backdrops. The animals are handled and portrayed similarly to Lassry's smiling, motionless young women and men; they also resemble the objects in his still lifes. The rather small sizes of the framed photographic pieces—mostly around 36 × 28 cm—together with a viewer's sense that connection or collaboration lies at the core of the image, suggests an intimate, often inscrutable encounter: between subject and photographer but also between viewer and picture. Lassry's insistent negation—his preference for a limited vocabulary, and his aversion to large-scale, loud, digital imagery—could be seen as a response to a time in which images are as unstable as they are ubiquitous. The carefully considered relationship of the frames' colors to the pictures gives the artworks the solid feel of objects rather than the transparency desired by large, face-mounted images. They are picture-objects, reminiscent of jewelry boxes or small vitrines, or perhaps of Joseph Cornell's boxes or Allan McCollum's collections of objects.

But beyond these physical aspects lies the quietness of Lassry's work, its restraint and self-imposed limitation. Robert Bresson noted, "Be sure of having used to the full all that is communicated by immobility and silence,"[4] and the quotation speaks to Lassry's stillness, sensuality, and restrained vocabulary. Despite their fervent colors, his works are quiet, with a sense of pause. Time barely passes. I am put in mind of Jack Goldstein's films, which share certain aspects: protagonists staged in composed and theatrical isolation, bright monochromatic backdrops that flatten the image, a formal and repetitive character, an avoidance of clear narrative in favor of open-ended situations. Both Goldstein and Lassry emerge during moments of highly theoretical discussion around the status of pictures but, while reflecting these discussions, both artists have produced imagery that is decidedly accessible: stylized, humorous, mesmerizing. And both artists have worked with animals, and images of animals.

*Burmese Mother, Kittens* (2008) depicts a mother cat with soft, beach-blond fur nursing her nougat-brown litter, and is mounted within a similarly nougat-brown wooden frame. The intimate scene hovers on a white picture plane lit so as to remove all shadow and thus any sense of space or gravity. This commercial-studio-style lighting is one of the tools Lassry uses to produce his peculiarly flat imagery, but not the only one. The black-and-white photograph *Untitled (Herend)* (2009) depicts two collectible porcelain figurines—a doe and its fawn—reclining on velvet fabric. The animals have been covered with hand-painted black-and-white graphic patterns, an Op art effect in which the viewer is lost before even fully deciphering the scene. The deer seem to float on the fabric, indistinguishable from one another, merging into one emblem of closeness and protection. The artist has called his work an ongoing image-based investigation into questions regarding culture and ideas, and here showing also means concealing, representing means manipulating.

Lassry also works with the flatness of re-photography, searching image archives, bookstores, and libraries for pictures that might become the starting point for a collage (or a picture to simply inspire an image-idea, a restaging). The images he uses, often portraits from the 1960s or 1970s, are overprinted or overlaid with colored strips or foil to highlight or obscure the people they depict, and, in the following example, the collage is itself then set in a scene just like any of his other subjects. In *Laminated Structure (For Her and Him)* (2008), a close-cropped film still of an elated Goldie Hawn with a dog, their blond heads framed by a car window, adorns the upper third of a collage that Lassry has placed before a cream-colored backdrop. Hawn is thrilled, glancing over to share this moment with the dog who, alas, is busy with the sensation of the wind in its fur.

*Travis Parker and Chilean Flamingo, 90028* (2008), the only diptych in Lassry's oeuvre, plays with a different sort of animal-human bond (just try to envision the day the artist spent with an animal trainer, a flamingo, and an aspiring local actor in order to get these pictures). Parker holds exactly the same posture in each picture, but while in the right-hand image he gestures at a gracefully reserved creature, an ideal of a flamingo, almost taxidermic, the left-hand picture reveals that the bird is in fact alive: here its head is lifted, its beak open in protest. Lassry tips his hand. What might all the photographs look like that were rejected in order to get The One? Or, why is this the only occasion in which he needed two pictures to make a work? He has an interest in the relationship between photography and film, in particular the fact that film is made up of individual photographic images. Has he made the shortest possible filmic impression by joining two photos to suggest motion?

In some of his portraits, Lassry uses selective double exposure to multiply the eyes alone, an effect that seems designed to simultaneously disturb and emphasize a viewer's act of looking. In *Wolf (Blue)* (2008), however, he doubles the eyes and the back legs. A black wolf is posed before a deep blue backdrop, front paws on a low pedestal. Otherwise motionless, his doubled eyes and back legs make him (or her?) into an uncanny, shape-shifting six-legged and four-eyed creature. Why, in this vocabulary of doubling, the back legs—what do they signify? Does the blue backdrop suggest twilight? And if so, why have the back paws, the tip of the tail, and small patch on the chest been painted in the same metallic blue? As usual in Lassry's work, what in some sense appears to be "a simple picture" at the same time reveals its own curious set of decisions and processes. With *Felicia* (2008), Lassry has applied the double-printing effect to an entire photograph. A conventionally pretty young woman with a slightly guarded smile, reminiscent of a high school yearbook, is set in front of a backdrop of colored dots. Through the effect, psychological and metaphorical readings arise. It is as if the photograph demonstrates that the entire identity of a woman, or of the image itself, slips in a ghostly displacement.

Lassry's effects are initially produced through studio- and darkroom techniques, and his research and artworks have a strong relationship to the photographic conventions and experiments of an earlier time. However, the scans and finishes take place in the digital format. He uses any manipulation that comes in handy and has stated before that he does not see any difference between the different strategies or formats of manipulation. From photography's beginnings, the potential for manipulation, multiplication, and mobility was inscribed in the medium, and ghost photography is an example of the use of that slippage so characteristic of its early history: while the photograph can depict the world more realistically than ever before, it is also fraught with the potential for manipulation, and thus the potential to make visible the invisible as well as to hide that which we think we know.

Why would someone make a particular picture? Why do we make figurines of animals, and why do we then photograph them? Why do we stare at these mute objects, where is the communication, how does the shared language work? Since we do not share a language with animals, our encounters happen largely through vision, through the meeting of eyes. Eye contact marks another curious aspect of the relationship between animals and humans: full of expectation and attentiveness. In the end the gaze is based on a certain kind of indifference, one coming from the animal's existence in another place. There is no gaze especially reserved for humans; animals presumably look at us just as they would at other animals, and this is a strange equivalence. Viscerally it makes little sense to us, and leaves us suspended in self-reflection. While we may share our space with animals, they will always remain in another place altogether, one that is beyond our reach, unknown and unknowable. We can transpose the question, "Why do we look at animals?" onto Lassry's carefully controlled images, and ask: "Why do we look at pictures? " A photograph opens into a private world that may have no use for us, or may touch us deeply, mysteriously. Unknowability must be one of the main reasons for our attraction to animals, and perhaps also has something to do with our attraction to art.

1. John Berger, *Why Look at Animals* (1977), Penguin Books, London 2009.
2. Elad Lassry, "Artists Dictionary: Elad Lassry," *FlashArtonline.com*, October 2009, http://www.flashartonline.com/interno.php?pagina=artisti_det&id_art=374&det=ok&nome_artista=LASSRY-ELAD (last accessed: June 17, 2010).
3. Berger, *Why Look at Animals*.
4. Robert Bresson, *Notes on Cinematography*, Urizen Books, New York 1977, p. 11.

Bettina Funcke

# Während sie also in einem gewissen Sinne einen Raum mit dem Tier teilt, tut sie dies in einem anderen nicht

„Tiere haben Geheimnisse, die anders als die Geheimnisse von Höhlen, Bergen und Meeren ausdrücklich an den Menschen und seine Einsamkeit als Spezies gerichtet sind. […] Alle Geheimnisse drehen sich um das Tier als Fürsprecher und Mittler zwischen dem Menschen und seinem Ursprung."
–John Berger[1]

„Mein Werk ist eine Untersuchung der Unmöglichkeiten wie der Möglichkeiten, die Bilder umgeben."
–Elad Lassry[2]

Erst vor etwa 150 Jahren haben wir damit begonnen, Tiere aus unserem intimen häuslichen Leben zu entfernen. Jahrtausendelang befanden sie sich aus ökonomischen oder produktionstechnischen Gründen und als spirituelle Botschafter und Orakel mitten unter uns. Eines der ersten Bilder der Menschheitsgeschichte zeigt ein Tier, und vermutlich zählte Tierblut zu den ersten Farben, mit denen man Bilder machte. Doch sobald Tiere die traditionellen häuslichen Gebrauchs- und Nahrungsfunktionen mehr oder weniger eingebüsst hatten, konnte die Frage aufkommen: Warum *schauen* wir Tiere an?

Wir sind den Tieren nicht durch eine gemeinsame Sprache verbunden, zumindest keiner symbolischen oder gesprochenen, sondern wir pflegen, John Berger zufolge, eine „nicht sprechende Kameradschaft"[3] mit ihnen, einen primär visuellen oder physischen Austausch: Augen, Lippen, der ganze Körper, eine Reaktion, die durch Klang, Geruch oder Berührung zum Ausdruck gebracht wird, mit denen Tiere ihre Emotionen und Anliegen deutlich machen. Wir betrachten diese Geschöpfe, um die Geheimnisse unserer Verbindung mit und unseres Unterschieds zu ihnen in Erwägung zu ziehen, um über ihre symbolische Verbindung zu unserem Leben nachzudenken, wie sie sich in Fabeln, Allegorien, Bildern äussert. Inwiefern sind wir wie sie? Können sie uns etwas mitteilen, zu dem wir auf anderem Wege keinen Zugang haben? Was könnte der Vorteil davon sein, über keine gemeinsame Sprache zu verfügen, wie ist es wohl ohne Sprache?

In seinen Werken richtet der Künstler Elad Lassry sein Augenmerk häufig auf Tiere: Katzen, Wölfe, Zebras, Flamingos oder Stinktiere. Aus ihrer natürlichen Umgebung entfernt und von einer künstlichen Stille durchdrungen, stehen sie in einer kontrollierten Atelierszenerie, eingefroren wie unbelebte Gegenstände in Arrangements mit Requisiten und Kulissen, alle in ähnlicher Nahsicht fotografiert, häufig vor einem markanten monochromen Hintergrund. Die Tiere werden auf ähnliche Weise behandelt und porträtiert wie Lassrys lächelnde, unbewegte junge Frauen und Männer. Sie erinnern aber auch an die Objekte in seinen Stillleben. Die eher kleinen Formate der gerahmten Fotoarbeiten, die meist um die 36 × 28 cm messen, in Verbindung mit dem Gefühl des Betrachters, dass Kontakt oder Kooperation den Kern des Bildes ausmachen, legen eine intime, häufig unergründliche Begegnung nahe: zwischen dem Sujet und dem Fotografen, aber auch zwischen dem Betrachter und dem Bild. Lassrys beharrliche Negation, seine Vorliebe für ein begrenztes Vokabular und seine Ablehnung grossformatiger, lauter, digitaler Motive könnte man als Reaktion auf eine Zeit auffassen, in der Bilder ebenso unstet wie allgegenwärtig sind. Die sorgfältig abgewogene Beziehung der Farben der Rahmen zu den Bildern verleiht den Kunstwerken die robuste Anmutung von Objekten statt der von grossen, en face montierten Bildern erwünschten Transparenz. Es sind Bildobjekte, die an Schmuckkästchen oder kleine Vitrinen erinnern, vielleicht aber auch an Joseph Cornells Kästen oder Allan McCollums Sammlungen von Objekten.

Doch jenseits dieser physischen Aspekte liegt die Ruhe von Lassrys Werk, seine Zurückhaltung und selbstauferlegte Begrenzung. Robert Bresson riet einmal, „Sorgen Sie dafür, dass Sie alles, was sich durch

Unbeweglichkeit und Schweigen mitteilen lässt, vollständig ausgeschöpft haben“[4], und dieses Zitat bringt Lassrys Stille, Sinnlichkeit und zurückhaltendes Vokabular vollkommen auf den Punkt. Trotz ihrer glühenden Farben sind seine Werke ruhig, vermitteln den Eindruck einer Pause. Die Zeit schreitet darin so gut wie nicht voran. Mir kommen dabei Jack Goldsteins Filme in den Sinn, mit denen sie einiges gemeinsam haben: Protagonisten, die in einer arrangierten, theatralischen Isolation in Szene gesetzt werden, lichte monochrome Hintergründe, die das Bild flacher erscheinen lassen, ein formaler und repetitiver Charakter, das Vermeiden einer eindeutigen Erzählung zugunsten von Situationen mit offenem Ausgang. Goldstein wie Lassry treten zu einer Zeit hochtheoretischer Diskussionen über den Status von Bildern auf den Plan, doch auch wenn sie diese Diskussionen reflektieren, haben beide Künstler doch Bildwelten geschaffen, die durchaus zugänglich sind: stilisiert, humorvoll, faszinierend. Und beide Künstler haben mit Tieren und Bildern von Tieren gearbeitet.

*Burmese Mother, Kittens* (2008) zeigt eine Katzenmutter mit weichem, strandblondem Fell, die ihren nugatbraunen Wurf säugt, und ist in einem ähnlich nugatbraunen Holzrahmen montiert. Die intime Szene schwebt über einer weissen Bildebene, die so ausgeleuchtet ist, dass es darin keinen Schatten und damit auch keine Andeutung von Raum oder Schwerkraft gibt. Diese Beleuchtung im Stil kommerzieller Fotostudios ist eines der Instrumente, deren sich Lassry bedient, um seine eigentümlich flachen Bilder zu produzieren, aber es ist nicht das einzige. Die Schwarz-Weiss-Aufnahme *Untitled (Herend)* (2009) zeigt zwei als Sammelobjekte fungierende Porzellanfigürchen, eine Rehgeiss und ihr Kitz, die auf einem Samtstoff liegen. Die Tiere sind mit einem handgemalten grafischen Schwarz-Weiss-Muster überzogen, ein Op-Art-Effekt, in dem sich der Betrachter verliert, noch ehe er die Szene völlig entschlüsselt hat. Ununterscheidbar voneinander scheinen die Rehe auf dem Stoff zu schweben und verschmelzen so zu einem Emblem von Nähe und Schutz. Der Künstler hat sein Werk als fortlaufende, bildbasierte Untersuchung von Fragen bezeichnet, welche Kultur und Ideen betreffen, und „zeigen“ bedeutet hier zugleich „verbergen“, „repräsentieren“ zugleich „manipulieren“.

Lassry arbeitet jedoch auch mit der Flachheit der Re-Fotografie und sucht in Bildarchiven, Buchläden und Bibliotheken nach Bildern, die Ausgangspunkt für eine Collage werden können (oder aber ein Bild, das ihn einfach zu einer Bildidee, einer Nachinszenierung inspiriert). Die Bilder, die er benutzt, häufig Porträts aus den 1960er und 1970er Jahren, sind mit Farbstreifen oder Folie übermalt oder überzogen, um die dargestellten Personen hervorzuheben oder zu verdecken. Beim folgenden Beispiel wird die Collage dann selbst in Szene gesetzt, so wie alle seine anderen Sujets. In *Laminated Structure (For Her and Him)* (2008) ziert ein nahansichtiges Standfoto einer beschwingten Goldie Hawn mit Hund – ihre blonden Köpfe werden von einem Autofenster umrahmt – das obere Drittel einer Collage, die Lassry vor einem cremefarbenen Hintergrund platziert hat. Hawn ist bester Dinge und schaut hinüber, um diesen Augenblick mit dem Hund zu teilen, der jedoch völlig mit dem Gefühl des Windes in seinem Fell beschäftigt ist.

*Travis Parker and Chilean Flamingo, 90028* (2008), das einzige Diptychon in Lassrys Œuvre, spielt mit einer anderen Form der Beziehung zwischen Tier und Mensch. (Man versuche sich einfach mal den Tag vorzustellen, den der Künstler mit einem Tiertrainer, einem Flamingo und einem aufstrebenden jungen Schauspieler verbrachte, um diese Bilder machen zu können.) Parker nimmt auf jedem der Bilder genau dieselbe Pose ein, doch während er seine Geste auf dem rechten Bild in Richtung einer anmutig zurückhaltenden Kreatur vollführt, einem nahezu taxidermischen Flamingoideal, zeigt das linke Bild, dass der Vogel tatsächlich lebt, denn hier hat er den Kopf erhoben und den Schnabel protestierend geöffnet. Lassry enthüllt seine Absicht ungewollt. Wie wohl all jene Fotos ausgesehen haben mögen, die um dieses einen willen verworfen wurden? Oder warum ist dies das einzige Mal, dass der Künstler zwei Bilder für ein Werk benötigte? Er interessiert sich für die Beziehung zwischen Fotografie und Film, nicht zuletzt für den Umstand, dass der Film aus einzelnen fotografischen Bildern besteht. Hat er den kürzestmöglichen filmischen Eindruck erzielt, indem er zwei Bilder miteinander verband, um auf diese Weise Bewegung anzudeuten?

Bei einigen seiner Porträts verwendet Lassry eine selektive Doppelbelichtung, mit der er nur die Augen vervielfältigt, ein Effekt, der offenbar darauf abzielt, den Akt des Schauens seitens des Betrachters zugleich zu stören und zu betonen. In *Wolf (Blue)* (2008) aber verdoppelt er sowohl die Augen als auch die Hinterläufe des Tiers. Ein schwarzer Wolf steht vor einem dunkelblauen Hintergrund, die Vorderpfoten auf einem niedrigen Sockel. Ansonsten regungslos wird er (oder sie?) durch die verdoppelten Augen und Hinterläufe zu einer unheimlichen, ihre Form verändernden sechsbeinigen und vieräugigen Kreatur. Warum, in diesem Vokabular der Verdoppelung, die Hinterläufe: Was sollen sie bedeuten? Deutet der blaue Hintergrund die Dämmerung an? Und wenn ja, warum wurden dann die Hinterpfoten, die Schwanzspitze und ein kleiner Fleck auf der Brust im selben metallischen Blau bemalt? Wie üblich in Lassrys Werk macht das, was in einem gewissen Sinne als „ein einfaches Bild" erscheint, zugleich seine eigene eigentümliche Reihe von Entscheidungen und Prozessen sichtbar. Bei *Felicia* (2008) wendet Lassry den Effekt des Doppelabzugs auf eine ganze Fotografie an. Man sieht das Bild einer im konventionellen Sinne hübschen jungen Frau mit einem verhaltenen Lächeln, das an das Jahrbuch einer High School erinnert, vor einem Hintergrund aus farbigen Punkten. Dieser Effekt legt psychologische und metaphorische Lesarten nahe. Es wirkt, als wolle die Fotografie demonstrieren, dass die gesamte Identität einer Frau, oder des Bildes selbst, in eine gespenstische Verschiebung gleitet.

Lassrys Effekte werden zunächst mit Hilfe der Studio- und Dunkelkammertechnik erzielt, und seine Recherchen und Kunstwerke zeugen von seiner intensiven Beziehung zu den fotografischen Konventionen und Experimenten einer früheren Zeit. Doch die Scans und die Schlussbearbeitung erfolgen im digitalen Format. Lassry benutzt jedes Manipulationsmittel, das seinen Zwecken entgegenkommt, und hat schon früher erklärt, für ihn gäbe es keinen Unterschied zwischen den verschiedenen Strategien oder Formen der Manipulation. Seit ihren Anfängen ist der Fotografie das Potenzial zur Manipulation, Vervielfältigung und Mobilität eingeschrieben, und die Geisterfotografie ist ein Beispiel für den Einsatz dieses für die Frühgeschichte des Mediums so charakteristischen Gleitens: Zwar kann die Fotografie die Welt auf realistischere Weise abbilden als je zuvor, doch zugleich birgt sie ein erhebliches Manipulationspotenzial und damit die Möglichkeit, Unsichtbares sichtbar zu machen, aber auch das zu verbergen, was wir zu wissen meinen.

Warum macht jemand ein bestimmtes Bild? Warum machen wir Tierfigürchen, und warum fotografieren wir sie dann? Warum starren wir diese stummen Gegenstände an? Wo ist die Kommunikation, wie funktioniert die gemeinsame Sprache? Da wir und die Tiere keine gemeinsame Sprache haben, spielen sich unsere Begegnungen grösstenteils auf visueller Ebene ab, durch die Begegnung unserer Augen. Der Blickkontakt stellt eine weitere seltsame Seite der Beziehung zwischen Tieren und Menschen dar: Voll von Erwartung und Aufmerksamkeit beruht der Blick letztlich auf einer Art Indifferenz, die daher rührt, dass das Tier an einem anderen Ort existiert. Es gibt keinen eigens dem Menschen vorbehaltenen Blick: Tiere schauen uns vermutlich genauso an, wie sie andere Tiere anschauen, und das ist eine seltsame Entsprechung. Instinktiv erkennen wir keinen besonderen Sinn darin und werden daher auf unsere Selbstreflexion zurückgeworfen. Auch wenn wir unseren Raum mit Tieren teilen mögen, werden diese doch immer an einem völlig anderen Ort bleiben, der sich jenseits unserer Reichweite befindet, unbekannt und unerkennbar. Wir können die Frage „Warum schauen wir Tiere an?" auf Lassrys sorgfältig kontrollierte Bilder übertragen und fragen „Warum schauen wir Bilder an?" Eine Fotografie eröffnet eine private Welt, für die wir keine Verwendung haben mögen oder die uns auf intensive, geheimnisvolle Weise berührt. Unerkennbarkeit muss einer der Hauptgründe dafür sein, dass wir uns von Tieren angezogen fühlen, und vielleicht ist sie auch einer der Gründe für unsere Anziehung durch die Kunst.

1. John Berger, *Why Look at Animals*, London 2009 (1977).
2. Elad Lassry, „Artists Dictionary: Elad Lassry", auf: *FlashArtonline.com*, Oktober 2009, http://www.flashartonline.com/interno.php?pagina=artisti_det&id_art=374&det=ok&nome_artista=LASSRY-ELAD (Stand: 17. Juni 2010).
3. Berger, *Why Look at Animals* (Anm. 1).
4. Robert Bresson, *Notes on Cinematography*, New York 1977, S. 11.

Fionn Meade

# Picture Perfect

"In the cinema, a society that has lost its gestures seeks to reappropriate what it has lost while simultaneously recording that loss."
—Giorgio Agamben[1]

The extended reach of a laughing woman grasping after a crawling baby is shot from above; set against soft white bedsheets and oriented so as to capture the restless motion of an infant, it conveys a domesticated Eden where the bond between a young mother and child is fresh and bare. Having once adorned the cover of *Life Magazine* in 1970, it is an impression of life as unfettered and resolutely optimistic. And yet in Elad Lassry's photograph *Joanna and Trace A1* (2007) (ill. 6), the vintage image is repurposed, undergoing a unique form of visual redaction as background blocks of typographic red and white meant to underscore taglines and prompt consumer desire are inverted and overlaid, obscuring the headlines beneath. Leaving only the tab of the original subscriber's address clearly legible, Lassry shifts the editorial and economic conventions at play here, orphaning this once idyllic portrait of American family life and returning it to the more anonymous world of gesture. In the process, the commercial viability of the image is both recalled and revoked. Context, source, and circulation are ghosted into background concerns and the implied motion of the image is brought forth. Similar encounters with unsettled photographic tropes characterize much of Lassry's image redirection, as when the winsome smile of a male model's headshot is vexed by doubly exposed eyes in *Man 071* (2007), or the benign schoolgirl charm of *Felicia* (2008) is likewise impaired by the noise and jitter of superimposition, an adjacency often amplified by matching the frame with a prominent color in the photograph's background, further destabilizing the figurative subject.

Placeholders meant to be readily legible lapse into a stuttered motion in Lassry's pictures as the conventions of studio photography—portraiture, still life, fashion, and product set-ups—are collaged, recast, and mimicked to uncanny effect. Unmoored from illustrative fidelity—a shift accentuated by the pull toward objecthood in their framing—Lassry's image repertoire departs from the marketing diegesis of advertising and Hollywood that it trades upon. Perfect human faces, animal specimens, and unblemished fruit look on imploringly—no products to adhere to—just as erstwhile protagonists, often collaged from or modeled upon Lassry's predilection for 1970s pop culture ephemera, conjure up a range of moods and expressions decoupled from plot and target audiences. In doing so, Lassry departs from now familiar appropriation tactics, adopting and modifying the clichéd, nostalgic, and artificial through impressions of staccato movement, misprint effects, and further evacuations of long instrumentalized imagery. Eschewing a critique of the iconic or representative persona, product, or conflict—as was often the case with many so-called "Pictures Generation" appropriation strategies—Lassry traffics in a secondary register of lesser familiarity and circulation.[2] Not dissimilar to Claude Lévi-Strauss' description of the bricoleur who always "references some extraneous movement: a ball rebounding, a dog straying, or a horse swerving from its direct course to avoid an obstacle,"[3] there is rather a sense of peripheral discord brought into syncopated focus in Lassry's pictures. Building up a recursive kinship between once utilitarian prompts and the exhausted stagecraft of product and audition scenarios, Lassry evokes the loss of a certain image efficacy in our increasingly cross-referenced, sortable digital age. The oscillation that results in a grouping of Lassry's mute yet entreating pictures extends to his films as they likewise borrow from multiple sources and embrace a process of crossing eras and abstracting cultural references.

Derived from an array of textbooks, magazines, and photography books, Lassry's films often begin with a questioning of pictures culled from contradictory contexts.

In translating the overlap and boundary conditions into moving images, Lassry insists upon the consciousness of the still frame, often returning to and repeating sequences that delay movement and withhold ready recognition or identification; setting up failed tableaux vivants and fragmented views of heightened physicality and choreography, Lassry emphasizes the time of registration over the time of narrative and direct quotation, choreographing what Annette Michelson identifies as "the instant of arrest and release, of reversal, of movement"[4] that structural filmmaking, in particular, makes possible. *Untitled* (2007), for example, takes its cues from a 1958 manual called *The Art of Making Dances*, published by choreographer Doris Humphrey. A pioneer of modern dance—who, like Martha Graham and Louise Brooks, got her start in the popular traveling shows of the 1920s Denishawn Dance Company—Humphrey's instructional approach proposed a method of breaking down expressionistic dance movements by identifying weak and strong areas of the stage. By adapting Humphrey's scheme (ill. 7) in relation to a pas de deux passage from George Balanchine's neoclassical ballet *Agon* (1957), Lassry imagines an unlikely collaborative moment that never existed, displacing the austere lyricism of Balanchine's balletic forms with a transported schematic, and vice versa. Prototypical of Lassry's approach, the outmoded is warped into the arena of the highly skilled or virtuosic, creating a dynamic of rupture and repetition that inflects each of his films.

Borrowing from structuralist film tactics of the 1960s—fixed camera positions, predetermined sequencing, and simplified action—Lassry delineates the limitations of the film camera's frame within a lexicon of views proposed by Humphrey's book, invoking his own version of what Deleuze termed the "out-of-field," that which "refers to what is neither seen nor understood, but is nevertheless perfectly present."[5] Specifically, in Lassry's case, the out-of-field is that of command and prowess, a charged atmosphere of directive that is partially withheld through the absence of sound in his films. Just as his photographs extract themselves from evicted but nevertheless insinuated editorial and design connotations, Lassry's films imply the presence of a directorial voice impelling each version and variation from off camera. For *Untitled*, Lassry adopts something like the répétiteur's role in an opera or ballet company—repeating a choreographed sequence and breaking it down step by step until it becomes rote for the performers and proxy viewer. Interpolating a silenced yet procedural ethos onto a climactic moment from Balanchine impedes the moment of catharsis even as it siphons from its aura.

Following a 1959 performance of *Agon* at the New York City Ballet, dance critic Edwin Denby wrote that "the emotion is that of scale"[6] as Balanchine's choreography worked to upend conventions and introduce a ballet that proceeded by gesture and rhythm, evading plot signatures, and taking instead "the form of a small entertainment."[7] Employing professional dancers Megan LeCrone and Ask la Cour, Lassry accordingly recreates the last minute of Balanchine's seminal work in a New York City Ballet rehearsal space, beginning each shot from a predetermined vantage point borrowed from the Humphrey book. As the dancers break their initial equipoise and cross before the camera, repeatedly filling the frame with fragments of studied movement, they cease to be merely performers embodying a duet and become the subjects of an elaborate study in visual contrast and embodied memory. Shot from different angles, the demands of executing a highly technical movement are heightened by partial views of the dancers' bodies, as the frame repeatedly fragments the choreography, simultaneously deciphering and annulling the delivery. The grid-like outline of the barre, Balanchine's trademark black-and-white costuming, and the immediate legibility of the neutral dance studio, are offset by Lassry's capturing the dancers' awkward bearing just prior to and after they repeat the routine's closure—a collapse wherein the dancers fall into each other and form a figurative abstraction.

Held within the frame just long enough to include the moment when the performers step in and out of their roles, thereby releasing the choreography's final symbolic image, Lassry here interprets scale as emotion via the moment when the individuated body steps from the rigor of the routine at the end of each variation. Similarly, the close-ups that bookend the film further reveal Lassry's interest in an estrangement of codified gesture; trained upon each dancer's head and shoulders, the dip, nod, and sway of transition moves across their faces as they envision the upcoming sequence, dilating their visual focus and punctuating time with the presence of memory and training. Not unlike an athlete imagining a series of maneuvers or a course that must be run, transitions stored in muscle memory flash across the mind's eye and ripple through the dancer's body. The result is that a condensation of bodily inscription occurs before the camera. Montage appears to be inverted here and attain a fleeting yet corporeal presence in the gestures of pre-enactment that occur in these long shots. Placed alongside the transient, unnerving appeal of his pho-tographs, Lassry's deliberate style of filmmaking recalls French critic Raymond Bellour's notion of "the pensive spectator" who vacillates before a film due to an awareness of the still image(s) that lie within and an awareness of the potential to pause the action and add to or interrupt the impending linearity of a given sequence.[8]

With *Zebra and Woman* (2007), Lassry further exacerbates the tension between still and moving images by engaging a conventional scenic device, in the form of a black backdrop, that erases depth of field and accentuates gesture and motion—a tactic used to emphasize the act of viewing that extends back to Eadweard Muybridge's motion studies (ill. 8) and Étienne-Jules Marey's chronophotography (ill. 9), but also early time-lapse films of plant and insect behavior, as well as W.K.L. Dickson's first experiments filming traveling players, pugilists, Buffalo Bill's revue, Sioux Ghost Dances (ill. 10), and other highly charged pantomimes in Edison's Black Maria laboratory. That this neutral backdrop would also become a standard mise-en-scène for film and photo shoots—from Warhol's screen tests to countless music videos and fashion spreads—is evoked in Lassry's dual portrait of a bemused artifice. Comprised of slow left-to-right panning shots, the film begins with the twitch of a zebra's tail, proceeds along the black-and-white sheen of the animal's flank, past its muzzle and skittish glance, to jump cut and end on the profile of an attractive blond woman absorbed in holding a far-off gaze. An exercise in the most basic principle of cinematic montage—the bringing together of contrasting or seemingly out-of-sequence images as an associative stimulus to the viewer—Lassry's use of the steady pan distorts our expectation of a beautiful woman's pose while also fluently referencing what film historian Tom Gunning has termed an "aesthetic of astonishment," which characterized so many spectators' incredulous response to early moving pictures.

The illusion of an exotic tableau vivant falters almost immediately in the zebra's quivered response to off-camera handlers, even turning to confront the camera, while the model—played by Hollywood actress Radha Mitchell—nearly manages her empty stare throughout before a slight pucker troubles her mouth as she passes slowly out of the frame. Stand-ins for a failed illustration of seemingly surrealist juxtaposition, the scenario attains instead a demonstrative tonality in keeping with early cinematic experiments. An awareness of the apparatus is amplified by the anticipation of the tracking shot along with subjects both reluctant and self-conscious, enfolding what Giorgio Agamben offers as definitive of cinema, namely a re-inscription of gesture that calls attention to its enervated status. In elaborating the paradoxical nature of cinema's returning the viewer to the realm of gesture, Agamben clarifies that "what characterizes gesture is that there is neither production nor enactment but undertaking and supporting."[9] For it is the sphere of the rehearsal, outtake, and mountable episode that differentiates cinema from theater, the ability to return to, parcel out, and synthesize the "anima" or vital force of a given gesture along with the knowledge that what transpires before the camera is imprinted for the material appeal of the apparatus rather than a reciprocated audience relationship. Existing forever alongside a time of whole and unitary performance—and so outside the immersion of ritual and the dénouement of theater or opera—cinema both mourns and ridicules linearity, duration, and continuity. And yet, as Agamben further intimates, perhaps it is exactly the phenomenological gap opened here by cinema and filmmaking that maintains a reserve of mimetic capability long exhausted in the still image's embedded subservience to logo, slogan, and column.[10]

A trio of recent films employs the white background of a stripped down soundstage in construing more elaborate investigations of perception, gesture, and past cultural achievements. *Untitled* (2008) (ill. 4), for instance, departs from a *trompe l'oeil* photograph found in a 1971 science textbook intended to show how visual depth perception works. Replicating the floor diagram of a house-like structure from the photograph—painted in a Josef Albers-esque combination of light blue and yellow—Lassry engages three young women and a man to interact with the optical illusion. The depthless white backdrop acts to highlight contour rather than motion, making the figures seem like cutouts. Negotiating their positions in order to maintain the illustrative effect, the models hold poses and repeat gestures for the camera in episodic scenes that resemble a series of commercial auditions. Employing what appear to be industry professionals, Lassry accumulates empty gestures and highly staged interactions in durations that disrupt their potential as static images: a windowpane frames a man and woman mouthing melodramatic dialogue; a woman struggles to hold her pose in the illusion's doorway, falling in and out of character with nervous laughter; while another model flashes a perfect smile over and over. *Untitled* (2009), continues Lassry's use of recognizable faces as actor Eric Stoltz pantomimes a series of explanatory gestures on a soundstage populated with oversized Minimalist columns finished in gleaming green, yellow, and black. The gravity of the man's authorial directives are ostensibly received by a boyish female dancer—always pictured separately—who attentively listens before enacting a series of spritely maneuvers, including the torso-down view of an aerial special effect that crosses back and forth before a stationary camera. Lassry's interpretation of the exaggerated production stills of a television adaptation of *Peter Pan* (ill. 5), originally choreographed by Jerome Robbins and played by Mary Martin, is collapsed with the gestalt effects of Minimalism's primary structures here made into props. The "kinesthetic demands" on the viewer, to use Robert Morris' oft-quoted phrase regarding Minimalist sculpture, including an "awareness of scale (that) is a function of the comparison between the constant, one's body size, and the object,"[11] are comically transformed into a Broadway-style backdrop.

Lassry's most recent film, *Untitled (Passacaglia)* (2010), returns to modern dance for inspiration as it restages sections of a Doris Humphrey composition from 1938 that was later filmed for American public television in 1966. Shot on Super-16mm—a film format with a wide aspect ratio originally designed for broadcast television and used by Lassry in three of his five films—the ensemble piece is transposed from black and white into color and challenges members of the New York City Ballet to interpret a somber yet assertive choreography considered radical for its time. By choosing a recreation in and of itself as a starting point and inviting performers with a different vocabulary and training, Lassry pushes the degree of remove and artifice to newfound lengths. The dance for camera aspect is heightened with long tracking shots, vertiginous angles, and close-up views that interrupt any continuity, refusing any overview or intimation of periodicity. Rather, the overtly expressionistic Humphrey movements get boxed in and made claustrophobic here. Offset by a methodical opening shot of a prop painting meant to mime Robert Delaunay's *La grande Portugaise* (1916) (ill. 11), the counterbalance offered by Lassry is not release, but yet another false movement. A mock-up of Delaunay's post-Cubist departure into rhythmic and colorful abstraction is filmed according to the sleight of hand conventions of filming painting. Long panning shots over the prop's surface move left to right and up and down, only to be supplanted onto the opening shot of the dancers as the film enacts an allusive collapse of once experimental styles. Eliding the styles of past innovations, Lassry underscores the loss of emphatic articulation even as he rehearses its renewal.

1 Giorgio Agamben, "Notes on Gesture," *Infancy and History: The Destruction of Experience*, Verso Press, London/New York 1993, p. 137.
2 Lassry's tactics of appropriation differ from such well-known examples as Cindy Sherman's *Untitled Film Stills* (1977–1980), or Richard Prince's re-photographing of Marlboro advertisements and Barbara Kruger's signature use of the Futura Bold Oblique font in that Lassry largely repurposes provisional imagery.
3 Claude Lévi-Strauss, *The Savage Mind*, University of Chicago Press, Chicago 1966, p. 19.
4 Annette Michelson, "From Magician to Epistemologist. Vertov's *The Man With a Movie Camera*," *The Essential Cinema. Essays on Films in the Collection of Anthology Film Archives*, ed. P. Adams Sitney, New York 1975, p. 104.
5 Gilles Deleuze, *Cinema 1. The Movement-Image*, University of Minnesota Press, Minneapolis 1986, p. 17.
6 Edwin Denby, "Three Sides of *Agon*," Roger Copeland, Marshall Cohen (eds.), *What Is Dance? Readings in Theory and Criticism*, Oxford University Press, New York 1983, p. 453.
7 Ibid, p. 446.
8 Raymond Bellour, "The Pensive Spectator," *Wide Angle*, Ohio, vol. 9, no. 1, 1987, p. 6–10.
9 Agamben, "Notes on Gesture," p. 140.
10 Ibid.
11 Robert Morris, "Notes on Sculpture, Part 2," *Continuous Projected Altered Daily. The Writings of Robert Morris*, MIT Press, Cambridge 1993, p. 13.

Fionn Meade

# Traumhafte Perfektion

„Im Kino versucht eine Gesellschaft, die ihre Gesten verloren hat, sich das Verlorene wieder anzueignen, und registriert zugleich den Verlust."
—Giorgio Agamben[1]

Eine Frau, die mit weit ausgestreckten Armen lachend nach ihrem krabbelnden Baby greift: Das Bild ist von oben aufgenommen, vor dem Hintergrund weicher weisser Bettwäsche, mit dem Ziel, die rastlose Krabbelei des Babys einzufangen. Es vermittelt den Eindruck einer häuslichen Variante des Gartens Eden, ein Zustand, in dem das Band zwischen Mutter und Kind noch ganz spontan und unverbrämt ist. Das preisgekrönte Bild – es zierte 1970 das Titelblatt des *Time Life Magazine* – zeigt ein uneingeschränkt und entschieden optimistisches Bild des Lebens. In Elad Lassrys Fotoarbeit *Joanna and Trace A1* (2007) (Abb. 6) wird das Originalbild jedoch umfunktioniert und einer speziellen Bildbearbeitung unterzogen. Die roten und weissen Blöcke, die in der Typografie zur Unterlegung von Titeln und Schlagzeilen dienen, um den Leser zu ködern, werden zweckentfremdet und über die Schrift gelegt, sodass diese dahinter verschwindet. Indem Lassry lediglich die Adressetikette des einstigen Heftabonnenten lesbar stehen lässt, verschiebt er die bestehenden redaktionellen und ökonomischen Konventionen; er macht das ehemals idyllische amerikanische Familienporträt quasi zum Waisenkind und versetzt es zurück in die anonymere Welt der Gesten. In diesem Prozess wird die kommerzielle Nutzbarkeit des Bildes zugleich bewusst gemacht und aufgehoben. Kontext, Herkunft und Verbreitung treten schemenhaft in den Hintergrund und die im Bild selbst enthaltene Bewegung rückt ins Zentrum. Ähnliche Begegnungen mit fotografischen Tropen, die ihrem ursprünglichen Zusammenhang entfremdet sind, charakterisieren viele von Lassrys Bildneubearbeitungen, so etwa, wenn das gewinnende Lächeln in der Porträtaufnahme eines männlichen Models – in *Man 071* (2007) – durch die Doppelbelichtung der Augen gestört, oder der gutmütige Schulmädchen-Charme von Felicia – in *Felicia* (2008) – durch den Lärm und das Flirren einer Überlagerung in Mitleidenschaft gezogen wird. Die enge Nähe dieser Überlagerungen wird dabei oft noch durch die farbliche Anpassung des Rahmens an eine auffällige Farbe im Hintergrund des ursprünglichen Fotos verstärkt, was das gegenständliche Sujet zusätzlich destabilisiert.

In Lassrys Bildern geraten normalerweise leicht entschlüsselbare Platzhalter in eine Stotterbewegung, weil die Konventionen der Studiofotografie – Porträt, Stillleben, Mode- und Produktpräsentationen – derart collagiert, umgestaltet und parodiert werden, dass die Bilder unheimlich wirken. Jeder anschaulichen Wiedergabetreue entbunden – ein Umstand, der durch den Sog zum Objekthaften in der Bildeinstellung noch unterstrichen wird – geht Lassrys Bildrepertoire auf Distanz zum Marketingkontext der Werbung und des Hollywoodfilms, mit dem es spielt. Perfekte menschliche Gesichter, exemplarische Tiere und makellose Früchte blicken uns, ohne dass sie an irgendwelchen Produkten festzumachen wären, inständig entgegen und rufen, genau wie alte Filmstars – häufig Lassrys Vorliebe für Eintagsfliegen der Popkultur der 1970er Jahre gemäss zusammengestiefelt oder diesen nachempfunden – ein breites Spektrum von Stimmungen und Ausdrucksformen abseits jedes Handlungszusammenhangs und Zielpublikums wach. In diesem Punkt weichen Lassrys Bilder von uns mittlerweile vertrauten Appropriationstechniken ab; sie übernehmen das Klischee und variieren es, lassen es nostalgisch und künstlich wirken, indem sie, anhand eines längst instrumentalisierten Bildvokabulars, den Eindruck von zuckenden Stakkatobewegungen, Fehlern im Druck und weiteren Entleerungseffekten vermitteln. Dadurch dass er eine Kritik der ikonischen oder stellvertretenden Funktion der dargestellten Figuren, Produkte oder Konflikte vermeidet – im Gegensatz zu manchen Appropriationsstrategien der sogenannten

„Pictures"-Generation –, begibt sich Lassry auf Nebenwege, die weniger vertraut und gängig sind.[2] Entsprechend der bei Claude Lévi-Strauss geschilderten, ursprünglichen Bedeutung des Verbs „bricoler" (basteln), das immer verwendet wird, „um eine nicht vorgezeichnete Bewegung zu betonen: die des Balles, der zurückspringt, des Hundes, der Umwege macht, des Pferdes, das von der geraden Bahn abweicht, um einem Hindernis aus dem Weg zu gehen"[3], wecken Lassrys Bilder eher das Gefühl einer peripheren, synkopisch aufblitzenden Unstimmigkeit. Indem er eine rekursive Beziehung zwischen einst zweckmässigen Informationen und der erschöpften Bühnenwirksamkeit von Produkt- und Probeszenarien herstellt, weist Lassry auf den Verlust einer gewissen Bildwirksamkeit in unserem zunehmend kreuz und quer vernetzten, sortierbaren digitalen Zeitalter hin. Die schillernde Wirkung, die eine Auswahl von Lassrys stummen und doch inständigen Bildern hervorruft, zeigt sich auch bei seinen Filmen, denn auch diese entlehnen ihr Material aus vielerlei Quellen, gehen gern epochenübergreifend zu Werke und reduzieren kulturelle Anspielungen aufs Wesentliche.

Die aus einer bunten Mischung von Drehbüchern, Zeitschriften und Fotobüchern hervorgegangenen Filme Lassrys beginnen oft mit einer Befragung von Bildern aus widersprüchlichen Kontexten. Beim Übersetzen von Überlappungs- und Grenzphänomenen in bewegte Bilder beharrt Lassry auf der Denkweise der Standaufnahme; dabei kommt er oft auf bewegungsverzögernde und nicht ohne weiteres erkennbare und identifizierbare Sequenzen zurück und wiederholt sie. Durch das Arrangieren missglückter Tableaux vivants und aufgebrochener Ansichten von betont körperlichem und choreografischem Charakter, unterstreicht Lassry die Zeit der Aufnahme auf Kosten der Zeit des narrativen Zusammenhangs und des direkten Zitats und setzt damit das, was Annette Michelson als „den Augenblick des Innehaltens und Loslassens, der Umkehr, der Bewegung"[4] bezeichnet, choreografisch um, was insbesondere durch den strukturalistischen Film möglich wurde. *Untitled* (2007) etwa ist von einem Handbuch der Choreografin Doris Humphrey aus dem Jahr 1958 inspiriert [(Abb. 7)]. Humphrey war eine Pionierin des modernen Tanzes, die – wie Martha Graham und Louise Brooks – ihre ersten Erfolge im Rahmen der beliebten Tourneeauftritte der Denishawn Dance Company in den 1920er Jahren feierte; ihr Lehransatz schlug eine Methode zur analytischen Aufgliederung moderner Ausdruckstanzbewegungen vor, indem sie die Bühne in schwache und starke Zonen aufteilte. Durch die Verbindung von Humphreys Schema mit einer Pas-de-deux-Szene aus George Balanchines neoklassischem Ballet *Agon* (1957), stellt sich Lassry einen unwahrscheinlichen Moment der Zusammenarbeit vor und verfremdet dadurch den strengen Lyrizismus von Balanchines tänzerischen Formen mit Anleitungsbildern und umgekehrt. Geradezu prototypisch für Lassrys Ansatz ist es, dass etwas längst Überholtes quasi auf die Bühne der Hochleistung oder Virtuosität „gewarpt" wird, um jene Dynamik zwischen Bruch und Wiederholung zu erzeugen, die alle seine Filme auszeichnet.

Durch Anleihen bei strukturalistischen Filmtechniken der 1960er Jahre – feste Kamerapositionen, vorgegebene Sequenzierung, vereinfachte Handlung – umreisst Lassry die Grenzen des Filmkamerabildes innerhalb jenes Lexikons möglicher Ansichten, das Humphreys Buch liefert, und deutet seine eigene Version dessen an, was Gilles Deleuze „hors-champ" nannte, „im Off", jenes also, was auf das verweist, „was man weder hört noch sieht und was trotzdem völlig gegenwärtig ist".[5] In Lassrys Fall ist es so, dass dieses „Off" eines der Macht und Kompetenz ist, eine knisternde Atmosphäre des Verfügens, die durch das Fehlen des Tons in seinen Filmen teilweise zurückgebunden wird. Genau wie seine Fotografien von zwar getilgten, aber nichtsdestoweniger angedeuteten redaktionellen und grafischen Konnotationen leben, implizieren Lassrys Filme das Vorhandensein einer Regie führenden Stimme, die jede Version und Variation aus dem Off antreibt. Bei *Untitled* schlüpft Lassry in eine Rolle, die der des Repetitors eines Opern- oder Ballett-Ensembles gleicht: Er wiederholt eine choreografische Sequenz und zerlegt sie Schritt für Schritt, bis sie für Darsteller und Zuschauer reine Routine werden. Dieses Einbringen eines gedämpften, aber für den äusseren Ablauf entscheidenden Ethos an einem Höhepunkt in Balanchines Choreografie verhindert deren kathartische Wirkung und schöpft zugleich selbst Kraft aus ihrer Aura.

Im Anschluss an eine Aufführung von *Agon* im New York City Ballet 1959 schrieb der Tanzkritiker Edwin Denby, dass es ein Gefühl von Grösse vermittle, wenn Balanchines Choreografie Konventionen auf den Kopf stelle und ein Ballett einführe, das auf Geste und Rhythmus setze, alle Merkmale einer Handlung meide und stattdessen die Form anspruchsloser Unterhaltung annehme.[6] Lassry verpflichtete die Tanzprofis Megan LeCrone und Ask la Cour um die letzte Minute von Balanchines bahnbrechendem Werk auf einer Probebühne des New York City Ballet angemessen nachzuspielen; dabei beginnt jede Einstellung mit einer in Humphreys Buch vorgegebenen Perspektive. Wenn die Tanzenden sich aus ihrer anfänglichen Gleichgewichtspose lösen und vor der Kamera vorübertanzen, wobei sie das Bild wiederholt mit Bruchstücken einstudierter Bewegungen ausfüllen, hören sie auf, lediglich Darsteller zu sein, die ein Duett verkörpern, und werden zu Subjekten einer raffinierten Studie über visuelle Kontraste und verkörperte Erinnerung. Aus verschiedenen Blickwinkeln aufgenommen, werden die Anforderungen an die Ausführung der technisch anspruchsvollen Bewegungen durch Teilansichten der Körper der Tanzenden gesteigert; die Einstellungen fragmentieren dabei immer wieder die Choreografie, sodass das Gezeigte laufend zugleich entziffert und annulliert wird. Der rasterartige Umriss der Ballettstange, Balanchines charakteristische Kostüme in Schwarz-Weiss und die unvermittelte Deutlichkeit des neutralen Tanzstudios werden aufgehoben durch Lassrys Einfangen der seltsamen Haltung der Tänzer unmittelbar bevor und nachdem sie den Schluss der Übung wiederholen – quasi ein Kollaps, bei dem die Tanzenden ineinanderfallen und zu einer figürlich-abstrakten Form verschmelzen.

Die Einstellung dauert genau so lange, dass der Moment, in dem die Tanzenden in ihre Rolle hinein- und wieder herausschlüpfen, miteinbezogen ist, und löst dadurch das symbolische Schlussbild der Choreografie aus. Lassry deutet hier das Gefühl von Grösse durch den Moment an, in dem der individuelle Körper am Ende jeder Variation aus der Strenge der Übung heraustritt. Ähnlich lassen auch die Nahaufnahmen am Ende des Films Lassrys Interesse am Verfremden normierter Gesten erkennen. Gezielt auf Kopf und Schultern jedes Tänzers gerichtet, zeigen sie das Neigen, Nicken und die Übergangsbewegung in ihren Gesichtern, wenn sie die kommende Sequenz in Angriff nehmen, ihr Blickfeld erweitern und der Zeit kraft der Präsenz ihres Erinnerungsvermögens und ihrer Übung eine Struktur geben. Ähnlich wie bei einem Athleten, der sich eine Reihe von Bewegungsabläufen oder ein bevorstehendes Rennen innerlich vergegenwärtigt, treten hier die im Muskelgedächtnis gespeicherten Abläufe vor das geistige Auge und überziehen den Körper des Tänzers mit einer Art Kräuseln. Dadurch kommt es vor der Kamera zu einer verdichteten Körperschrift. Die Montage scheint hier eine Umkehrung zu erfahren und in den Gesten unmittelbar vor der eigentlichen Ausführung, die in diesen langen Einstellungen sichtbar werden, eine flüchtige und doch physisch erlebbare Präsenz zu erreichen. Neben dem flüchtigen, verunsichernden Appell seiner Fotografien betrachtet, erinnert die bewusste Machart von Lassrys Filmen an den Begriff des „nachdenklichen Betrachters" des französischen Kritikers Raymond Bellour: Dieser Betrachter kommt vor einem Film ins Wanken, weil er um die einzelnen Standbilder weiss, aus denen der Film zusammengesetzt ist, und um die Möglichkeit, die Handlung jederzeit anzuhalten und die lineare Abfolge jeder beliebigen Sequenz zu erweitern oder zu unterbrechen.[7]

Bei *Zebra and Woman* (2007) verschärft Lassry die Spannung zwischen Standaufnahmen und bewegten Bildern noch durch einen konventionellen szenischen Kunstgriff in Gestalt eines schwarzen Hintergrundes, der dem Raum die Tiefe nimmt, hingegen Gesten und Bewegungen hervortreten lässt – eine Strategie zur emphatischen Betonung des Sehvorganges, die bis in die Zeit von Eadweard Muybridges Bewegungsstudien (Abb. 8) und Etienne-Jules Mareys Chronofotografie (Abb. 9) zurückreicht, aber auch bis zu frühen Zeitrafferfilmen über Pflanzenwachstum und das Verhalten von Insekten oder W.K.L.Dicksons ersten Experimenten mit Filmen über reisende Spieler, Boxer, Buffalo Bills Wildwest-Revue, Sioux-Geistertänze (Abb. 10) und weitere spannungsgeladene Pantomimen aus Thomas Edisons Black-Maria-Experimentalstudio. Dass dieser neutrale Hintergrund auch zur Standardszenerie für Film- und Fotoaufnahmen werden sollte – von Andy Warhols Probeaufnahmen bis zu zahllosen Musikvideos und Modeseiten – kommt in Lassrys Doppelporträt mit verblüffender Raffinesse zum Ausdruck. Aus langsamen Kameraschwenks von links nach rechts bestehend, beginnt der Film mit dem Zucken eines Zebraschwanzes, führt weiter der schwarz und weiss schimmernden Flanke des Tieres entlang, vorbei an seiner Schnauze und seinem nervösen Blick, um mit einem plötzlichen Schnitt auf dem Profil einer attraktiven Blondine zu enden, die ganz damit beschäftigt ist, ihren entrückten

Blick beizubehalten. Als Übung im einfachsten Prinzip der filmischen Montage – der Kombination von gegensätzlichen oder scheinbar unzusammenhängenden Bildern, um die Assoziationskraft des Betrachters zu wecken – stört Lassrys Verwendung des langsamen Schwenks unsere Erwartung an die Haltung einer schönen Frau und spielt zugleich geschickt auf etwas an, was der Filmhistoriker Tom Gunning „Ästhetik der Verblüffung" nannte und was die ungläubige Reaktion vieler Betrachter auf die ersten Filme absolut treffend umschreibt.

Die Illusion eines exotischen Tableau vivant fällt fast sofort in sich zusammen durch die nervöse Reaktion des Zebras auf die im Bild nicht sichtbaren Kameraleute; es dreht sich sogar frontal zur Kamera, während es dem Model – gespielt von der Hollywood-Schauspielerin Radha Mitchell – beinahe gelingt, ihren leeren Blick durchzuhalten; erst als sie langsam aus dem Bild gleitet, umspielt ein leichtes Kräuseln ihren Mund. Als Ersatz für die gescheiterte Illustration einer scheinbar surrealistischen Gegenüberstellung erreicht das Szenario eine Tonalität, die demonstrativ im Einklang mit frühen Filmexperimenten steht.
Das Bewusstsein um den technischen Apparat wird noch verstärkt durch die Antizipation der Kamerafahrt, deren Sujets widerspenstig und befangen sind, und umfasst, was Giorgio Agamben als definierendes Merkmal des Films beschreibt, nämlich eine Wiederaneignung der Gesten, die auf deren geschwächten Status verweist. Indem er den paradoxen Charakter der Tatsache herausarbeitet, dass das Kino dem Betrachter das Reich der Gesten wieder zurückgibt, macht Agamben deutlich, dass die Geste sich dadurch auszeichnet, „dass man in ihr weder etwas hervorbringt bzw. macht noch ausführt bzw. handelt, sondern etwas übernimmt und trägt."[8] Denn es ist die Sphäre der Probeaufnahme, des Herausschneidens und der montierbaren Episode, die das Kino vom Theater unterscheidet, die Fähigkeit auf etwas zurückzukommen, das Ganze aufzubrechen und die „anima" oder den „élan vital" einer Geste synthetisch herzustellen, im Wissen darum, dass das, was vor der Kamera passiert, eher vom handfesten Appell des Apparats geprägt ist als von einer reziproken Beziehung zum Publikum. Da es für immer zu einer Existenz ausserhalb der Zeit der ganzen und einheitlichen Aufführung verurteilt ist – und damit ausserhalb des rituellen Eintauchens und der dramatischen Entwicklung von Theater und Oper –, trauert das Kino der Linearität, Dauer und Kontinuität zugleich nach und macht sich über sie lustig. Und doch ist es vielleicht, wie Agamben weiter andeutet, genau diese phänomenologische Lücke, die Kino und Film hier auftun, die einen Rest mimetischer Kapazität bewahrt, die sich im Falle des Standbildes durch die Abnutzung in Logos, Slogans und Zeitungsspalten längst erschöpft hat.[9]

Drei neue Filme verwenden den weissen Hintergrund eines demontierten Film-Tonstudios, um ausgeklügelte Untersuchungen zu Wahrnehmung, Gestik und älteren kulturellen Errungenschaften durchzuführen. *Untitled* (2008) (Abb. 4) etwa geht von einer Trompe-l'Œil-Fotografie aus einem wissenschaftlichen Buch von 1971 aus, die zeigen soll, wie die optische Tiefenwahrnehmung funktioniert. Mit Hilfe einer Replik des auf dieser Fotografie abgebildeten Bodenmusters eines hausähnlichen Gebildes – in einer an Josef Albers erinnernden Kombination von Hellblau und Gelb gemalt – lässt Lassry drei junge Frauen und einen Mann mit der optischen Täuschung interagieren. Der weisse Hintergrund ist ohne jede Tiefe und betont eher die Umrisse als die Bewegung, was die Figuren wie ausgeschnitten wirken lässt. Ihre Positionen bedachtsam abwägend, um die Wirkung der Illustration nicht zu beeinträchtigen, halten die Models bestimmte Posen und wiederholen gewisse Gesten für die Kamera in episodischen Szenen, die fast wie eine Serie von Werbefilm-Probeaufnahmen wirken. Anscheinend mit Profis aus eben dieser Szene arbeitend, sorgt Lassry für eine Anhäufung leerer Gesten und äusserst inszenierter Interaktionen, die so lange dauern, dass sie das Potenzial statischer Bilder sprengen: Hinter einer Fensterscheibe führen ein Mann und eine Frau einen melodramatischen Dialog; eine Frau versucht krampfhaft ihre Pose unter der Tür der Bildillusion zu halten, wobei sie immer wieder nervös lachend aus der Rolle fällt; gleichzeitig lässt ein anderes Model ein durch und durch perfektes Lächeln aufblitzen. In *Untitled* (2009) setzt Lassry seine Arbeit mit bekannten Gesichtern fort, wenn Eric Stoltz pantomimisch eine Reihe erläuternder Gesten auf einer Tonstudiobühne mit übergrossen minimalistischen Säulen vollführt, die grün, gelb und schwarz glänzend lackiert sind. Das Gravitätische der autoritären Anweisungen des Mannes wird von einer – immer separat gezeigten – knabenhaften Tänzerin aufgenommen, die jeweils aufmerksam zuhört, bevor sie eine Reihe quirliger

Manöver ausführt, einschliesslich der vom Torso an abwärts gefilmten Ausführung eines luftigen Spezialeffekts, bei dem sie vor einer unbeweglichen Kamera vor und zurück springt. Lassrys Interpretation der übertriebenen Standbilder einer Fernsehadaptation des – ursprünglich von Jerome Robbins choreografierten und von Mary Martin gespielten – *Peter Pan* (Abb. 5) wird mit den Gestalt-Effekten der Grundformen des Minimalismus, hier zu Kulissenelementen degradiert, überblendet. Die kinästhetischen Anforderungen an den Betrachter, die – um Robert Morris' oft zitierten Satz über die minimalistische Skulptur zu verwenden – ein „Wissen um die Grösse als Funktion des Vergleichs zwischen der Konstanten, der eigenen Körpergrösse, und dem Objekt"[10] mit einschliessen, werden hier durch komische Verzerrung zur Broadway-Kulisse.

Lassrys jüngster Film, *Untitled (Passacaglia)* (2010), kehrt zum modernen Tanz als Inspiration zurück, insofern er Teile einer Komposition von Doris Humphrey aus dem Jahr 1938 reinszeniert, die 1966 für das öffentlichrechtliche amerikanische Fernsehen verfilmt wurde. Der im Format Super-16-mm gedrehte Film – ein Breitbildformat, das ursprünglich für das Fernsehen gedacht war und von Lassry in dreien seiner fünf Filme verwendet wird – wurde zur Gänze von Schwarz-Weiss in Farbe übertragen und verlangt von Mitgliedern des New York City Ballet, eine düstere, aber bestimmte Choreografie zu interpretieren, die seinerzeit als radikal galt. Allein schon indem er eine Pause als Ausgangspunkt wählt und Tänzer mit einem ganz anderen tänzerischen Vokabular und Training einlädt, treibt Lassry die Distanz und Künstlichkeit in neue Extreme. Der Aspekt des Tanzens für die Kamera wird noch stärker hervorgehoben durch lange Kamerafahrten, Schwindel erregende Blickwinkel und Nahaufnahmen, die jede Kontinuität zerstören, indem sie jeden Überblick und jede Andeutung einer Periodizität verweigern. Stattdessen werden die bei Humphrey betont expressionistischen Bewegungen hier eingeschlossen, bis sie klaustrophobisch wirken. Der Kontrast zu einer bewusst raumöffnenden Einstellung auf eine Bühnenmalerei, die Robert Delaunays *La grande Portugaise* (1916) (Abb. 11) nachbilden soll, erweist sich nicht als befreiend, sondern lediglich als ein weiterer trügerischer Schachzug. Modellhaft wird Delaunays postkubistischer Aufbruch in die rhythmische und farbenfrohe Abstraktion nachgestellt, mit allen konventionellen Raffinessen des Filmens von Malerei. Lange Kamerafahrten über die Kulissenfläche streifen von links nachrechts, nach oben und unten, nur um schliesslich über die Eingangssequenz mit den Tänzerinnen gelegt zu werden, wenn der Film den Kollaps der einst experi-mentellen Stile inszeniert. Indem er so die innovativen Stile der Vergangenheit gleichsam annulliert, unterstreicht Lassry den Verlust emphatischer Ausdrucksformen noch im selben Moment, in dem er ihre Erneuerung probt.

1 Giorgio Agamben, „Noten zur Geste", in: ders., *Mittel ohne Zweck*, Berlin/Freiburg 2001, S. 56.
2 Lassrys Appropriationstaktiken unterscheiden sich durch die weitgehende Verwendung von unprätentiösem Bildmaterial deutlich von so bekannten Beispielen wie Cindy Shermans *Untitled Film Stills* (1977–1980), Richard Prince' nachgestellten Marlboro-Reklamebildern oder Barbara Krugers Verwendung des Schriftsatzes „Futura fett kursiv" als Markenzeichen.
3 Claude Lévi-Strauss, *Das wilde Denken*, Frankfurt am Main 1973, S. 29.
4 Annette Michelson, „From Magician to Epistemologist: Vertov's *The Man With a Movie Camera*", in: P. Adams Sitney (Hg.), *The Essential Cinema*, New York 1975, S. 104. (Zitat aus dem Engl. übers.)
5 Gilles Deleuze, *Kino 1: Das Bewegungs-Bild*, Frankfurt am Main 1997, S. 31–32.
6 Edwin Denby, „Three Sides of *Agon*", in: Roger Copeland, Marshall Cohen (Hg.), *What Is Dance? Readings in Theory and Criticism*, New York 1983, S. 446, 453.
7 Raymond Bellour, „The Pensive Spectator", in: *Wide Angle*, Ohio, Jg. 9, Nr. 1, 1987, S. 6–10.
8 Agamben, „Noten zur Geste" (Anm. 1), S. 59.
9 Agamben, „Noten zur Geste" (Anm. 1), S. 140.
10 Robert Morris, „Notes on Sculpture, Part 2", in: *Continuous Projected Altered Daily. The Writings of Robert Morris*, Cambridge 1993, S. 13.

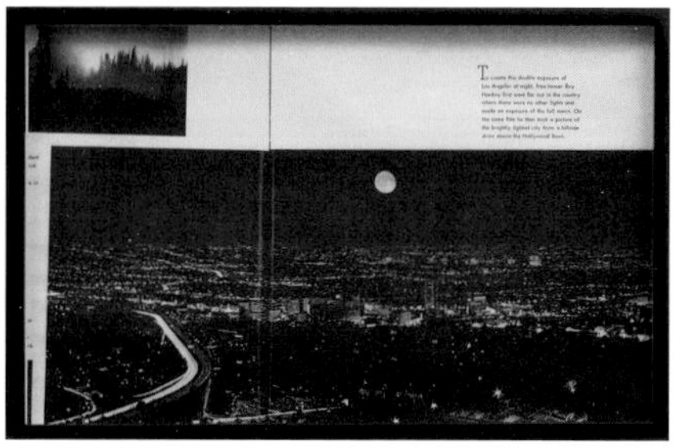

Ill. / Abb. 1
Elad Lassry
*Los Angeles at Night*, 2006
Xerox image / Fotokopie
27.9 × 45.7 cm
Courtesy David Kordansky Gallery,
Los Angeles, CA

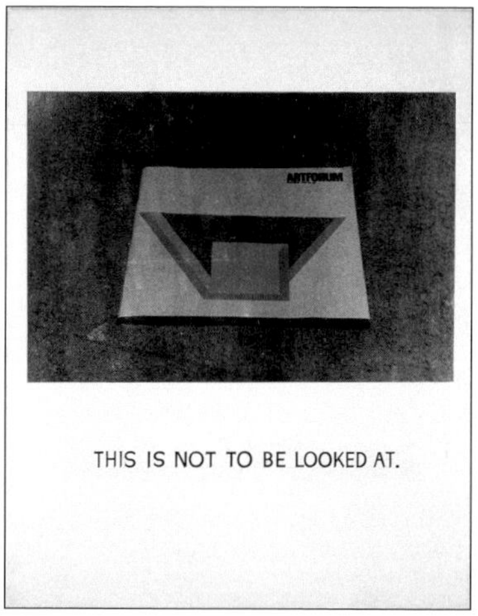


Ill. / Abb. 2
John Baldessari
*This is Not To Be Looked At*, 1966–1968
Acrylic, photo-emulsion on canvas /
Acryl, Fotoemulsion auf Leinwand
149.9 × 114.3 cm
Courtesy John Baldessari

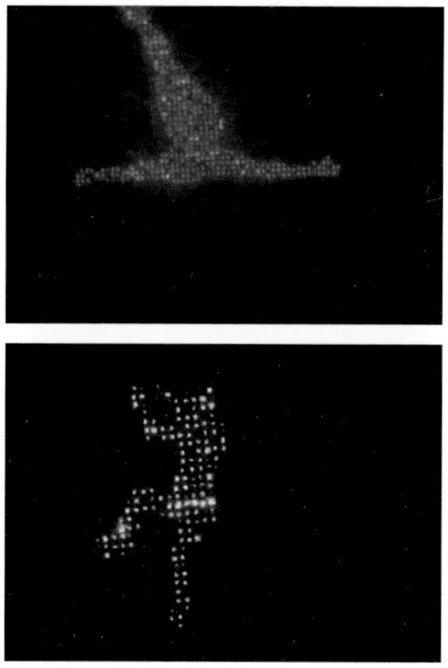

Ill. / Abb. 3
Jack Goldstein
*The Jump*, 1978
16mm film, color, silent / 16mm-Film, Farbe, ohne Ton
0:51 min.
Courtesy Galerie Daniel Buchholz, Cologne/Berlin
& The Estate of Jack Goldstein

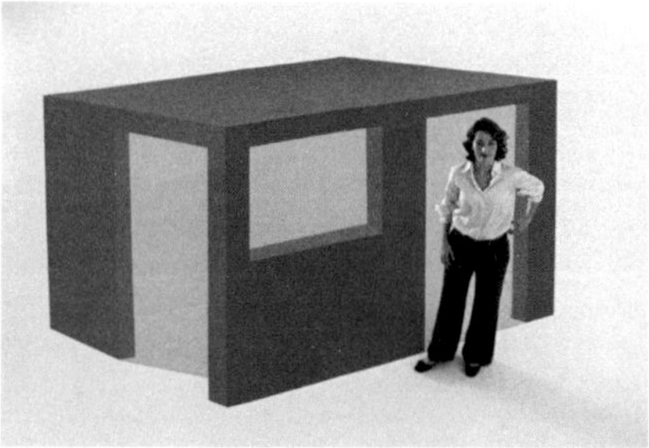

Ill. / Abb. 4
Elad Lassry
*Untitled*, 2008
16mm film, color, silent / 16mm-Film,
Farbe, ohne Ton
9:20 min.
Courtesy David Kordansky Gallery,
Los Angeles, CA

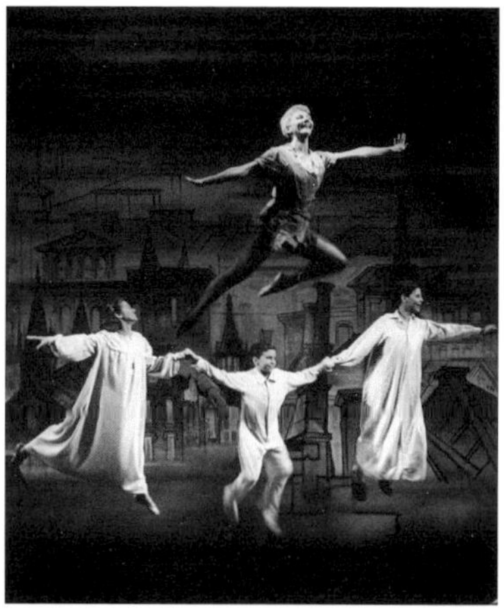

Ill. / Abb. 5
Actress Mary Martin as Peter Pan flying over the heads
of the three children as she gives them a flying lesson
in the Broadway production of the musical *Peter Pan*. /
Die Schauspielerin Mary Martin in der Figur des Peter Pan
in der gleichnamigen Broadway-Musicalproduktion,
wie sie über die drei Kinder hinwegschwebt, als sie
diesen Flugunterricht gibt.
1954
Photo: Allan Grant//Time Life Pictures/Getty Images

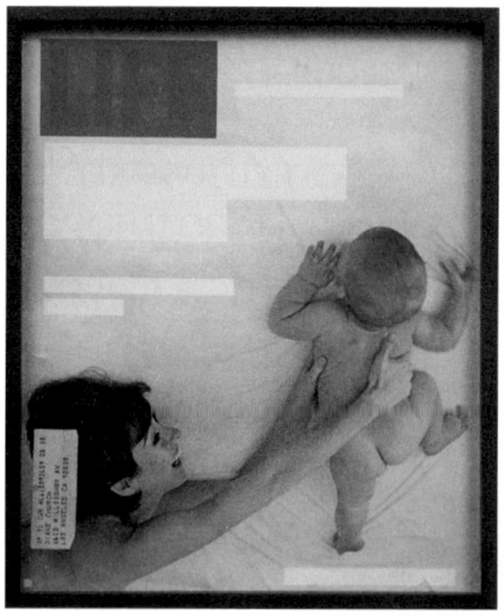

Ill. / Abb. 6
Elad Lassry
*Joanne and Trace A1*, 2007
Silkscreen on magazine paper / Siebdruck
auf Magazinseite
34.9 × 27.9 cm
Courtesy David Kordansky Gallery,
Los Angeles, CA

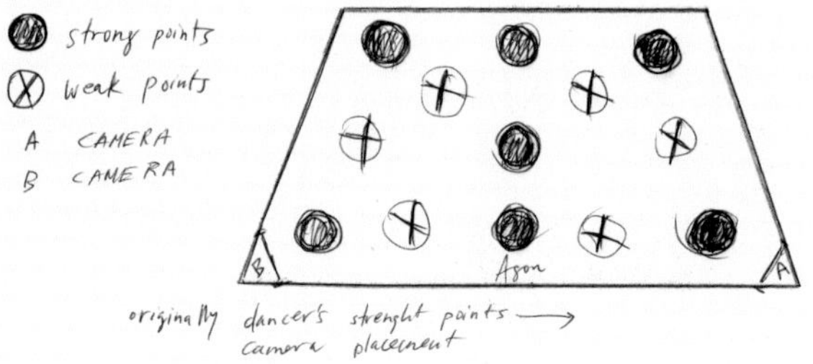


Ill. / Abb. 7
Elad Lassry
Sketch for *Untitled* (2007) based on a diagram by Doris Humphrey /
Skizze zu *Untitled* (2007), basierend auf einem Diagramm von Doris Humphrey

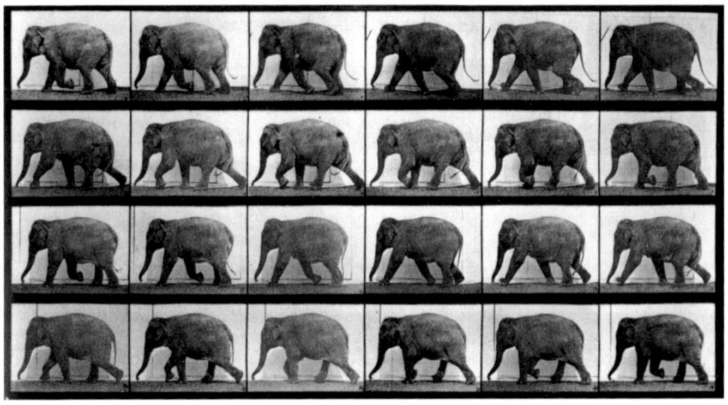

Ill. / Abb. 8
Eadweard Muybridge
*Walking Elephant*, August 1885, plate 733 from the series /
Tafel 733 aus der Serie *Animal Locomotion*
Collotype / Farblichtdruck
20.5 × 37.8 cm

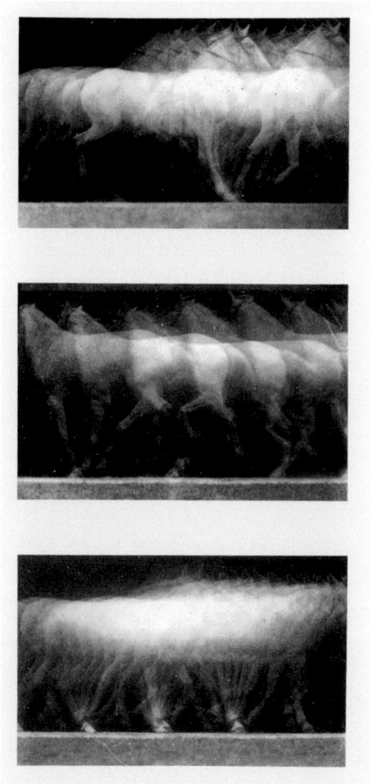

Ill. / Abb. 9
Étienne-Jules Marey
*Movements of a White Horse*, 1885–1886
Collège de France

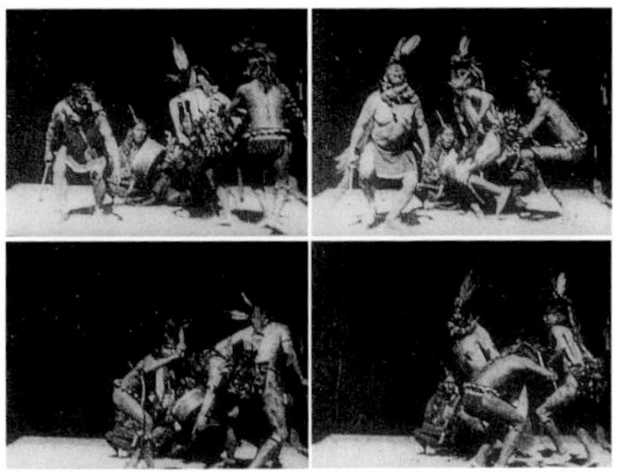

Ill. / Abb. 10
Thomas A. Edison
*Sioux Ghost Dance*, 1894
b/w film, silent, filmed in Edison's Black Maria studio /
s/w-Film, ohne Ton, gefilmt in Edisons Black-Maria-Studio
0:21 min. at 20 fps / mit 20 Bildern pro Sekunde

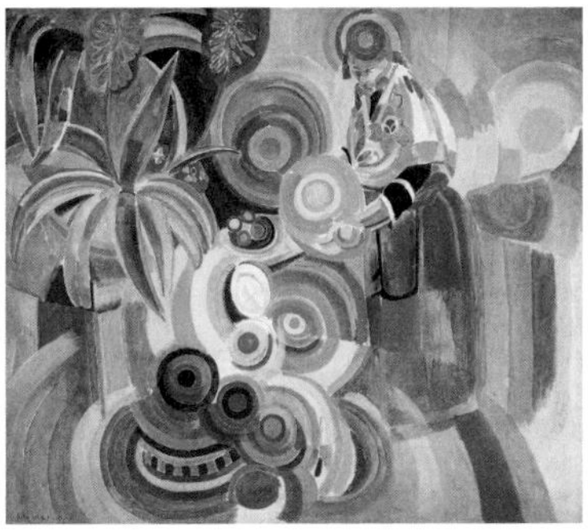

Ill. / Abb. 11
Robert Delaunay
*La grande Portugaise*, 1916
Wax on canvas / Wachs auf Leinwand
180 × 205 cm
Colección Carmen Thyssen-Bornemisza en depósito
en el Museo Thyssen-Bornemisza

# List of Illustrations/ Abbildungsverzeichnis

38 *Ropes*, 2009
C-print
27.9 × 35.6 cm
Sammlung Ringier, Schweiz

39 *Czech Girl*, 2009
C-print
36.8 × 29.2 cm
Sammlung Ringier, Schweiz

40 *Boys*, 2009
C-print
20.3 × 25.4 cm
Sammlung Ringier, Schweiz

41 *Living Room*, 2010
C-print
21.6 × 26.7 cm
Courtesy David Kordansky Gallery, Los Angeles, CA, & Galleria Massimo De Carlo, Milan

42 *High Heel, Purse*, 2009
C-print
35.6 × 27.9 cm
The Carol & Arthur Goldberg Collection

43 *Wolf (Blue)*, 2008
C-print
29.2 × 36.8 cm
Collection of David Kordansky & Mindy Shapero, Los Angeles, CA

44–45 *Untitled*, 2008
16mm film, color, silent / 16mm-Film, Farbe, ohne Ton
9:20 min.
Courtesy David Kordansky Gallery, Los Angeles, CA

46 *Baguette, Croissant*, 2008
Silver gelatin print / Silbergelatineabzug
36.8 × 29.2 cm
Sammlung Ringier, Schweiz

47 *Untitled (Red Cabbage 1)*, 2008
C-print
[illegible] cm
Collection Thomas Stauffer, Muri b. Bern, Switzerland

48 *Dustin Christenson*, 2010
C-print
36.8 × 29.2 cm
Courtesy David Kordansky Gallery, Los Angeles, CA, & Galleria Massimo De Carlo, Milan

49 *Two British Shorthair Cats (BSH)*, 2009
C-print
27.9 × 35.6 cm
The Eugene Sadovoy Collection, Los Angeles

50 *Kitchen*, 2010
Silver gelatin print / Silbergelatineabzug
36.8 × 29.2 cm
Courtesy David Kordansky Gallery, Los Angeles, CA, & Galleria Massimo De Carlo, Milan

51 *Harry Potter*, 2010
C-print
36.8 × 29.2 cm
Courtesy David Kordansky Gallery, Los Angeles, CA, & Galleria Massimo De Carlo, Milan

52 *Soccer Ball*, 2007
C-print
24.1 × 27.9 cm
Courtesy David Kordansky Gallery, Los Angeles, CA

53 *Felicia*, 2008
C-print
35.6 × 27.9 cm
Collection of Carlo Bronzini Vender

54 *Tomatillos*, 2010
C-print
36.8 × 29.2 cm
Courtesy David Kordansky Gallery, Los Angeles, CA, & Galleria Massimo De Carlo, Milan

55 *Textile (For Him and Her)*, 2009
Silver gelatin print / Silbergelatineabzug
27.9 × 35.6 cm
Sammlung Ringier, Schweiz

56 *Untitled (Two Purple Bars)*, 2010
Foil on C-print / Folie auf C-Print
20.3 × 25.4 cm
Courtesy David Kordansky Gallery, Los Angeles, CA, & Galleria Massimo De Carlo, Milan

57 *Horn Structure (For Massage and Collectable)*, 2009
Paper on C-print / Papier auf C-Print
35.6 × 27.9 cm
Sammlung Ringier, Schweiz

58–59 *Zebra and Woman*, 2007
Super-16mm film, color, silent / Super-16mm-Film, Farbe, ohne Ton
5:21 min.
Courtesy David Kordansky Gallery, Los Angeles, CA

60 *Cityscape (Burbank)*, 2009
Silkscreen on magazine paper / Siebdruck auf Magazinseite
34.3 × 50.8 cm
Private Collection / Privatsammlung

61 *Three Bottles*, 2009
C-print
36.8 × 29.2 cm
John Morace & Tom Kennedy, L. A.

62 *2000*, 2009
C-print
27.9 × 35.6 cm
Sammlung Ringier, Schweiz

63 *Eggs*, 2010
C-print
36.8 × 29.2 cm
Courtesy of David Kordansky Gallery, Los Angeles, CA, & Galleria Massimo De Carlo, Milan

64 *Lipstick*, 2009
C-print
36.8 × 29.2 cm
Sammlung Ringier, Schweiz

65 *Chocolate Factory*, 2007
C-print
27.9 × 35.6 cm
Helen N. Lewis & Marvin B. Meyer, Beverly Hills, California

66 *Persian Cucumbers, Shuk Hakarmel*, 2008
C-print
24.1 × 27.9 cm
Courtesy David Kordansky Gallery, Los Angeles, CA

67 *Woman (Puzzle)*, 2010
C-print
36.8 × 29.2 cm
Courtesy David Kordansky Gallery, Los Angeles, CA, & Galleria Massimo De Carlo, Milan

68 *Guinevere*, 2009
C-print
35.6 × 27.9 cm
The Eugene Sadovoy Collection, Los Angeles

69 *Joanne and Trace, No Distractions*, 2007
Silkscreen on magazine paper / Siebdruck auf Magazinseite
34.3 × 54 cm
Collection of David Kordansky & Mindy Shapero, Los Angeles, CA

# Biography & Bibliography / Biografie & Bibliografie

Born 1977 in Tel-Aviv. Lives and works in Los Angeles.
Geboren 1977 in Tel-Aviv. Lebt und arbeitet in Los Angeles.

## Education / Ausbildung

2007
Master of Fine Arts, University of Southern California, Los Angeles

2003
Bachelor of Fine Arts, California Institute of the Arts, Valencia

## Selected Solo Exhibitions / Einzelausstellungen (Auswahl)

2010
Luhring Augustine, New York
*Sum of Limited Views*, Contemporary Art Museum, St Louis
Galleria Massimo De Carlo, Milan
Kunsthalle Zürich

2009
David Kordansky Gallery, Los Angeles
*Elad Lassry: Three Films*, Whitney Museum of American Art, New York

2008
Art Institute of Chicago
*The Artist Moving Image Exhibition* (with / mit Daria Martin), Bath Film Festival

2007
*She Takes These Pictures of His Wife Silhouetted on a Hillside*, Cherry and Martin, Los Angeles

## Selected Group Exhibitions / Gruppenausstellungen (Auswahl)

2010
*Triumphant Carrot: The Persistence of Still Life*, Vancouver Contemporary Art Gallery, Vancouver
*Photos and Phantasy, Selections from the Fredrik R. Weisman Foundation*, Beverly Hills Municipal Gallery, Beverly Hills
*New Photography 2010*, MoMA – The Museum of Modern Art, New York
*Les Rencontres d'Arles 2010 / Edition 41*, Arles
*Permanent Mimesis: An Exhibition on Realism and Simulation*, GAM – Galleria Civica d'Arte Moderna e Contemporanea, Turin
*At Home/Not at Home, Works from the Collection of Martin and Rebecca Eisenberg*, Center for Curatorial Studies, Bard College, Annandale-on-Hudson

2009
*The Perpetual Dialogue*, Andrea Rosen Gallery, New York
*Beg, Borrow, and Steal*, Rubell Family Collection, Miami
Carlson/Massimo De Carlo, London
*Berlin-Los Angeles: A Tale of Two (Other) Cities*, Galleria Massimo De Carlo, Milan
*The Reach of Realism*, Museum of Contemporary Art, North Miami
*Pete and Repeat*, 176, London
*Dance with Camera*, Institute of Contemporary Art, Philadelphia
*Superficiality and Superexcrescence*, Ben Maltz Gallery at Otis College of Art and Design, Los Angeles
*The Generational: Younger Than Jesus*, New Museum, New York

2008
Front Room, Museum of Contemporary Art, St Louis
*Half-Life*, Los Angeles Contemporary Exhibitions, Los Angeles
*2008 California Biennial*, Orange County Museum of Art, Newport Beach
*Photos and Phantasy*, Carnegie Art Museum, Oxnard
*Past Forward*, 176, London
*You, Whose Beauty Was Famous in Rome*, Mandarin Gallery, Los Angeles

2007
*I Am Eyebeam*, Gallery 400, University of Illinois at Chicago

2006
*LA25*, Skadden, Los Angeles

2005
*Defense—Body and Nobody in Self Protection*, Sweeney Art Gallery, UC Riverside

## Artist's Projects / Künstlerprojekte

2010
*Frieze*, London, no. 132, June/July/August 2010, p. 146–149.

2009
*X-TRA Contemporary Art Quarterly*, vol. 11, no. 3, Spring 2009.

## Bibliography / Bibliografie


2010
Aram Moshayedi, "Work in Progress: Elad Lassry," *Bidoun*, New York, no. 21, Summer, p. 34–35.
Daphne Javitch, "Elad Lassry," *L'Officiel Hommes*, Paris, no. 20, June–August, p. 100–103.
Hans Ulrich Obrist, "Kunst im 21. Jahrhundert – Kuratiert von Hans Ulrich Obrist," *Du Magazin*, Zurich, no. 807, June.
*At Home/Not at Home: Works from the Collection of Martin and Rebecca Eisenberg*, Annandale-on-Hudson: Center for Curatorial Studies, Bard College, New York.
"Hijacked in a Winter Garden Moment, Cay Sophie Rabinowitz with Erin Tao in conversation with Elad Lassry," *Fantom*, Cinisello Balsamo / New York, no. 03, Spring, p. 84–95.
Simon Baier, "Elad Lassry," *Spike*, Vienna, no. 23, Spring, p. 133.
Brian Sholis, "Dance With Camera," *Aperture*, New York, Spring, p. 14.
Yvonne Ziegler, "Elad Lassry," *Kunstbulletin*, Zurich, no. 4, p. 72–73.
Branko B. Gabriel, "Branko B. Gabriel triff ...," *Cruiser*, Zurich, March 1, p. 34–35.
Gerhard Mack, "Zarte Annäherung," *NZZ am Sonntag*, Zurich, February 28, p. 55.
Feli Schindler, "Retrokitschiger Bilderfries von Elad Lassry," *Tages Anzeiger*, Zurich, February 22, p. 28.
Brigitte Ulmer, "Bildparasiten aus der kollektiven Bilderbank," *Neue Zürcher Zeitung*, Zurich, February 19, p. 17.
David Velasco, "White Columns Annual," *Artforum*, New York, vol. 48, no. 6, February, p. 204–205.
Nicolas Trembley, "Au-delà du réel," *Numéro*, Paris, no. 110, February, p. 60.
Shane Lavalette & Michael Bühler-Rose (ed.), *Lay Flat 02: Meta*, February, p. 90–91.
Caoimhin Mac Giolla Léith, "Looking Back: Emerging Artists," *Frieze*, London, no. 128, January/February, p. 90.
Alessandro Rabottini, "Looking Forward," *Frieze*, London, no. 128, January/February, p. 93.
Holland Cotter, "The Perpetual Dialogue," *The New York Times*, New York, January 8, p. 32.
Alex Israel, "Myths of Decline," *Artforum*, New York, vol. 48, no. 5, January, p. 67–70.
*Blind Spot*, New York, no. 41.

2009
Heidi Zuckerman Jacobson, Karl Haendel, Thomas Houseago & David Moos, *Beg, Borrow and Steal*, Rubell Family Collection, Miami.
Lisa Kraus, "Dancing through the lens," *The Philadelphia Inquirer*, Philadelphia, December 22, http://www.philly.com/inquirer/magazine/79879367.html#axzz0r7G5GDrZ (last accessed: June 17, 2010).
David Pagel, "Art Review: 'The Newest' at Phil," *LosAngelesTimes.com*, Los Angeles, December 18, http://latimesblogs.latimes.com/culturemonster/2009/12/art-review-the-newest-at-phil.html (last accessed: June 17, 2010).
Christopher Bollen, "Rated ART," *Interview*, New York, December 2009/January 2010, p. 149.
Aimee Walleston, "Elad Lassry's New Show," *The Last Magazine*, New York, no. 3, p. 10.
Michael Ned Holte, "Best of 2009," *Artforum*, New York, vol. 48, no. 4, December, p. 192.
Elad Lassry, "The Artists' Artists," *Artforum*, New York, vol. 48, no. 4, December, p. 88.
Stefan Heideinreich & Thomas Lawson, *Berlin-Los Angeles. A Tale of Two (Other) Cities*, Mousse Publising, Milan.

Lucy Davies, "Pete and Repeat at 176 Gallery: review," *The Telegraph*, London, October 29, http://www.telegraph.co.uk/culture/art/art-reviews/6455469/Pete-and-Repeat-at-176-Gallery-review.html (last accessed: June 17, 2010).

Christopher Miles, "Elad Lassry at Kordansky Gallery," *LA Weekly*, Los Angeles, October 22, http://www.laweekly.com/2009-10-22/art-books/elad-lassry-at-david-kordansky-gallery/ (last accessed: June 17, 2010).

Christopher Knight, "Art review: Elad Lassry at the David Kordansky Gallery," *Los Angeles Times*, Los Angeles, October 16, http://latimesblogs.latimes.com/culturemonster/2009/10/art-review-elad-lassry-at-the-david-kordansky-gallery.html (last accessed: June 17, 2010).

Sahra Lehrer-Graiwer, "Openings: Elad Lassry," *Artforum*, New York, vol. 48, no. 2, October, p. 218–221.

Alex Gartenfeld, "Elad Lassry's Material Context," *ArtInAmerica.com*, September 23, http://www.artinamericamagazine.com/news-opinion/conversations/2009-09-23/elad-lassry/ (last accessed: June 17, 2010).

*Metropolis M*, New York, August/September, p. 41–42, 85.

Lisa Dorin, *Film. Video. New Media at the Art Institute of Chicago With the Donna and Howard Stone Gift*, Yale University Press, New Haven/London, p. 104–105.

Paul Young, "Direct to Video!," *Angeleno*, Los Angeles, September, p. 75–76.

Merrily Kerr, "The Generational. Younger Than Jesus," *Flash Art*, Milan, July/September, p. 27–28.

Anat Ebgi, "Elad Lassry," *artisrael.org*, June, http://www.artisrael.org/feature/press/elad-lassry-june-2009 (last accessed: June 17, 2010).

Holly Myers, "Superficiality and Superexcrescence at Ben Maltz Gallery," *Los Angeles Times*, Los Angeles, July 8.

Alex Gartenfeld, "The Liste List," *ArtInAmerica.com*, June 15, http://www.artinamericamagazine.com/news-opinion/finer-things/2009-06-15/liste-/ (last accessed: June 17, 2010).

Nicolas Trembley, "Time Is Money," *Artforum.com*, June 15, http://artforum.com/diary/id=23101 (last accessed: June 17, 2010).

Kelly Crow, "Window Shoppers," *Wall Street Journal*, New York, June 12, http://online.wsj.com/article/SB124475192106507443.html (last accessed: June 17, 2010).

Christopher Bedford, Kristina Newhouse, & John Welchman, *Superficiality and Superexcrescence*, Otis College of Art and Design, Los Angeles, p. 72–75.

Holland Cotter, "Framing the Message of a Generation," *The New York Times*, New York, May 31, p. 1, 25.

Alessio Ascari, "Elad Lassry and Adrien Missika," *Kaleidoscope*, Milan, no. 2, Summer, p. 92–97.

Simon Castets, "Splitting Image," *Vman.com*, April 12, http://www.vman.com/blog/splitting-image/ (last accessed: June 17, 2010).

Lauren Cornell, Massimiliano Gioni, & Laura Hoptman, *Younger Than Jesus: The Generational Book*, New Museum & Steidl, New York, p. 49, 124–125.

Walead Beshty, Elad Lassry, Carter Mull, & Erika Vogt, "After Materiality and Style," *Art in America*, New York, April, p. 130–139, 162.

"A Concerted Overview," *Kaleidoscope*, Milan, no. 1, March/April, p. 46, 54.

Fionn Meade, "Elad Lassry: Three Films," *Bidoun*, New York, Spring, p. 167–168.

2008

Sarah Lehrer-Graiwer, "Studio Visit," *FlashArtonline.com*, November 18, http://www.flashartonline.com/interno.php?pagina=studio_det&id_art=210&det=ok&title=Elad-Lassry (last accessed: June 17, 2010).

Christopher Bollen, "Elad Lassry," *Interview*, New York, November, p. 42.

Joshua Decter, Lauri Firstenberg & Rene Peralta, *2008 California Biennial*, Orange County Museum of Art, Newport Beach, p. 136–139.

Andrew Hunt, Michael Ned Holte, Ilsa Colsell, Raimundas Malasauskas, & Ben Borthwick, *Past-Forward*, Zabludowicz Art Projects, London.

Michele D'Aurizio, "The Better Craftsman," *Mousse*, Milan, no. 12, January, p. 26–29.

Michael Ned Holte, "Elad Lassry," *Artforum*, New York, vol. 46, no. 5, January, p. 290–291.

"Graduate Directory. Elad Lassry," *Wallpaper*, London, January, p. 94.

2007

Ed Schad, "A Look at Lassry," *Artslant.com*, November, http://www.artslant.com/la/articles/show/594 (last accessed: June 17, 2010).

David Grosz, "Weekend Picks. Elad Lassry in LA," *Artinfo.com*, November 16, http://www.artinfo.com/news/story/26094/elad-lassry-in-la/ (last accessed: June 17, 2010).

Sarah Donaldson, "Zoo is the fair with flair," *Guardian Unlimited: Arts blog*, October 15, http://www.guardian.co.uk/artanddesign/artblog/2007/oct/15/zooisthefairwithflair (last accessed: June 17, 2010).

Brian Sholis, "Deep Frieze," *Artforum.com*, October 14, http://artforum.com/diary/id=18753 (last accessed: June 17, 2010).

Louisa Buck & Melanie Gerlis, "Zoo's move out of the zoo is a success," *The Art Newspaper*, London/New York/Turin/Paris/Athens, October 12, p. 4.

Melanie Gerlis, "And the champagne goes to ..." *The Art Newspaper*, London, October 12, p. 4.

Sharon Lockhart, "An Email Conversation," *Roski School of Fine Arts*, MFA catalogue, Los Angeles, p. 33–35.

2006

Suzanne Muchnic, "Giving local artists a good first shot," *Los Angeles Times*, Los Angeles, July 7, p. 27.

2004

Alix Lambert, "Top Ten," *Artforum*, New York, vol. 39, no. 3, November, p. 92.

# Colophon / Impressum

This book is published on the occasion of the exhibition / Diese Publikation erscheint anlässlich der Ausstellung:

*Elad Lassry*
Kunsthalle Zürich
13.2.–25.4.2010

## Exhibition / Ausstellung

Kunsthalle Zürich
Limmatstrasse 270
CH–8005 Zürich
T +41 (0)44 272 15 15
F +41 (0)44 272 18 88
www.kunsthallezurich.ch

Director & Curator / Direktorin & Kuratorin
Beatrix Ruf
Administration & Secretariat / Administration & Sekretariat
Suncana Sipek
Assistant Curator / Assistenzkuratorin
Katharina Pilz, Rahel Blättler
Members & Patrons, Sponsors, Limited Editions, Events / Mitglieder & Gönner, Sponsoren, Editionen, Events
Susanne Stortz
Exhibition Assistant & Press / Assistenz Ausstellungen & Presse
Isabelle Messina
Website, IT, & Graphics / Webseite, IT & Grafik
Alfonso Negri
Chief Technician / Cheftechniker
Attila Panczel
Technical Team / Technisches Team
Corina Enzler, Silvan Goette, Rachel Goette, Boris Knorpp, Nella Lombardi, Roland Rüegg
Cashiers / Kasse
Alexandra Hermann, Nella Lombardi, Konstantinos Manolakis, Maya Minder
Invilgilation / Aufsicht
Nadja Crola, Claire Geyer, Livia Di Giovanna, Daniel Herràn, Raphael Zürcher

## Publication / Publikation

Editor / Herausgeberin
Beatrix Ruf
Editorial Coordination / Redaktion
Rahel Blättler, Salome Schnetz
Copyediting & Proofreading / Lektorat & Korrektorat
Rahel Blättler, Clare Manchester, Salome Schnetz
Translations / Übersetzungen
Nikolaus G. Schneider (Funcke), Suzanne Schmidt (Maede, Kotz), Susan Cox (Ruf)
Graphic Design / Grafische Gestaltung
Gavillet & Rust/Eigenheer, Geneva
Color Separation & Print / Lithografie & Druck
Musumeci S.p.A., Quart (Aosta)

Dustjacket / Schutzumschlag
*Untitled (Passacaglia)*, 2010, Filmstill / Standbild

Photo Credits / Fotonachweis
Fredrik Nilsen (8–9, 11, 13, 15–16, 20, 23–27, 30, 31–33, 36–43, 48–51, 54–57, 60–64, 67–68),
Robert Wedemeyer (6–7, 10, 12, 14, 17, 21–22, 34–35, 46–47, 52–53, 65–66, 60, 69)

## Acknowledgments / Danksagung

We are grateful to the generous exhibition lenders / Wir danken den grosszügigen Leihgebern der Ausstellung:

Collection of Carlo Bronzini Vender
Collection of David Kordansky & Mindy Shapero, Los Angeles, CA
Collection of Dean Valentine & Amy Adelson, Los Angeles
Collection of Larry Sanitsky
Collection of Nathan Mabry & Tia Pulitzer
Collection Shelley Fox Aarons & Philip Aarons, New York
Collection Thomas Stauffer, Muri b. Bern, Switzerland
David Kordansky Gallery, Los Angeles, CA
Helen N. Lewis & Marvin B. Meyer, Beverly Hills, California
John Morace & Tom Kennedy, Los Angeles
Martin & Rebecca Eisenberg
Private Collection, Geneva
Sammlung Thomas & Cristina Bechtler
The Eugene Sadovoy Collection, Los Angeles
The Carol & Arthur Goldberg Collection

As well as to the private lenders who do not wish to be named. / Und den privaten Leihgebern, die nicht genannt werden wollen.

Elad Lassry and the Kunsthalle Zürich very much appreciate the help and support of / Elad Lassry und die Kunsthalle Zürich danken herzlich für die Hilfe und Unterstützung:

Stefan Altenburger, Rahel Blättler, Lionel Bovier, Massimo De Carlo, Nadja Crola, David Kordansky Gallery/Los Angeles, CA, Jessica De Ruiter, Lisa Dorin, Galleria Massimo De Carlo/Milan, Claire Geyer, Livia Di Giovanna, Rachel Goette, Silvan Goette, Bettina Funcke, Alexandra Hermann, Daniel Herràn, Chrissie Illes, Joya Indermühle, Marcel Isler, Samuel Kahn, Boris Knorpp, David Kordansky, Liz Kotz, Ask la Cour, Megan LeCrone, Sarah Lehrer-Graiwer, Sharon Lockhart, Alice Lodge, Nella Lombardi, Konstantinos Manolakis, Hedia Maron, Kevin McHugh, Fionn Meade, Isabelle Messina, Maya Minder, Aram Moshayedi, Alfonso Negri, Lucia Noyce, Olaf Saeger|filmkunsttechnik Berlin, Attila Panczel, Francesca Pia, Katharina Pilz, Ronald Rüegg, Anke Schiller, Salome Schnetz, Suncana Sipek, Brock Smith, Frances Stark, Susanne Stortz, Studio 2M Filmtechniek Amsterdam, Elena Tavecchia, Yon Thomas, Melissa Tolar, Nicholas Trikonis, Ana Vejzovic Sharp, Lisa Williamson, Raphael Zürcher

Kunsthalle Zürich would like to thank for their continuous support / Kunsthalle Zürich dankt für die kontinuierliche Unterstützung:

Präsidialdepartement der Stadt Zürich
Swiss Re
LUMA Foundation

And a very special thanks to Elad Lassry. / Und ein ganz besonderer Dank an Elad Lassry.

Published by / Publiziert von:

JRP|Ringier
Letzigraben 134
CH–8047 Zürich
T +41 (0) 43 311 27 50
F +41 (0) 43 311 27 51
E info@jrp-ringier.com
www.jrp-ringier.com

ISBN 978-3-03764-152-1

JRP|Ringier books are available internationally at selected bookstores and from the following distribution partners / JRP|Ringier Bücher sind international in ausgewählten Buchhandlungen und bei den folgenden Vertriebspartnern erhältlich:

Switzerland / Schweiz
Buch 2000, AVA Verlagsauslieferung AG, Centralweg 16, CH–8910 Affoltern a.A., buch2000@ava.ch, www.ava.ch
France / Frankreich
Les presses du réel, 35 rue Colson, F–21000 Dijon, info@lespressesdureel.com, www.lespressesdureel.com
Germany and Austria / Deutschland und Österreich
Vice Versa Vertrieb, Immanuelkirchstrasse 12, D–10405 Berlin, info@vice-versa-vertrieb.de, www.vice-versa-vertrieb.de
UK and other European countries / Grossbritannien und andere europäische Länder
Cornerhouse Publications, 70 Oxford Street, UK–Manchester M1 5NH, publications@cornerhouse.org, www.cornerhouse.org/books
USA, Canada, Asia, and Australia / USA, Kanada, Asien und Australien
D.A.P./Distributed Art Publishers, 155 Sixth Avenue, 2nd Floor, USA–New York, NY 10013, dap@dapinc.com, www.artbook.com

For a list of our partner bookshops or for any general questions, please contact JRP|Ringier directly at info@jrp-ringier.com, or visit our homepage www.jrp-ringier.com for further information about our program. / Für eine Liste der Partnerbuchhandlungen oder allgemeine Fragen kontaktieren Sie bitte JRP|Ringier direkt unter info@jrp-ringier.com oder besuchen Sie unsere Webseite www.jrp-ringier.com für weitere Programminformationen.